"The American Statesmen Series was a pathbreaking venture in its time; and the best proof of its continuing vitality for our time lies in the testimony of the introductory essays written by eminent scholars for the volumes of the Chelsea House edition—essays that not only explain the abiding value of the texts but in many cases represent significant scholarly contributions on their own.

"Chelsea House is contributing vitally to the scholarly resources of the country—and, at the same time, helping us all to understand and repossess our national heritage."

—Professor Arthur M. Schlesinger, jr.

American Statesmen Series

The Home of Salmon P. Chase

Other titles in this Chelsea House series:

CHARLES FRANCIS ADAMS, *Charles Francis Adams, Jr.*
JOHN ADAMS, *John Quincy Adams and Charles Francis Adams*
JOHN QUINCY ADAMS, *John T. Morse, Jr.*
SAMUEL ADAMS, *James K. Hosmer*
JUDAH P. BENJAMIN, *Pierce Butler*
JOHN C. CALHOUN, *Hermann E. von Holst*
LEWIS CASS, *Andrew C. McLaughlin*
HENRY CLAY, *Carl Schurz*
ALBERT GALLATIN, *Henry Adams*
ALEXANDER HAMILTON, *Henry Cabot Lodge*
PATRICK HENRY, *Moses Coit Tyler*
ANDREW JACKSON, *William Graham Sumner*
JOHN JAY, *George Pellew*
THOMAS JEFFERSON, *John T. Morse, Jr.*
JAMES MADISON, *Sydney Howard Gay*
JOHN MARSHALL, *Albert J. Beveridge*
JAMES MONROE, *Daniel Coit Gilman*
GOUVERNEUR MORRIS, *Theodore Roosevelt*
JOHN RANDOLPH, *Henry Adams*
CHARLES SUMNER, *Moorfield Storey*
MARTIN VAN BUREN, *Edward M. Shepard*
GEORGE WASHINGTON, *John Marshall*
DANIEL WEBSTER, *Henry Cabot Lodge*

Forthcoming titles in this Chelsea House series:

JOHN P. ALTGELD, *Harry Barnard*
THOMAS HART BENTON, *Theodore Roosevelt*
JAMES G. BLAINE, *Edward Stanwood*
DANIEL BOONE, *Reuben G. Thwaites*
WILLIAM JENNINGS BRYAN, *M. R. Werner*
AARON BURR, *James Parton*
PETER COOPER, *R. W. Raymond*
STEPHEN A. DOUGLAS, *Allen Johnson*
DAVID FARRAGUT, *Alfred Thayer Mahan*
ULYSSES S. GRANT, *Louis A. Coolidge*
NATHANIEL GREENE, *Francis Vinton Greene*
MARCUS ALONZO HANNA, *Herbert D. Croly*
SAM HOUSTON, *Marquis James*
HENRY KNOX, *Noah Brooks*
LUTHER MARTIN, *Paul S. Clarkson and R. Samuel Jett*
ROBERT MORRIS, *Ellis Paxson Oberholtzer*
FRANKLIN PIERCE, *Nathaniel Hawthorne*
WILLIAM H. SEWARD, *Thornton K. Lothrop*
JOHN SHERMAN, *Theodore E. Burton*
WILLIAM T. SHERMAN, *B. H. Liddell Hart*
THADDEUS STEVENS, *Samuel W. McCall*
ROGER B. TANEY, *Carl Swisher*
TECUMSEH, *Glenn Tucker*
THURLOW WEED, *Glyndon G. VanDeusen*

SALMON P. CHASE

ALBERT BUSHNELL HART

INTRODUCTION BY

G. S. BORITT

American Statesmen Series

GENERAL EDITOR

ARTHUR M. SCHLESINGER, JR.

ALBERT SCHWEITZER PROFESSOR OF THE HUMANITIES

THE CITY UNIVERSITY OF NEW YORK

CHELSEA HOUSE

NEW YORK, LONDON

1980

Cover design by Zimmerman Foyster Design

Printed and bound in the United States of America

Library of Congress Cataloging in Publication Data

Hart, Albert Bushnell, 1854-1943.
Salmon P. Chase.

(American statesmen)
Reprint of the 1899 ed. published by Houghton, Mifflin, Boston, which was issued as v. 28 of American statesmen, under title: Salmon Portland Chase.
Includes index.
1. Chase, Salmon Portland, 1808-1873. 2. United States--Politics and government--1849-1877. 3. Legislators--United States--Biography. 4. United States. Congress. Senate--Biography. 5. Ohio--Governors--Biography. 6. Judges--United States--Biography. I. Title. II. Series: American statesmen (New York) III. Series: American statesmen ; v. 28.
E415.9.C4H28 1980 973.7'092'4 [B] 80-21705
ISBN 0-87754-191-4

Chelsea House Publishers
Harold Steinberg, Chairman & Publisher
Andrew E. Norman, President
Susan Lusk, Vice President
A Division of Chelsea House Educational Communications, Inc.
133 Christopher Street, New York 10014

TO

ALBERT GAILLARD HART

ABOLITIONIST

UNDERGROUND-RAILROAD CONDUCTOR

LIBERTY MAN, FREE-SOILER

UNION SOLDIER

A SON'S GRATITUDE

CONTENTS

ILLUSTRATIONS

FOLLOWING PAGE 196

General Introduction

BLAZING THE WAY

Arthur M. Schlesinger, jr.

THE ORIGINAL AMERICAN STATESMEN SERIES consisted of thirty-four titles published between 1882 and 1916. Handsomely printed and widely read, the Series made a notable contribution to the popular appreciation of American history. Its creator was John Torrey Morse, Jr., born in Boston in 1840, graduated from Harvard in 1860 and for nearly twenty restless years thereafter a Boston lawyer. In his thirties he had begun to dabble in writing and editing; and about 1880, reading a volume in John Morley's English Men of Letters Series, he was seized by the idea of a comparable set of compact, lucid and authoritative lives of American statesmen.

It was an unfashionable thought. The celebrated New York publisher Henry Holt turned the project down, telling Morse, "Who ever wants to read American history?" Houghton, Mifflin in Boston proved more receptive, and Morse plunged ahead. His intention was that the American Statesmen Series, when complete, "should present such a picture of the development of the country that the reader who had faithfully read all the volumes would have a full and fair view of the history of the United States told through the medium of the efforts of the men who had shaped our national career. The actors were to develop the drama."

In choosing his authors, Morse relied heavily on the counsel of his cousin Henry Cabot Lodge. Between them, they enlisted an impressive array of talent. Henry Adams, William Graham Sumner, Moses Coit Tyler, Hermann von Holst, Moorfield Storey and Albert Bushnell Hart were all in their early forties when their volumes were published; Lodge, E. M. Shepard and Andrew C. McLaughlin in their thirties; Theodore Roosevelt in his twenties. Lodge took on Washington, Hamilton and Webster, and Morse himself wrote five volumes. He offered the authors a choice of $500 flat or a royalty of 12.5¢ on each volume sold. Most, luckily for themselves, chose the royalties.

Like many editors, Morse found the experience exasperating. "How I waded among the fragments of broken engagements, shattered pledges! I never really knew when I could count upon getting anything from anybody." Carl Schurz infuriated him by sending in a two-volume life of Henry Clay on a take-it-or-leave-it basis. Morse, who had confined Jefferson,

John Adams, Webster and Calhoun to single volumes, was tempted to leave it. But Schurz threatened to publish his work simultaneously if Morse commissioned another life of Clay for the Series; so Morse reluctantly surrendered.

When a former Confederate colonel, Allan B. Magruder, offered to do John Marshall, Morse, hoping for "a good Virginia atmosphere," gave him a chance. The volume turned out to have been borrowed in embarrassing measure from Henry Flanders's *Lives and Times of the Chief Justices.* For this reason, Magruder's *Marshall* is not included in the Chelsea House reissue of the Series; Albert J. Beveridge's famous biography appears in its stead. Other classic biographies will replace occasional Series volumes: John Marshall's *Life of George Washington* in place of Morse's biography; essays on John Adams by John Quincy Adams and Charles Francis Adams, also substituting for a Morse volume; and Henry Adams's *Life of Albert Gallatin* instead of the Series volume by John Austin Stevens.

"I think that only one real blunder was made," Morse recalled in 1931, "and that was in allotting [John] Randolph to Henry Adams." Half a century earlier, however, Morse had professed himself pleased with Adams's *Randolph.* Adams, responding with characteristic self-deprecation, thought the "acidity" of his account "much too decided" but blamed the "excess of acid" on the acidulous subject. The book was indeed hostile but nonetheless stylish. Adams also wrote a life of Aaron Burr, presumably for the Series. But Morse thought Burr no statesman, and on his advice, to Adams's extreme irritation, Henry Houghton of Houghton, Mifflin rejected the manuscript. "Not bad that for a damned bookseller!" said Adams. "He should live for a while at Washington and know our *real* statesmen." Adams eventually destroyed the work, and a fascinating book was lost to history.

The definition of who was or was not a "statesman" caused recurrent problems. Lodge told Morse one day that their young friend Theodore Roosevelt wanted to do Gouverneur Morris. "But, Cabot," Morse said, "you surely don't expect Morris to be in the Series! He doesn't belong there." Lodge replied, "Theodore . . . *needs the money,*" and Morse relented. No one objected to Thomas Hart Benton, Roosevelt's other contribution to the Series. Roosevelt turned out the biography in an astonishing four months while punching cows and chasing horse thieves in the Badlands. Begging Lodge to send more material from Boston, he wrote that he had been "mainly evolving [Benton] from my inner consciousness; but when he leaves the Senate in 1850 I have nothing whatever to go by. . . . I hesitate to give him a wholly fictitious date of death and to invent all the work of his later years." In fact, T.R. had done more research than he pretended; and for all its defects, his *Benton* has valuable qualities of vitality and sympathy.

Morse, who would chat to Lodge about "the aristocratic upper crust in which you & I are imbedded," had a fastidious sense of language. Many years later, in the age of Warren G. Harding, he recommended to Lodge that the new President find someone "who can clothe for him his 'ideas' in the language customarily used by educated men." At dinner in a Boston club, a guest commented on the dilemma of the French ambassador who could not speak English. "Neither can Mr. Harding," Morse said. But if patrician prejudice improved Morse's literary taste, it also impaired his political understanding. He was not altogether kidding when he wrote Lodge as the Series was getting under way, "Let the Jeffersonians & the Jacksonians beware! I will poison the popular mind!!"

Still, for all its fidelity to establishment values, the American Statesmen Series had distinct virtues. The authors were mostly from outside the academy, and they wrote with the confidence of men of affairs. Their books are generally crisp, intelligent, spirited and readable. The Series has long been in demand in secondhand bookstores. Most of its volumes are eminently worth republication today, on their merits as well as for the vigorous expression they give to an influential view of the American past.

Born during the Presidency of Martin Van Buren, John Torrey Morse, Jr., died shortly after the second inauguration of Franklin D. Roosevelt in 1937. A few years before his death he could claim with considerable justice that his Series had done "a little something in blazing the way" for the revival of American historical writing in the years to come.

New York
May, 1980

INTRODUCTION
TO THE
CHELSEA HOUSE EDITION

G. S. Boritt

"I did not say to you: 'I put you upon your honor, Prof. Hart', because I considered that the use of those words 'Upon honor' might have somewhat jarred upon your ear." In the summer of 1898 John T. Morse, Jr., editor of the much acclaimed American Statesmen Series, aimed these sharp barbs at a seemingly dilatory Harvard professor of history who had promised to deliver a biography of Salmon P. Chase in the early part of that decade. The outraged editor's communication to Albert Bushnell Hart contained five typewritten pages, with the most insulting remarks inserted by hand, and with a demand and a dire threat in conclusion:

Now you will permit me to say that you are under obligation to furnish this book immediately, an obligation of such a nature that, if you are an honorable gentleman, you *must fulfil it*, no matter at what cost of labor and sacrifice to yourself. It seems idle to ask you what you intend to do, or what you will agree to do, yet you *must determine and act promptly*, and, I hope, also honestly. If you furnish the book by the end of the summer, (which you can do if you choose to,) the past disgraceful record may be forgotten; but if you fail to do this, I shall consider myself at liberty to express freely my opinion of you and of your conduct whatever and whenever I see fit, and it will be an opinion not likely to afford you gratification.

Seven and a half years earlier, at the end of 1890, it had been Hart who requested the assignment of the life of Chase. The fame of the American Statesmen Series, or the considerable financial rewards it was bringing to some of its contributors, probably had much less to do with the request than the young professor's desire to write a new kind of study. He was later recognized as a founding father of professional history in the United States, and the *Chase,* we can be sure, he viewed as a possible step to such an exalted station. Also, Hart was eager to help "scientific history" triumph over the patrician school that still dominated the field with elegant literary creations the young professionals saw as bad, unfaithful history.

Editor Morse anticipated no such battle between the old and the new. Hart's Ohio background, his antislavery sympathies (characteristics he shared with Chase), and his Harvard appointment were recommendations enough for making the assignment. The addition of Chase extended the Series to the figures of the Civil War period, but Morse had been considering such a possibility, and his publisher, the respected Houghton, Mifflin and Company, was eager for it. He expected the venture to be "difficult" because too short a time had elapsed since the war to provide perspective. Neither he nor Hart foresaw how difficult it would be.

Eighteen ninety-two arrived before Hart managed to get a real start. Fully familiar with the printed literature of the period from his teaching, he concentrated his energies on systematically assembling primary sources. He enlisted the aid of colleagues in the profession, amateurs, friends, strangers; he traveled, talked with old-timers, searched through the proverbial musty records, and conducted a substantial correspondence. The net result was a valuable cache of information including Chase's letters and diaries.

Along the way Hart came face to face with a large problem: Chase's ungodly handwriting. Though he had to hire someone to help with the deciphering, his book would generously say no more than that Chase's "handwriting, never remarkably legible, at last became difficult to read." Hart maintained his enthusiasm, however, and began to think not only in terms of a two-volume biography with footnotes and a bibliography (scholarly impedimenta the American Statesmen Series had dispensed with) but also of a multivolume edition of Chase's collected works. Hart had always thought highly of the Ohio abolitionist. Now he was sure that Chase was a great man.

The publishers were not cooperative. Though for a time they humored him about notes and bibliography, the life, he was told, had to be a single volume. As for the collected works of Chase, among the many merits conceded to the project by various houses, the most crucial one, potential for profit, was missing. These frustrations must have encouraged Hart to find time for other historical undertakings, popular as well as academic. Editor Morse began to worry.

In early 1891 Hart had hoped to complete the work in two years. Morse had expressed dread at the prospect of such an extended deadline. After all, he knew that a gentleman historian like Theodore Roosevelt had written most of his biography of Thomas Hart Benton in three months. Understandings for delivery in six months to a year were common. Morse did acquiesce in Hart's desire for "a liberal allowance" of time, but the years began to go by and produced only promises—for later and later delivery of the *Chase*. In 1892 Morse sent a polite request for a progress report. In 1893 he could understand that Hart's success in obtaining source materials meant a postponement. "Is it ready, or nearly so?" went the query in 1894. And in 1895: Can Houghton, Mifflin "announce your Life of Chase in their list of autumn publications?" In 1896: "How comes the Life of Chase?" Though most of Hart's replies do not seem to have survived, it is clear that with disturbing consistency he only reported "slow progress" and argued the hardships of scholarship. In the winter of 1896 a personal confrontation took place between author and editor. Hart offered to give up the project and his painfully collected materials. Morse realized, however, that the professor preferred to be given more time. Thus an agreement was struck, with Hart promising delivery at what Morse saw as an "inconveniently distant" date.

A year and a half later, in the summer of 1898, Morse finally exploded. They had made, he wrote Hart "what is called 'an agreement between gentleman,' and at the time I supposed that it would prove to be such." Morse's outrage and his long and bitter assault on Hart's character appear to have worked. The following spring Hart handed over his manuscript. Even then, when he found that the volume would not be published until the fall, he retrieved the manuscript from the printer to make final revisions.

Such a curious performance from a "founding father" raises intriguing questions. Hart's problems included Chase's terrible handwriting, a desire for a more substantial work than publishers were willing to finance, and perhaps such lesser matters as waiting for the publication of relevant volumes by colleagues. Above all, Hart pleaded that the "essential" cause of his long failure to complete *Chase* was the "students, who must be a first charge on the intellectual funds of an instructor." But surely something more fundamental had blocked the progress of the only biography he wrote in a long and productive lifetime.

Hart was a leading member of the first generation of professional historians in this country whose forte was institutional history. As befitted the triumph of realism over romanticism in American culture, they wanted their studies to provide an impersonal framework for the actors and events of the past. For these scientific historians, biography could only be a stepchild. When they descended into that genre, they tried to remake it into a body of formal works heavily buttressed with the objective circumstances of a period. Not surprisingly, their biographical studies were also models of discretion.

Hart consciously set out to write in this new mold. It mattered not to him that his editor preferred the established pattern of the Series and looked for "the whole" of Chase, private and public, in a Life. From the professional's standpoint, a sharp contrast between the *Chase* and much of the American Statesmen Series would benefit the study of history. To create such a contrast, to write the new kind of biography, however, turned out to be very difficult —as Hart's nearly decade-long struggle testifies. In time he resolved the tension between the art of biography and the new science of history by writing a book that instead of telling a traditional Life, portrayed Chase as "the central figure in three episodes . . . of great historic importance:" the antislavery movement in Western politics, Civil War finance, and the judicial phase of Reconstruction.

The principles of scientific history were reinforced by the Victorian sensibilities of the times. Accordingly, Hart concentrated on the public life of Chase and reserved his most critical comments for an earlier official biographer of his subject, who "knew no other use to make" of the masses of original Chase materials "than to print the most private and sacred passages with the rest." In contrast, Hart said very little about the man who was "fond of the ladies, and . . . liked to tell his diary what he thought of them"; who married and buried three wives in the space of eighteen years, between 1834 and 1852; buried five of his seven children during the same period; struggled through the great successes, and the great failures, of his next twenty years; and reared two daughters, one of whom, Kate Chase Sprague, was overenthusiastically described by Hart as "a political force of magnitude . . . the only woman in the history of the United States who has had such public influence." The *Political Science Quarterly*'s reviewer could thus conclude smugly in 1900 that the "type of readers whose curiosity is satisfied only with the spicy and fanciful gossip of clubs and the small tittle-tattle of drawing-rooms" would be sorely disappointed by Hart's *Chase.* Romanticism had run its course, and the Freudian age that could find intimate scholarly connections between a "spicy" private and an austere public man lay far in the future.

Eighty years later *Salmon Portland Chase* still displays the force of its author's clear analytic mind. It shows an earnest and to no small degree successful striving for balance. If William A. Dunning, Hart's colleague at Columbia University, could aptly call him a "pre-natal abolitionist," if Hart was too much a fiscal conservative, if he had no use for even a whiff of debunking, still the latter-day historian cannot help but regard with filial pride the high level of professionalism displayed by Hart in 1899. In the intervening years much new material has been unearthed about the middle period of American history. The field has benefited from the changing perspectives of successive generations of scholars, perspectives that sometimes double back to Hart's. We have learned a freer use of the historical imagination and are willing to dig deeper for insights. We have also abandoned the early academics' deep distrust of literary style, which, minor concessions notwithstanding, Hart, too, shared. "The founding fathers of professional history," as John Higham has said, "lacked the faith that writes epics"; but they did possess "the faith that moves mountains." The gentlemen of letters who wrote subjective and often very romantic stories in the guise of history—and, more important, the outlook they represented in the realm of learning—were the fathers' mountain. That old mountain had its fine features. Historians owe something to it; they should borrow more. But historical scholarship in the last quarter of the twentieth century owes much more to the faith that moved the mountain. Hart's *Chase* is a fine example of that faith.

When the book appeared Hart was well on his way to being considered one of the leading historians of America. *Chase* added measurably to his stature. His work continued and honors awaited him—the presidencies of the American Historical Association and the American Political Science Association, and an endowed chair at Harvard. Among the testimonials contained in his papers is a 1909 telegram from patrician historian and old classmate then in Nairobi:

> Bully for good old Hart '80
> tell him bagging elephants beats
> writing or making history
> best wishes Theodore Roosevelt.

Hart also carried a very large share of professional labors and attendant heartaches. If his most lasting contribution was to help make history a central element of the curriculum of the American university, his substantial number of publications appears as a more palpable monument to him. These include, in addition to monographs such as *Slavery and Abolition, 1831-1841* or *The Formation of the Union,*

1750-1829, a popular American history text; a pioneering anthology, *American History Told by Contemporaries,* in five volumes; and the equally pioneering *Harper's Atlas of American History.* Among other things, while working on *Chase,* Hart brought out in cooperation with his Harvard colleague and rival, Edward Channing, the first edition of the influential *Guide to the Study of American History.* It continues today as the *Harvard Guide.* Most important, in the early 1900s Hart edited the first professional synthesis of American history, the American Nation Series. Its twenty-five volumes appeared between 1904 and 1907. Hart himself wrote one of the volumes (and later one of the three supplementary volumes) and served not only as a rigorous editor but also as a tough and immensely successful enforcer of deadlines. He even managed to obtain a complete book from Frederick Jackson Turner—the only one of Turner's career. Hart had evidently learned much from his battles with John T. Morse, Jr., during the previous decade.

The battles about the *Chase* continued for another generation. In 1911, for example, the newly appointed Eaton Professor of Government at Harvard wrote to his publisher about royalties: "7-1/2 cents a copy (although I undoubtedly contracted to receive it) is not a fair proportion to the author. I make no appeal for revision . . . but I want to place on record the conviction of years that Houghton, Mifflin & Co, squeezed me on that agreement." The publisher was not amused. In the following decade the granddaughter of Flamen Ball, Chase's old law partner, took offense at Hart's description of her ancestor as a man who "failed in business . . . much inferior to Chase in abilities, character, and habits." Hart, then in his seventies, apprehended a lawsuit but was not about to change his history. Nothing came of the matter.

There had been a hint of legal action even vis-à-vis Morse. But eleven days after Hart signed and dated the Preface to *Chase,* his editor became more conciliatory: "I was neither so vindictive nor so foolish as to contemplate an assault upon your character or reputation," he wrote to Hart. "I have had no special occasion to refer to the matter, & probably never shall have in the future." Morse had the last word, however. Some thirty years later, discussing the American Statesmen Series before the Massachusetts Historical Society, with Hart perhaps in attendance, he recalled how he had "waded among the fragments of broken engagements, shattered pledges!" An agreement with historians ("literary men," he called them) "is marvelously different from a promissory note made by a merchant to pay dollars. . . . The sheriff can't distrain the goods of the cheerful gentleman who has only pledged himself to have a book finished at a certain date." Whomever else he had in mind, we can be sure Hart was prominent among them.

At that time, in 1931, *Chase* was still the standard biography. It still is, in 1980, the year of its reissue, the only full-length academic treatment. The quality of Hart's book long served as a deterrent to new works by younger scholars. So did perhaps Chase's less than lovable personality and handwriting. But today the most difficult obstacle facing the student is academic specialization. It frightens ordinary mortals away from a man who trod through such disparate fields of American history.

And with what aplomb Chase had traversed the political and moral landscape of the mid-nineteenth century. He was not so great a man as Hart portrayed. But unlike any other during the first century of the United States, he served prominently in all three branches of the national government. He made a most significant contribution to the formation of the ideology and organization of the Republican party. He reached the height of his public distinction as the hardworking Secretary of the Treasury in

Lincoln's cabinet and, after the Civil War, as the Chief Justice of the United States who presided over the impeachment of Andrew Johnson, helped sidetrack the trial of Jefferson Davis, and left his mark on both the Supreme Court and Reconstruction.

His greatest failing, so evident in the pages of Hart's book, was an unbounded belief in his own superiority. That in the 1850s it led him to begin to contemplate the "picture of 'President Chase'" was well enough. But the picture came back to haunt him "every year during the rest of his life." Lincoln was supposed to have said of him that the Secretary was "about one and a half times bigger than any other man that I ever knew." The compliment, of course, was not entirely complimentary. Yet though Chase never reached the White House, though he never abandoned the pursuit, his life was triumphant. He had always insisted that principles must be placed far above personal ambitions. The passionate antislavery principles of his youth succeeded beyond all hope. He did not. Life had taken him at his word.

Bolton, Massachusetts
August, 1980

BIBLIOGRAPHICAL NOTE

Hart's hope for a collected works of Chase has not been fulfilled. Hart's influence, however, led to the publication of a portion of the Chase diaries and many of his important letters in the somewhat hastily prepared *Annual Report of the American Historical Association for 1902.* Half a century later David Herbert Donald edited *Inside Lincoln's Cabinet: The Civil War Diaries of Salmon P. Chase* (1954). The principal depositories of Chase's unpublished papers are the Library of Congress and the Historical Society of Pennsylvania. There are scattered papers and minor collections in Ohio and elsewhere.

The most useful study of Chase during the antebellum period is Eric Foner, *Free Soil, Free Labor, Free Men: The Ideology of the Republican Party Before the Civil War* (1970). Like Hart, Foner gives Chase a central role in the creation of a Republican ideology, placing him above William A. Seward and Abraham Lincoln in importance. For overviews see Reinhard H. Luthin, "Salmon P. Chase's Political Career Before the Civil War," *Mississippi Valley Historical Review* 29 (1943):517-40; and Robert H. Gruber, "Salmon P. Chase and the Politics of Reform," Ph.D. dissertation, University of Maryland, 1969. The most telling aspect of Chase's pre-Republican career is considered in Frederick J. Blue, *The Free-Soilers: Third Party Politics, 1848-1854* (1973). Blue's forthcoming "Salmon P. Chase and the Governorship: Steppingstone to the

Presidency," *Ohio History* (1981), highlights Chase's use of the Ohio Governor's office to attempt to obtain the Republican presidential nomination for 1856. The transition to Republican politics is also considered in Eugene H. Roseboom, "Salmon P. Chase and the Know Nothings," *Mississippi Valley Historical Review* 25 (1938):335-50; and in two careful articles by Dick Johnson, "The Role of Salmon Portland Chase in the Formation of the Republican Party" and "Along the Twisted Road to the Civil War: Historians and the Appeal of the Independent Democrats," both in the *Old Northwest* 3 (1977):23-38, 4 (1978):119-41. For Chase's formative years see Arthur M. Schlesinger, "Salmon Portland Chase, Undergraduate and Pedagogue," *Ohio Archeological and Historical Quarterly* 28 (1919):119-61.

For the Civil War, Donald's substantial introduction to *Inside Lincoln's Cabinet* is the best work. Donald goes beyond Hart to depict Chase as "the great Civil War Secretary of the Treasury." G. S. Boritt, *Lincoln and the Economics of the American Dream* (1978) is of some use. British criticism of Chase's stewardship is documented in A. Curtis Wilgus, "Some 'London Times' Comments on Secretary Chase's Financial Administration, 1861-1864," *Mississippi Valley Historical Review* 26 (1939):395-99. Donnal V. Smith, *Chase and Civil War Politics* (1931), also attacks the ambitious and radical cabinet officer. Louis A. Gerteis, "Salmon P. Chase, Radicalism, and the Politics of Emancipation, 1861-1864," *Journal of American History* 60 (1973): 42-62, however, sees in the collapse of Chase's presidential hopes a measure of the radicals' failure to provide necessary aid to the freedmen. Chase's use of the Treasury patronage is examined in Harry J. Carman and Reinhard H. Luthin, *Lincoln and the Patronage* (1943), and in Ovid Futch, "Salmon P. Chase and Civil War Politics in Florida," *Florida Historical Quarterly* 32 (1954):163-88. Useful documents appear in Annie A. Nunns, "Some Letters of Salmon P. Chase, 1848-1865," *American Historical Review* 34 (1929):536-55; and in Charles R. Wilson, "The Original Chase Meeting and *The Next Presidential Election*," *Mississippi Valley Historical Review* 23 (1936):61-79.

For the final, judicial phase of Chase's career the student must turn to a pair of unpublished doctoral dissertations: David F. Hughes, "Salmon P. Chase: Chief Justice," Princeton University, 1963; and Harold M. Hollingsworth, "The Confirmation of Judicial Review under Taney and Chase," University of Tennessee, 1966. Hughes also published "Salmon P. Chase: Chief Justice," *Vanderbilt Law Review* 18 (1964-65):569-614. On the whole these works underscore Hart's highly complimentary evaluation of the Chief Justice. That valuation is moderated by Leon Friedman, "Salmon P. Chase," in Friedman and Fred L. Israel, eds., *The Justices of the United States Supreme Court, Their Lives and Major Opinions* (1969), 1113-49. More critical estimates can be found in the general literature on the legal and constitutional history of the period. Charles Fairman, *Reconstruction and Reunion, 1864-88*, Part 1 (1971), is a massive compilation about the Chase Court. James E. Sefton, "Chief Justice Chase as an Advisor on Presidential Reconstruction," *Civil War History* 12 (1967):242-64, contains letters to Andrew

Johnson written by Chase during his 1865 tour of the South.

For brief sketches see the articles on Chase by J. G. Randall in the *Dictionary of American Biography* 4 (1930):27-34; and in Mark E. Neely, Jr., *The Lincoln Encyclopedia* (forthcoming, 1981). A short but perceptive chapter in Peter F. Walker, *Moral Choices: Memory, Desire, and Imagination in Nineteenth-Century American Abolition* (1978) connects the private and public man.

Biographies preceding Hart's include J. T. Trowbridge's 1864 campaign tract, which was based in part on autobiographical letters by Chase: *The Ferry Boy and the Financier.* Chase selected Robert B. Warden as an authorized biographer, and his book appeared in 1874 over the bitter objections of Chase's daughters and friends: *An Account of the Private Life and Public Services of Salmon Portland Chase.* A somewhat better contemporary history was the volume by Jacob W. Shuckers, one of Chase's secretaries, also published in the year after the death of the Chief Justice: *The Life and Public Services of Salmon Portland Chase* (1874). Subsequent to Hart, several more or less popularly oriented accounts of varying craftsmanship appeared, with the focus on Chase's older daughter–difficult undertakings because of the paucity of primary materials on her. They tend to accept, albeit not uniformly, Hart's view about the extraordinary political powers of Kate Chase Sprague: Mary Merwin Phelps, *Kate Chase, Dominant Daughter; The Life Story of a Brilliant Woman and Her Famous Father* (1935); Ishbel Ross, *Proud Kate: Portrait of an Ambitious Woman* (1953);

Thomas Graham Belden and Marva Robbins Belden, *So Fell the Angels* (1956); and Alice Hunt Sokoloff, *Kate Chase for the Defense* (1971). Thus Albert Bushnell Hart's 1899 *Salmon Portland Chase* remains the sole full-length biography by an academic historian. A modern study is much needed.

The principal source for this introduction is the Albert Bushnell Hart Papers, University Archives, Nathan Marsh Pusey Library, Harvard University.

AUTHOR'S PREFACE
TO THE
1899 EDITION

THE biographies of most of the American statesmen of the Civil War have been written by their contemporaries, who could supplement research by their own impressions and recollections. The work of preparing this volume and estimating the character and services of Salmon Portland Chase falls to one who never saw him; but though dependent upon written and printed materials and the reminiscences of others, I may perhaps claim some special interest in him as an exponent of that Western political anti-slavery movement which early stirred my blood through both heredity and training.

The life of Mr. Chase has already been told in three published biographies. J. T. Trowbridge's "The Ferry Boy and the Financier," although founded on valuable data furnished by Chase himself, is a romantic tale and really intended as a campaign document. R. B. Warden's long and elaborate "Life of Salmon P. Chase" is uncritical and unsatisfactory, and the mass of material which he had at his disposal was used neither with personal discrimination nor literary judgment. The third and best biography, by J. W. Schuckers, is written with historical perspective, but lacks the advantage of many valuable documents which have come to light in the twenty-five years following the death of Mr. Chase.

Perhaps, therefore, there is room for another briefer biography, in which Warden's and Schuckers's works may be used as collections of material, partly accessible in no other form, but of which the chief sources shall be three collections of manuscripts. The first is a file of letters to Chase, about eight thousand in number, running from 1824 to 1873, for the use of which I am indebted to the kind permission of Mr. Chase's daughters, Mrs. Kate Chase and Mrs. W. S. Hoyt, and to the courtesy of Mr. James Ford Rhodes, who recovered them from their place of deposit. The second collection, which came to me through the late Mr. C. S. Hamlin of Williamsburg, Virginia, includes most of Chase's original diaries, letter-books, and memoranda, together with three autobiographical sketches, written, dictated, or inspired by him at various times. The third set is a considerable body of Mr. Chase's own unpublished letters, kindly lent by many persons, but especially by Major Dwight Bannister of Ottumwa, Iowa, and the late Mr. Edward L. Pierce of Milton, Massachusetts, who also placed at my disposal the letters of Chase to Charles Sumner.

Besides this mass of contemporary material, professional, personal, and political, I have freely drawn on the few publications of Chase, on the debates and reports of Congress, and on the works of his fellow statesmen and their biographers. To Mr. Charles E. Ozanne I am much indebted for his patient and discriminating labor in deciphering and analyzing the diaries and letters of Chase. Professor James Bradley Thayer and Professor Charles F. Dunbar have done me the great kindness to read some of the proofs, and to make some suggestions on the chapters relative to finance and the constitutional decisions.

It is not the purpose of this volume to give a detailed account of Mr. Chase's private life, nor even to describe fully his long, eventful, and varied public career, but rather to present him as the central figure in three episodes which are of great historic importance,—the Western political anti-slavery movement, the financial measures of the Civil War, and the process of judicial reconstruction. The biography is therefore intended to be a brief history of these three epochs as seen through the activity of the anti-slavery leader, the financier, and the jurist.

ALBERT BUSHNELL HART.

CAMBRIDGE, April 1, 1899.

SALMON P. CHASE

CHAPTER I

EARLY LIFE

IN the course of the sixty-five years of his life, from 1808 to 1873, the lot of Salmon Portland Chase was cast in many places. In his boyhood his family lived successively in two towns in New Hampshire, and he went to school and college in three others; as a lad he lived in Ohio, first in a village and then in a city; his earliest manhood and much of his senatorial term he spent in Washington; his professional years, in Cincinnati; his four years' service as governor, in Columbus; and during the last twelve years of his life he had his permanent home in or near Washington.

Few American public men have had so multifarious an experience, and few illustrate so many types of national character. Chase was endowed with a New England tradition of learning and statesmanship, a Western knowledge of the power of organization, and a national insight into the meaning of the American system of government. His abilities, courage, and good fortune gave him many opportunities to show his powers: as leader of the political abolitionists of Ohio from 1841 to 1849, as Ohio senator from 1849 to 1855, as governor of Ohio from 1856 to 1860, as secretary of the treasury from 1861 to 1864, and as chief justice of the United States from 1864 to 1873, he moved in the midst of great events, which he helped to make and to modify.

The Chase family was of the purest American stock. In 1660 Aquila Chase, an Englishman, came to Newbury, Massachusetts, and there built and commanded a ship. He left a son Moses, from whom sprang Daniel; and from Daniel, Samuel, who married Mary Dudley. Their son Dudley emigrated in 1763 from Sutton, Massachusetts, with his wife, Alice Corbett, and seven children, to the wilds of the upper Connecticut, and helped to found the new town of Cornish, named by the Chases for the English town or county from which their ancestors sprang. From the loins of Dudley sprang nine stout sons, of whom Ithamar, born in 1763, married Janet Ralston, daughter of a Scotch settler of Keene, and on January 13, 1808, became the father of Salmon Portland Chase.

Few families have given to their communities such a proportion of energetic leaders. Chase's father, Ithamar, was a man of substance, a farmer and small manufacturer, for years a stout Federalist and member of the governor's council. The most noted of the kindred were uncle Dudley, twice a United States senator, and uncle Philander, one of the most striking figures in the development of the West. The boy, Salmon, was heir to a noble tradition of learning, of public spirit, and of usefulness. Chase's birthplace, in what one of his friends once called "hill-ridden New Hampshire," lies in the last roll of the mountain billows which sweep from Monadnock and Kearsage down westward to the fertile river bottoms of the Connecticut. From these hill and valley towns have sprung numerous rugged men of affairs, who have made their fortunes in other States; and near by was Dartmouth College, nursery of many great men, and among them of Daniel Webster, with whom Chase once touched elbows for a few weeks in the Senate.

About 1816 his father removed to Keene, New Hampshire; but when the boy was nine years old the father died, leaving to his widow a slender property and ten children, the oldest of whom was a son of twenty-five years. The boy's education had already begun in 1816: a dame school; a district school in Keene; a better school in Windsor, Vermont, where he began Latin, a language which he always liked to quote; a tutor in Keene, with whom he began Greek, — under such training passed the years till 1820. At this time an influence came in which probably determined Chase's career: Uncle Philander appeared as the good genius of the family and took the boy out to his Ohio frontier bishopric "*in partibus*." Later generations know a great deal about the ruder side of the religious development of the West, — about camp-meetings and Peter Cartwright; they do not remember the gentle, more refined, yet upbuilding work of Bishop Chase and his coadjutors. He was poor as Jean Valjean's bishop, so that he almost envied a friend his "good fat living of $1000 a year as clerk in the Navy Department;" he had an official ecclesiastical income which did not pay his postage; yet he was a man who knew how to unite the secular with the religious, to carry on farms and mills side by side with his school and his churches.

In the bishop's school at Worthington, near Columbus, the boy simultaneously did farm work and studied Greek. Two years passed in monotonous life, for which the boy had no love. In 1822 Bishop Chase was appointed president of Cincinnati College. Evidently the requirements of Cincinnati College were not exacting, for the fifteen-year-old lad quickly became a sophomore. The bishop's new activity, however, gave him so little satisfaction that he resigned at the end of a year, and young Chase returned to his New England home in Keene. He never expressed any enthusiasm over his boyhood experience in the West, and the only important direct effect from it that can be traced is that it probably led him later to settle in Ohio.

On his return to New Hampshire, at sixteen years of age, the boy forthwith became a man, for he began to support himself, at least in part. One of many children, and much away from home, Chase felt his mother's influence less than most boys; but her shrewd and affectionate character is revealed in some letters of the period written to him. She struggled hard to get her children started in life, and in 1824 put Salmon into Dartmouth College. Entering as junior, he taught in country schools during the long winter vacations, and in 1826 he was graduated.

Dartmouth College was a wholesome school, in which young men studied a little classics, mathematics, and *belles-lettres*, and got good from each other and from the characters of their instructors. A fellow collegian of Chase said of it in 1826: "We meddled little with the history, government, or politics of our country; I think not enough to prepare us for the active side of life." Certainly none of Chase's college teachers seem to have impressed him, and of President Tyler there is not a mention in his reminiscences. Chase was only a moderate student and took no high rank in college. Of his private reading, the "Mysteries of Udolpho" was all that stood in his memory in after life. On the whole, his intellectual advantages were unusual for that time, and in the end he got an excellent education, though it came chiefly from men and books after he had left college; at least, throughout his life he had the enjoyment of academic brotherhood with men everywhere who had been stamped with the same collegiate training as his own.

The next step in his life was of especial consequence, for it was to make a cultivated man of the world out of the country boy. When he graduated he had already made up his mind to study law; but he could no longer accept his mother's sacrifices, and the readiest way to earn his living for the time was to teach school. Uncle Philander, like a genius of the lamp, appeared at the right moment to give him guidance and letters of introduction; and Chase went to Washington. There he had no better resource than to announce "a select classical school," for which but one pupil was entered. In discouragement he applied to his uncle, Senator Dudley Chase, to get him a government clerkship, and received a warning never to enter government service, with the offer of "fifty cents to buy a spade." The good bishop's letters were more serviceable, however, for through his influence Chase became the proprietor of an established boys' school, and for three years he was a schoolmaster.

By this time some of the habits of Chase's life were forming: fondness for good company; love of reading; a habit of letter-writing; interest in affairs; a share in the financial burdens of his family; acquaintance with public men; and the keeping of a diary. He even spoke to some friends of "a wonderful vision of meeting in the halls of legislation." Chase's later life was distinctly serious, for he was then absorbed in the moral side of existence, and in the hard, practical work of social and political organization. These three years in Washington, however, have an altogether different tone; the young man's writings are light and almost frivolous. Perhaps the episode of Parisian gayety in a Puritan life was chiefly due to the family of Chase's patron, nominal preceptor, and friend, William Wirt of Virginia, attorney-general of the United States. In Wirt's family were several lively daughters, whose Southern archness and banter were very agreeable to the young Yankee. In praise of two of them he published a poem, which was no worse than the stock material of the annuals of the day, and closed with fashionable gloom: —

> "Even so —
> I thought, and with the thought a heavy sigh
> Came from my inmost heart — must fade away
> All that the earth of the beautiful inherits,
> And so must these bright creatures pass from earth."

In the warmth of this delightful family, this "pure and gentle and refined and cultivated circle," the young man basked, and it was a keen disappointment to him when they left Washington in 1829, at the end of Wirt's term of office. All his life long he remembered Mr. Wirt, "one of the handsomest men and one of the completest gentlemen of his time;" and in the furious debates of 1854 in the Senate, Chase paid him a tribute as a type of the lovable slaveholder.

Through the Wirts, his uncle Dudley, and Henry Clay, Chase entered into the pleasant society of the national capital. The town was still raw, ugly, and unclean; but it was a period of much refined hospitality, and he was welcomed by members of the cabinet and at presidential levees. Thus he went to Secretary Porter's, where, as he notes, Daniel Webster tossed off a full glass of whiskey, supposing it to be wine; and he was invited to "the scene of ceremonious frivolity at Mr. Clay's." The picture of Washington society thus drawn in a contemporary diary is on the whole pleasing, and makes one wish that Mrs. Trollope could have had access to the Wirt household.

Chase's record of the political conditions of the time is interesting, and especially important because it covers the transition period from Adams to Jackson, as seen by the young schoolmaster. An early entry in his diary, under the date of January 28, 1829, is as follows: —

"As Mr. Adams was soon to go out of office, his last Drawing-room was numerously attended. . . . The whole avenue to the palace-door was filled with carriages of those who had arrived before us, and we had only the meagre satisfaction of not being the last of the train. Nearly fifteen minutes elapsed before we were able to reach the door. At length we were set at liberty and entered the house. An immense crowd was present. Three rooms were full of guests. Music was heard in the great, and yet unfurnished, East-Room, inviting the dancers to engage in the cotillion. Many accepted the invitation, and soon many light feet were tripping over the floor. At ten o'clock, the dance broke off, and the supper room was thrown open.

Long tables were spread in a spacious apartment, covered with everything that could please the eye or gratify the taste. They were soon surrounded by a crowd by no means reluctant to disburden them of their load. As each company was satisfied and departed, others filled the vacant places, and the banquet did not end until after eleven o'clock. Then the dance was resumed for a little while, until, one by one, the gay group diminished, when the music played 'Home, Sweet Home,' as a finale, and the pleasures of the evening were ended."

It was the fortune of the young observer, who was of course an Adams man, to see the first reception of another President, and to be shocked at the uproar in the White House after the inauguration of Jackson. A few weeks later he notes that a "more savage spirit breathes in the administration, and as a natural consequence distrust has come in place of confidence." Of Jackson himself Chase wrote, "In his manners, he is graceful and agreeable, and much excels his predecessor in the art of winning golden opinions from all sorts of men." Van Buren, whom Chase was ardently to support for President in 1848, seemed to him, in 1829, "cold, selfish, base, and faithless. May he never," he exclaims, "reach the golden reward to which he so vehemently aspires." Chase notes the universal belief that Van Buren was really responsible for the policy of removals from office; and he relates that one of his own acquaintance was informed by

Jackson that the President could not conscientiously remove an incumbent in order to make a place for the applicant.

Chase's opinion of several other public men deserves record. He thought it strange that John Randolph was "allowed to exercise his fantastic humors in the House without check and almost without rebuke — an aristocrat at heart, and disordered in intellect, the scorn of the wise; the laughing-stock of the gay, and the abhorrence of the good." Calhoun was "an unfortunate politician, yet a very good man. Few men in our party are gifted with more splendid abilities — all that he does and utters and imagines is marked by his grand, characteristic, impetuous energy." When he heard Webster for the first time, in an argument before the Supreme Court, he observed: "He states his case with great clearness, and draws his inferences with exceeding sagacity. His language is rich and copious; his manner dignified and impressive; his voice deep and sonorous; and his sentiments high and often sublime. He argues generally from general principles, seldom descending into minute analysis where intricacy is apt to embarrass and analogy to mislead. He is remarkable for strength rather than dexterity, and would easier rend an oak than untie a knot. If I could carry my faith in the possibility of all things to labor, so far as to suppose that any degree of industry would enable me to reach his height, how day and night should testify of my toils!"

While thus interested in political events and public men, young Chase was learning his own tastes and was taking in the social world about him. He listened to concerts and felt sure that he understood why he enjoyed them. He hobnobbed with artists. He visited the first completed two miles of the Baltimore and Ohio Railroad, and mused on the new system, which "removes the Alleghanies," and "makes Cincinnati and Baltimore neighboring cities." Sometimes he indulged also in the natural dreams of a gifted youth. "Knowledge may yet be gained," he writes, "and golden reputation. I may yet enjoy the consciousness of having lived not in vain. Future scenes of triumph may be mine."

Already the road to distinction had been chosen, for in 1827 he began to study law, ostensibly as a student of William Wirt, but really as a neglectful private reader. Neither his diary nor his later reminiscences conceal the fact that his law studies were scanty, and that his preceptor Wirt had asked him only one question in the two years of their relation. Indeed, Chase frankly admits that "very seldom had any candidate for admission to the bar presented himself with a slenderer stock of learning;" and after the ordeal was over he lamented that the cramming process "had given strength to a habit of superficial reading." When he presented himself for admission to the bar, kindly Justice Cranch demurred, either at the weakness of the preparation or at the shortness of the time of study; but he gave way, and thus, on December 14, 1829, Chase became a lawyer.

With his admission to the bar closed the first period of Chase's life. In twenty-two years he had developed a handsome though still awkward person, an observant mind, a habit of reflection, and a clear though still somewhat artificial style. In this formative period are seen already the foundations of the strong and versatile character of the later man. He worked hard, if spasmodically; he read a little; he showed perseverance, address, and devotion to principle; he held himself well in hand; and his most intimate correspondence shows him to have been upright without priggishness. He had had opportunities of education and culture such as came to few young men of that period; he had been among men who could impress his character. Out of it all he had brought a wholesome sense of his own deficiencies, expressed in somewhat exaggerated self-examination in the closing entry of his diary for 1829. "I am almost twenty-two, and have, as yet, attained but the threshold of knowledge. I have formed few settled opinions, and have examined but few subjects. The night has seldom found me much advanced beyond the station I occupied in the morning, and the end of the year has at length come round and finds me almost in the very spot I was in at its commencement. I have learned little, and have forgotten much, and, really, to conclude of the future from the past, I almost despair of making any figure in the world."

CHAPTER II

THE WESTERN LAWYER

According to the statement of Chase himself, the argument which induced Justice Cranch to admit him to the bar was his declaration: "I have made all my arrangements to go to the Western country and practice law." As early as July, 1826, while he was still in college, a friend in Cincinnati wrote, advising him against a place where there were "about sixty lawyers, about thirty ministers, and doctors without number." In February, 1830, Judge Burnet, of Cincinnati, senator from Ohio, rather faintly counseled him to settle in Cincinnati, with the remark: "On the whole it offers to you stronger inducements than any other place in the West." With large expectations and a little money Chase left Washington in March, 1830, to make his fortune in the golden West.

The choice of Cincinnati as the place for the development of a young and ill-trained lawyer was of course influenced by Chase's Ohio relatives and boyhood experiences, but he sought it chiefly because he believed that it offered the largest opportunity for brains and ambition. It was no longer a rude frontier town, but the largest city in the

West, apparently destined to be the metropolis of the Mississippi Valley, on the axis of Eastern and Western commerce, and a terminus for important and growing trade from North to South. The Cumberland road to Wheeling and Zanesville and the road to Pittsburg across southern Pennsylvania were the great Western highways of the time; and from Pittsburg and Wheeling navigation reached to Cincinnati, St. Louis, St. Paul, and New Orleans. The Northwest was then an undeveloped section, far behind the Ohio River settlements.

Of all the cities of the West the most individual and the most foreign was Cincinnati. On the contracted plain above the high-water mark lay the business district; the rest of the city and suburbs straggled up over the confused hills, everywhere flanked by walls of squared limestone. Among the twenty-five thousand people of Cincinnati in 1830 were to be found four different elements, which were slowly and unwillingly combining in a common life: the Southerner, the New Englander and Middle State man, the foreigner, and the negro. The Southern element was on the whole the most numerous, for all the lower counties of Ohio, Indiana, and Illinois had a large number of Southern settlers, and in Cincinnati itself there were many people of distinctly Southern habits of mind. Indeed, in many respects Cincinnati was a Southern city on free soil: the Southern buyer gladdened the heart of the merchant; the Southern traveler and his family took the best rooms in the hotels;

and in times of crisis Southern sympathy for slavery was visible in the newspapers. New Englanders were numerous and contended for their familiar standards of education and intellectual life; but they were not here, as in northern Ohio, the dominant element. Foreigners had begun to straggle in; and Cincinnati became an early place of settlement for Germans, through whom, about 1825, the culture of the grape was introduced. The negro population was only about one fifteenth of the whole, but it was a source of some perplexities, for besides the influx of negroes from other Northern communities, free to shift for themselves, there was an infusion of freed slaves from Kentucky, and even of runaways.

Commercially Cincinnati was a place of growing importance. The artery which kept the city prosperous was the Ohio River, which in modern railway circles is said to be shallow and uncertain, but in 1830 was a natural street, for which pious travelers thanked the Almighty, even though a voyage from Pittsburg to Cincinnati might take a week. Besides having the direct river trade, Cincinnati was already becoming the centre of a rich countryside, and the exchange point for Northern and Southern products. On the north, however, the means of communication were still so poor that even so late as 1839 a traveler leaving Cincinnati on Thursday reported that he arrived at Columbus, a hundred miles away, on Monday. Canals from Portsmouth to Cleveland and from Cincinnati to Dayton were now almost completed; but not till the railroad came, in the early fifties, was Cincinnati really united to the shores of Lake Erie. Toward the south, however, it was otherwise. The navigable branches of the Ohio — the Kanawha, Licking, Kentucky, Cumberland, and Tennessee — gave access to Kentucky and the country farther south; and Cincinnati was already becoming a favorite supply point for provisions, especially for hog products. There was also some manufacturing, — in cotton, lumber, and machinery, — which cheap coal was later to develop.

The social life of Cincinnati has been much misrepresented by Mrs. Trollope's "Domestic Manners of the Americans." However accurately that author described the life which she saw, the diaries and letters of Chase, then living in the city, show that there was much which she did not see. To the mind of the cultivated Englishwoman, dirty streets, tobacco chewing, and the coarseness of a frontier town seemed incompatible with refined society; but such a society there was, and Chase at once found a share in it. In a few months he was the welcome friend of the Burnets and the Longworths, the social leaders in the city.

The first duty of the newcomer was to establish himself in his profession, and within four years and a half he had taken his place as one of the best and busiest lawyers in Cincinnati. During the first two years, however, progress was very slow. He was admitted to the Ohio bar in June, 1830, and in September set up his own office. He afterward said that his first client paid him half a dollar for drawing a deed, and the second client borrowed the half dollar and decamped.

It is a proof of the strength of character of the young man that this period of growth into his profession is also the period of greatest intellectual progress in his whole life: he read, he reflected, he analyzed, he pondered upon religion, he lectured, he wrote articles, he projected a literary magazine, and he began the only formal publication of his whole career. Chase was throughout his life a great reader, though in a rather haphazard fashion. But to read and reflect was not enough for the active young man; hence in the fall of 1830 he took a large part in founding the Cincinnati Lyceum, a system of popular lectures much like that of the modern "Institutes" in the great cities, to which he proposed to add the illustration of scientific discoveries by simple experiments; but only that part of the scheme which provided for lectures was carried out.

Of these lectures, Chase himself delivered four; and he was thus led directly to his first literary venture, the publication in the "North American Review" of two of his lectures, "The Life and Character of Henry Brougham" (July, 1831), and "Effects of Machinery" (January, 1832). The impulse to this latter article appears in an entry in his diary of March 2, 1831: "Perused an article in the Ed. Rev. on the effects of Machinery and accumulation and about 50 pages of the Wealth of Nations and about a dozen pages of Say." The article is a good wholesome statement of the orthodox doctrine of the real advance resulting from machinery, with a special statement of those American conditions which take away the force of the argument against factory towns. "Machinery," says Chase, "substitutes bodies of iron with souls of steam to do the work of living men."

From contributor to editor was a step which Chase longed to take, and in 1832 he was busily writing to his friends in behalf of a scheme for a "Western Quarterly Review." The plan was heroic, in a region where there were almost no booksellers, but it was not unexampled. Timothy Flint had for a year or two been issuing his "Western Monthly Review," and James Hall at Vandalia was editing an "Illinois Magazine and Western Souvenir." Some effort was made to consolidate these ventures, but the project lacked support, and the only result seems to have been that Hall gave the name of "Western Monthly Magazine" to his periodical in its later form of 1833–36.

The only literary careers in the thirties in which a man could make a living in the West were journalism and the writing of law books. For newspaper work Chase had some early inclination, and to some of the local papers he occasionally sent short unsigned articles or editorials. Law books, however, came more directly in the line of his profession; hence in September, 1832, he formed the project of publishing a collection of the laws of Ohio, for the use of lawyers and courts. The state judges took an interest in the plan, and lent him their aid; and he reprinted in his three volumes all the public acts in the four volumes of "adopted laws" for the Northwest Territory, the four volumes of territorial enactments, and the thirty-one volumes of state laws. He added abundant notes and references, and his "Laws" at once became the standard edition. Unfortunately, the legislature would buy only a hundred and fifty copies, and Chase's rewards were probably not over a thousand dollars for his immense labor; but the work at once gave him a solid reputation throughout the West. Chancellor Kent and Justice Story, in personal letters of much warmth, testified to its value and its learning.

From the beginning it had been Chase's intention to prefix to the "Laws" a brief historical sketch of Ohio, and the resulting forty pages remain one of the best accounts of the early constitutional history of the Northwest Territory and of the commonwealth of Ohio. The historical matter is sound; there are references to some sources, and a successful effort to choose the really interesting and significant events. The Ordinance of 1787 had already been the subject of a long disquisition in Chase's diary, in July, 1831, and his careful discussion of it in his historical sketch did much to call attention to its historical importance. The history is a plain, straightforward story, with little comment, for the editor avoided political and controversial questions; hence the book gives little indication of Chase's opinions. One of the few subjects on which the future governor of Ohio takes ground, however, is the administration of St. Clair in the Northwest, which afforded him opportunity for expressing his satisfaction that "the veto power, that anomaly in republican government, is not recognized by the Constitution of the State of Ohio." As a whole, the history shows Chase full of the spirit of historical investigation, and possessed of an unusual power of statement. He had the qualities of a good historian,—truth, patience, accuracy, impartiality, discernment, an interesting method, and a readable style.

Soon after the publication of the Ohio statutes, Chase married. The frank diary of a susceptible young man of twenty-two is certain to record much to vex the same man at forty and to amuse him at sixty. Chase was fond of the ladies, and liked to call on them and to tell his diary what he thought of them. A frequently recurring name is that of Catherine Jane Garniss, a young lady about three years Chase's junior. After a leisurely courtship they were married, March 4, 1834; on December 1, 1835, she died, leaving him a little girl, who lived only four years longer. To the very end of his life the statesman recalled with tenderness this wife of his youth, who seemed so well suited to be his helpmeet. The desolation of the young father intensified a strong religious feeling, to which he gave frequent expression in public and in his diary: the Puritan habit of withdrawal and meditation awoke in him; he constantly reviewed his own life, upbraided his few failings, and set himself forward in a new effort. Sincerity and uprightness speak out from the anguish of these months.

Four years later, September 26, 1839, Chase married his second wife, Eliza Ann Smith, of Cincinnati, then a girl of eighteen. Of the three children whom she bore to him, his daughter Kate (later Mrs. Sprague) was the only one who lived; and Mrs. Chase was taken from him September 29, 1845. She was a refined woman, who had much influence in moderating in her husband a tendency to harshness and aggressiveness; but it is evident that she had little connection with the exciting professional and political career in which Chase was busied during their whole married life.

A third marriage took place November 6, 1846, with Sarah Bella Dunlop Ludlow. This connection was in many respects different from the others. In the first place, Miss Ludlow belonged to one of the best-known families in Cincinnati, her grandfather, Israel Ludlow, having been one of the founders of the city; by the marriage of his wife's sister to Randall Hunt, of New Orleans, Chase gained a useful insight into Southern conditions; and his wife brought some property with her. Mrs. Chase was a woman of much dignity and force of character, showing a beautiful tenderness toward her husband, and sharing in his public life, though much of the time too ill to go about with him. She also brought him into close relations with her own anti-slavery family, and especially with her uncle by marriage, John McLean, later an associate justice of the United States Supreme Court. Two children were born to them, of whom the only one that lived was Jeanette Ralston (later Mrs. Hoyt). On June 13, 1852, Chase was again bereft of his wife, having thus in seventeen years stood at the biers of three wives and five children; thenceforward he lived a widower to the end.

While the sorrows of life thus descended upon Chase, his professional reputation steadily increased. In April, 1832, he was received into partnership on equal terms by General Edward King, and Timothy Walker, afterward author of the well-known "American Law." Seven months later Chase entered into a partnership with D. J. Caswell, the importance of which lay in the fact that Caswell was solicitor for the Cincinnati agency of the Bank of the United States, and divided this valuable employment with Chase. In July, 1834, he withdrew from Caswell, retaining the business of the Bank of the United States on his own account; and in November he was made the solicitor of the Lafayette Bank. These important trusts gave him so lucrative a practice that his literary pursuits were gradually thrust into the background, and finally ceased.

The estimates of Chase as a lawyer differ widely: to enthusiastic anti-slavery men he was a great lawyer because he made out so plausible a constitutional argument on their side; to the practitioner he seemed a very able and effective attorney, but by no means at the head of the Ohio bar. He prepared his cases with great care, sometimes making briefs on both his own and his opponent's side. Once in court, he made an impression by the force of his clear statement, but not by any impassioned appeal; in fact, he is said to have broken down on his first important argument; and he never had the art of winning over a reluctant jury. His learning was not great in this period of his life, and he depended on luminous principles rather than on authorities. As one of his friends puts it, "Chase was not a great lawyer, but a great man who had a knowledge of law."

To carry on his multifarious practice, Chase early felt the need of a partner who should take office work and detail. He first associated himself with Samuel Eels, in the firm of Chase & Eels; but in 1838 they separated, and Chase took up Flamen Ball, a man who had failed in business, had then studied law in Chase's office, and was now made a partner. As Chase from this time on was much away from home on legal or political business, Ball took most of the office work, for which he had some talent; but he was much inferior to Chase in abilities, character, and habits, and at times was very neglectful of the firm's business. In 1848, when Chase went to Washington, Horace Wells was taken into the new firm of Chase, Ball &

Wells; in February, 1849, George Hoadly was made a partner, under the firm name of Chase, Ball & Hoadly.

From about 1834, when Chase had gained a reputation as a lawyer, he always had in his office one or more law students. At that period law schools were few and feeble, and the approved method of legal education was to go into a lawyer's office, do his drudgery, read his books, and pick up crumbs of his wisdom. To Chase, however, the relation was much more serious than that of teacher to pupil, or of man of affairs to an unpaid employee: he felt a genuine interest in these able young men, cultivated their friendship, impressed them with his strong personality, and sent them out into the world to be good lawyers,—and to be "Chase men." Nothing more plainly speaks the real sanity and strength of Chase's character than the later success of many of these men in law and in public life. Among them were George Pugh, supporter of Chase for the Senate in 1849, and in 1855 his political rival and the successor to his seat; Stanley Matthews, Chase's confidential agent in the legislature of 1849, later senator from Ohio and justice of the United States Supreme Court; William M. Groesbeck, member of Congress from Ohio in 1857–59; Chase's nephew, Ralston Skinner, an officer in the Civil War; Edward L. Pierce, of Massachusetts, a strong anti-slavery man, and an official of the Treasury Department under Chase's secretaryship, later the biographer of Charles

Sumner; James Monroe, an Oberlin abolitionist, later sent as consul to Rio by Chase's influence, and afterward member of Congress; George Hoadly, judge of a superior court of Cincinnati, governor of Ohio, and the most eminent lawyer who ever came under Chase's influence; Jacob D. Cox, lawyer, historian, governor of Ohio, and Secretary of the Interior.

It was a fine thing to be patron and inciter to such spirits, but there was another side to this relation: with genuine love for his young friends, Chase expected that they would some day reciprocate his kindness, and he felt entitled to lay out for them a political future which would contribute to his own advancement. The testimony of several of them is that they felt a pressure put upon them to subordinate their plans to Chase's judgment; a few of them broke loose from him and eventually turned up on the other side of politics. Pierce wrote to him in 1856: "I have been in company with prominent men more than the majority of young men of my age, but at the same time have looked after my own independence, and avoided the appearance of being any one's parasite." Yet, though Chase's old students were sometimes his opponents, they were never his enemies, and those who are now living still carry for him a feeling of warm, admiring gratitude. Upon his own political fortunes these relations with young men were not altogether happy, for his urgency lost him the cordial aid of some of the strongest of these friends, and hence at critical times he was compelled to rest upon weaker men, whose counsel was not always wise or disinterested.

Chase's legal practice was chiefly commercial; he did, it is true, assist the State to prosecute the murderer Gedney in 1836; but outside of the famous fugitive slave cases it was not his lot to be concerned in any great causes. His argument in the telegraph case of *O'Reilly* v. *Morse*, in 1853, is said to have persuaded Taney to alter the received doctrines of patent law; but the court afterwards returned to its former ground.

The details of the business of Chase and Ball reveal a curious and interesting commercial system. All lawyers see the seamy side of life, but perhaps few knew so much as they of the intricacies of State banking, of the effects of "wild-cat" bank notes, of the difficulty of realizing on any real-estate collateral, of the devices to shore up the credit of despairing merchants, of the years necessary to straighten out the affairs of a debt-ridden estate. Few firms have less to fear from an examination of their records; in the recesses of his most intimate correspondence with his partner, Chase appears an upright man, an honest lawyer, and a faithful trustee. In 1841 Chase lost his valuable connection with the estate of the Bank of the United States, because his fees were considered too high, and the flood tide in the affairs of Chase and Ball seems to have been reached in 1845, when the firm's annual income was nearly ten thousand dollars.

It was perhaps this familiarity with banks and banking which caused Chase himself to become a man of affairs. In December, 1845, he figured out his debts at about eleven thousand dollars, against which he had holdings of undivided real estate, partly his own, partly in trust for his children; and with his good professional income and his rents he should speedily have cleared up his obligations. Instead, he held to his real estate, dribbling out taxes from year to year, and renewing his notes as they came due. At the end of twenty years of practice he had probably accumulated a net property of twenty thousand dollars, but he was still renewing his own paper. Had Chase cared to make corporation law the chief business of his life, he must have become rich, for he had the qualities of a great railroad lawyer and manager; but he gradually took up two interests which withdrew him from his regular practice, and kept him a comfortably poor man, — he threw himself into the unpopular anti-slavery movement, and he went into politics as the Ohio leader of the Liberty Party.

CHAPTER III

ANTI-SLAVERY IN OHIO

MANY of the States of the Union include two communities of widely different origin, interests, and standards; but even the upper and lower peninsulas of Michigan are not more diverse now than were northern Ohio and southern Ohio in the two decades from 1830 to 1850. The reason was very simple: the two great arteries of travel from the seacoast to the Northwest were by the Potomac valley and over the highlands of southern Pennsylvania to the Ohio River, and through the Mohawk valley and highlands of New York to Lake Erie. Over the southern road came settlers from the States of Maryland, Virginia, Delaware, even North Carolina; and immigrants through the ports of Baltimore, Alexandria, and Norfolk. By the northern route came New Englanders and their allies of central New York. Even the land grants were divided between North and South: to Connecticut fell the strip along the south side of Lake Erie, the so-called "Western Reserve" and "Fire Lands;" to Virginia were left the Military Bounty Lands in southern-central Ohio. The State was also the shortest bridge between the slave-holding territory of Virginia and Kentucky and the free shores of Canada. The northern counties knew negroes chiefly as panting fugitives; the southern counties looked across the river upon a mild form of negro slavery, and themselves had a plentiful sprinkling of freemen of the negro race. The northern counties turned eastward for their markets and their stocks of goods, while southern trade was the support of many communities on the Ohio River. It was inevitable that there should be jealousy and antagonism within the State, and that the rivalry of interests should some day find expression in politics; fortunately there were on the southern border a few men like Chase, who shared in the antagonism to slavery, and who eventually created a common political standpoint for both sections of the State.

It must not be forgotten that the negro question in Ohio was never extraneous, as it was in Massachusetts and Vermont. However little one might feel responsibility for slaves in Kentucky, it was impossible to dodge questions of the free-negro population in Ohio; and the majority of the people in the State liked that element as little as it was liked in the South. In 1830 there were about 7500 negroes in Ohio, of whom 2200 were in Cincinnati, and most of the others in towns. Most of the adults had been born slaves, had bought or received their freedom, and had then come across the borders, hoping to find better opportunity for themselves and their children than in the slave

States; but they were at the bottom of the communities from which they came, and most of them remained in a despised and degraded class in Ohio.

The general policy of the States on both sides of the river was to prevent such people from changing their domicile. In 1807 the Ohio legislature passed a stringent law for the registration of the free negroes, requiring them to give bonds that they would not become a public charge, and subjecting them to exclusion from the State if the security were refused or neglected; at the same time, any person who harbored an unregistered free negro was liable to a large fine. This law remained a dead letter, partly from the difficulty of administration, but chiefly because the community needed hewers of wood and drawers of water and seethers of flesh and fullers of fine linen; and when it came to the point, Cincinnati, like every Southern community which has ever faced the problem, preferred the free negro to no negro at all.

Under the constitution of Ohio, negroes were as a matter of course excluded from voting, and by statutes similar to those of all slave-holding, and of some free, States, they were put in a position of painful legal inferiority: thus their testimony could not be received against white persons, even to corroborate white witnesses; they had no right to public education, even though they paid school taxes; and where law did not reach, public sentiment came in, to prevent white people from employing colored mechanics, to keep the negroes out of the best quarters of the cities, and to prevent any kind of social intercourse.

The negro population was of various kinds. Many of the negroes had lost, or had never possessed, legal proofs of their freedom; many others knew that they were fugitives, and of these a considerable number were slowly buying their freedom. Indeed, a theological student is known to have provided for his education from the installments thus paid by a man for his own flesh, and to have charged the poor negro twelve per cent on deferred payments; and a negro child in a charitable school excused her absence by explaining, "I 'm staying at home to help buy father." Hence when, in 1829, an attempt was made in Cincinnati to enforce the registration law of 1807, the colored people in extremity sent a committee to see whether homes could be found in Canada. But before the emigration could be arranged, a mob descended upon them, and there were street fights, in which some of the assailants were killed. Eventually fright drove out 1100 of the 2200 negroes in the city, of whom many went to Canada. The whole incident is a proof that the prejudices against the negro race were as strong on the north bank of the Ohio as on the south, and that the ordinary principles of the right to labor, of movement from place to place, and of legal privileges did not apply to men and women of dark skins.

Side by side with the manifest distaste of the people of Ohio for free negroes stood the entire willingness of certain inhabitants, black and white, to harbor and aid fugitive slaves. The Ohio River was a barrier easily to be passed by anybody who could paddle a skiff, and on the northern side there had been, ever since 1787, forerunners of what came later to be called the "Underground Railroad." By the Ordinance of 1787, the right of masters to recover their slaves from the Northwest Territory was affirmed; by the Constitution, that right was to be continued in every State admitted to the Union; and by the federal statute of 1793 the method of search was defined. This statute recognized the right of a master, or of his agent, to lay hands upon his fugitive, found anywhere in a free State, and *proprio motu* to drag him back, provided any magistrate held that the person arrested was the escaped slave. It provided for no system of testimony, allowed no jury to determine even the question of identity, made no promise that the courts of the slave State should examine questions of disputed freedom, and gave the master the powers of an officer of the law in a State of which he was not a citizen. The statute was anomalous, because the existence of free and slave States in the same Union was an anomaly; it provided no proper security for the actual rights of free negroes, because those rights were little respected anywhere; and it ignored the fact that, while in the South the presumption was that a wandering negro was a slave, in the North the presumption in every case was that he was a freeman.

From the date of the Act of 1793 it proved useless in the New England States. The first case in Massachusetts, arising in that very year, led to a violent rescue in open court; and in 1796 President Washington was informed that he could not safely set the machinery of the law in motion to recover a slave woman from Portsmouth, N. H. In the States bordering on slave-holding regions the law had more force. In Pennsylvania, Ohio, Indiana, and Illinois fugitive-slave cases were common, and usually the seizure was unresisted. But many masters lost the trail, or would not go to the trouble and expense of pursuit; and there were many negroes (like an "Uncle Tom" whom the writer remembers in northern Ohio) who were well known in the whole countryside to be fugitives. The legal question was further complicated by the fact that the Ohio River was part of a direct highway from Virginia and Maryland to the far South, and that negroes in transit were often brought into ports on the Ohio side of the channel; hence the question might fairly be raised whether such persons were "fugitives."

By the operation of the Black Laws, by propinquity to slave-holding territory, and by the object lesson of fugitive slaves, the people of Ohio were compelled to know something of the institution and to take some responsibility for it. Both as a question of morals and as a question of political liberty, the startling contrast between slavery and Christian American civilization inevitably came before men's minds, and the result was the anti-slavery agitation, which swiftly developed into an abolition movement. Not only was Ohio a free State, it had never had any other than a free organization. The Ordinance of 1787, secured by Massachusetts men who desired to found a colony on the principles with which they were familiar, but also passed with the assent of every Southern member present, provided that "there shall be neither slavery nor involuntary servitude in the said Territory, otherwise than in the punishment of crimes whereof the party shall have been duly convicted." This clause did not apply to slaves already in the Territory; but, fortunately, as yet the only slaveholders in the Northwest were a few French settlers and some Southern squatters; and the slaves held in 1787 gradually died off, so that in 1840 slaves appear for the last time in the census list for Ohio. The state constitution of 1802 repeated the phrase of the Ordinance, with the result that there was, and could be, no state statute authorizing any person to restrain another of his liberty on the ground that he was a "slave," unless he had "fled" from "another State" and was "found" in Ohio.

From 1775 to 1830 the opinion of most thoughtful statesmen, North and South, was that slavery was a great evil, which good men ought to discountenance; and there was in most States of the Union some kind of organization which opposed slavery, with much the same feeling with which reformers might now oppose child labor. An anti-slavery society, founded at Ripley, Ohio, probably before 1810, continued to exist for more than twenty years; and so late as 1820 national anti-slavery conventions were held, usually in Southern States, and sent out appeals against the system, and memorials to Congress. The feeling on this subject was not very different in Ohio and Kentucky, and freedom of speech in criticism of slavery was about as great in one community as in the other. It was the Missouri Compromise debate of 1820 which roused the country to the fact that insensibly slavery had become so profitable that the South held it an unfriendly act to limit its extension. In that great contest the Ohio delegation in Congress was on the side of freedom for Missouri, but eventually consented to the Compromise.

Between 1820 and 1830 a change of feeling was visible in the South: instead of keeping to the view of men like Jefferson that slavery was an evil, and eventually must disappear, the trend of opinion was toward the doctrine that slavery was unfortunate, but could not be ended without ruin to the whole community. The next step, consciously taken only after the abolition movement gained headway, was to defend slavery as a good thing in itself. Slowly the idea gained ground in the North that slavery would not die a natural death, and that it behooved the friends of freedom to organize. An apostle of anti-slavery was found in Benjamin

Lundy, who worked in Tennessee and Missouri, organized an anti-slavery society in Ohio in 1817, and in 1821 began to publish his "Genius of Universal Emancipation" in that State. Other Ohio societies were founded in southern and southeastern counties, and the movement for an organized protest never wholly died out. In 1824 the Ohio legislature even passed resolutions in favor of emancipation.

Except for repeated attempts to get rid of slavery in the District of Columbia, there was between 1820 and 1830 no widespread Northern interest either in the attack on slavery or in its defense. William Lloyd Garrison took upon himself in 1831 the task of compelling his countrymen to face the question, and his success not only proved his own tremendous intensity, but also showed that thousands of men all over the country were aroused already and only waited for the kindling spark. Garrisonian abolition, however, always had three disadvantages: its seat was in a commonwealth not much affected by actual slavery; it was conducted almost entirely by men born in free States; and it abjured political action. Although Garrison made addresses in Ohio, his influence in the anti-slavery movement in the West was not direct, but was exerted through his disciples. Once aroused, the Ohio abolitionists had three powerful advantages: they knew the benumbing effect of slavery in neighboring States; they might call in the aid of anti-slavery men who had been slaveholders; and they did not underrate the method of political organization.

Most accounts of the slavery contest have been written by New England men, to whom the word "abolitionist" has brought up chiefly the figures of Garrison and Wendell Phillips; but instead of "the abolition movement" there were three different movements, working rarely together, though usually side by side, — New England abolition, Middle-State abolition, and Western abolition. The third, or Western, movement was from the beginning the most effective, because it was brought face to face with the actualities of slavery, and because it used political means to destroy the traces of the accursed system in its own communities.

From 1831 to 1835 the abolitionists in Ohio, as well as those elsewhere, were learning to forge their weapons for the tremendous task which they had undertaken. The movement would have had no more vitality than the contemporary anti-Masonic episode, but for one of those inherent weaknesses in slavery which were ultimately to set at naught the counsels of the ungodly. Upon the face of things, a man might say in Massachusetts or in Ohio that slavery was wrong, or even that slaveholders were criminals, as freely as he might say that judicial torture in China was wrong, or that the serf-owners of Russia were criminals; and an American citizen had as much right to petition for the abolition of slavery in the District of Columbia as for regulation of immigrant vessels. Indeed, the spirit and the letter of the laws all over the country allowed peaceable public meetings and criticisms by speakers and newspapers, even though acrid things were said about neighbors in other States. In the case of slavery, however, such attacks were held to destroy the value of property, and — what was even more serious — they tended to make the slaves discontented; moreover, it was generally believed in the South that they must lead to slave insurrections. None of these dangers dismayed the abolitionist; if free speech and slavery could not live in the same federal Union, that fact was to his mind an additional reason for giving up slavery, while to the startled slaveholder it seemed a reason for abolishing free speech.

In Ohio there was from 1830 to 1849 a specific objective point for the abolitionists in the repeal of the Black Laws, attainable by action of the legislature; but even in that State the main issue for some years was simply the right of a man to express his sentiments on a public question under protection of the state laws. Two centres of abolition agitation were speedily developed, one in the Connecticut Western Reserve in northern Ohio, and the other in and about Cincinnati. In that city was a group of the most powerful enemies who could be raised up against slavery, — sons of Southern slaveholders, or themselves former slaveholders, who out of their own experience had come to hate slavery and to fight it. Among them were Rev. Samuel Crothers; Dr. John Rankin, long pastor at Ripley on the Ohio, and agent of the Underground Railroad; the two Dickeys; Wallace; and the Quaker, Levi Coffin. There was also a group of men born or domiciled in Ohio, who hated slavery on their own responsibility, and early joined forces with the immigrants from the South.

What was now needed was agitation, organization, and persecution; and in 1834, 1835, and 1836 southern Ohio saw all these; and influences were then set at work which eventually drew Chase into the anti-slavery ranks. In 1829, at Walnut Hills, a new suburb of Cincinnati, Lane Seminary was founded, for the training of young men for the Presbyterian ministry. Of the one hundred students, more than half were Southerners; but the president was Lyman Beecher of Connecticut; his son-in-law, Stowe, was associated with him as professor, and one of the instructors was Theodore D. Weld of Massachusetts, who had brought a body of students from Oneida Institute, New York. Weld had already come under the influence of Garrison, and had thus become an intense abolitionist. In 1833 the young men of the Seminary began to talk on slavery as a natural topic of discussion, of special interest to the communities from which they came. In 1834 the two forces joined issue in a debate in the chapel, which lasted eighteen consecutive nights; a former slave was allowed to give his testimony, and the exciting discussion closed with the decision of some of the Southern students, notably Allan and Thome, that they were thenceforth enemies to slavery. Works went hand in hand with faith; the students began to start Sunday and day schools for negro children at Cincinnati, and to bring a pressure to bear on religious organizations.

This dangerous crisis was promptly met by the Trustees. In August, 1834, they voted that there should thenceforth be no discussion of slavery in any public room of the seminary, because it was a "political" subject; and they dropped John Morgan, one of the anti-slavery men, who had been principal of the preparatory department. One of the Trustees, Rev. Asa Mahan, at once resigned, but Beecher and Stowe were absent, and hence for the time accepted the situation. Not so the students, of whom fifty-one left the seminary in a body. Where were they to go? James C. Ludlow, whose daughter Chase married in 1846, lent them a building near the city, in which for five months they taught themselves, with the aid of some lectures by Dr. Bailey, who about this time became Chase's intimate friend. Thus the effort to save the seminary from the evil effects of controversy had led only to disruption. When, the next year, one of these students, Amos Dresser, was found in Tennessee with abolition documents in his possession, he was seized by a mob and brutally whipped; but this incident only called wider public attention to the troubles of Lane Seminary, and was a stock example of the barbarity of the system of slavery.

Meanwhile, in northern Ohio, a place was preparing for an anti-slavery seminary which might receive the Lane seceders and plant a new abolition stronghold. In 1833 it entered the minds of Rev. John J. Shipherd of Elyria, Ohio, twenty-five miles west of Cleveland, and Philo P. Stewart, manufacturer of cooking-stoves, to found in the backwoods of Ohio a Christian commonwealth, with "as perfect a community of interest as though we had a community of property." They deliberately chose a spot remote from other villages, in the township of Russia, and there in April, 1833, they set up the first house in Oberlin, so named from a philanthropic pastor of the Vosges Mountains. In December, 1833, a school was founded with forty-four students, under the name of "Oberlin Collegiate Institute," which, like many academies of the time, undertook to carry pupils "from the infant school up through a collegiate and theological course."

At the very beginning the founders took a pioneer step in college education by setting forth as a purpose of the institution "the elevation of female character by bringing within the reach of the misjudged and neglected sex all the instructive privileges which hitherto unreasonably distinguished the leading sex from theirs." The education of negroes, or even of anti-slavery agitators, was not a part of the original plan; but Mr. Shipherd was aroused by the news from Lane Seminary, went to Cincinnati, and reported, in December,

1834, that they must engage as professors Rev. Asa Mahan, and Morgan, the dismissed instructor; adding that those men would come to Oberlin only on condition that students should be admitted "irrespective of color."

There was an uproar in Oberlin, with many threats of withdrawal from the community and the school. There were as yet few, if any, out-and-out abolitionists in the place, and the Trustees at first voted not to take action which would put Oberlin on a different footing from other schools in Ohio. In a second meeting, however, they voted: "That the education of the people of color is a matter of great interest, and should be encouraged and sustained in the institution." Thereupon Mahan accepted the presidency and Morgan a professorship, and with them came thirty of the Lane seceders, including Amos Dresser, while others went to Western Reserve College. The school rapidly increased, though of two hundred and seventy-seven students in 1835 only one was colored. Theodore D. Weld now came to Oberlin as an abolitionist lecturer and converted the doubters, and from that time to the end of the Civil War, Oberlin was a radiating point for an incessant abolition propaganda. The Lane students and their successors went out as apostles all over the State; they lectured, they preached, they wrote, they endured persecutions; they scattered through the Northwest, and brought up their children to fight the slave power. In Oberlin the colored students became about a sixteenth of the whole number, and the colored population about a fourth; the place was a junction on the Underground Railroad, and a meeting-place for radical abolitionists; and since the Oberlinites never for a moment accepted Garrison's policy of non-intervention, they voted, and in 1848 their votes returned the man who came to hold the balance of power in the Ohio senatorial contest, and who cast his deciding ballot for Salmon P. Chase.

Oberlin was not the only anti-slavery centre of northern Ohio. For some years Elizur Wright and Beriah Green were professors in Western Reserve College at Hudson, — the Western Yale, — where they poured forth anti-slavery doctrine till they were compelled to resign. The Western Reserve was peopled chiefly by immigrants from Connecticut, a church-going and a reading folk, provided with good schools and able newspapers; hence the anti-slavery seed there fell upon good soil, and gradually there grew up a constituency massed in one congressional district, in which the anti-slavery men were predominant. From that district of the Western Reserve in 1838 came Giddings, the first Western anti-slavery member of the national House of Representatives; and he was steadily reëlected at every opportunity up to 1860.

The Lane Seminary and Oberlin movements came to a head early in 1835, and the next step was to form an organization of the anti-slavery men throughout the State. A state convention of more than one hundred delegates was held at Putnam in April, 1835, at which many of the Lane seceders were present, among them Weld, H. B. Stanton (later a life-long friend of Chase), and Horace Bushnell. The main work of the meeting was the foundation of the "Ohio Anti-Slavery Society," to be carried on in organic relation with the national society. Most of the few remaining old anti-slavery societies in Ohio affiliated themselves with the new society, and other auxiliaries were organized; so that at the end of the year there were a hundred and twenty societies, with more than ten thousand members. Another fruit of the meeting and the society was an able "Report on the Condition of the People of Color in the State of Ohio," which opened the eyes of the community to the character of the Black Laws.

No Cincinnati newspaper sympathized with the movement; hence the next step was to found a distinct abolition journal. At this point appears one of the most interesting figures in the whole Western abolition movement, James G. Birney, a Kentuckian by birth, once a slaveholder, who had by sheer force of his own conscience renounced the system and set free his remaining slaves. Birney felt that he understood the difficulties of slavery better than the Garrisonians did, and he planned an anti-slavery journal which should command respect by its studied moderation of tone and avoidance of hard language. Although a Kentucky state society was founded in 1835, he found it impossible to start his paper in that State; accordingly he crossed the river, and in 1836 set up the "Philanthropist" at a little town above Cincinnati; and the new state society afterward agreed to publish it in Cincinnati.

Precisely the issue was now made which caused the murder of Lovejoy at Alton in 1837, namely, the right to publish in a border town a paper censuring the institutions of the neighbor State; and substantially the same means were adopted to stop the paper as in Lovejoy's case. Cincinnati had at just that time, July, 1836, a number of Southern visitors, and it profited by Southern trade. Accordingly a public meeting was called to protest against the "Philanthropist." The mayor of the city presided, with various local dignitaries as vice-presidents, and resolutions were passed against the proposed paper. As this action had no effect, on July 12 the printing-office was broken into by a mob and badly damaged. The mayor issued a proclamation against the rioters, but he directed it also against the persistent abolitionists. Birney's rejoinder was to repair his press for the continuance of his paper. The next step, July 23, was a rousing anti-abolition meeting, which reprehended the violence of the abolitionists, and appointed a committee to advise Birney to desist. Judge Burnet, Lawrence (the president of the Lafayette Bank), and other friends of Chase accepted membership, and urged upon the executive committee of the Ohio society that such a paper was damaging to the city; not a single local newspaper defended the right of free speech or spoke out for its own inestimable privilege of a free press.

During the years of agitation in Ohio, and of especial excitement in Cincinnati, where was the ardent young New England lawyer, Chase? The question of slavery had several times come before his mind since he first went to Washington. The status of slavery in the District of Columbia was peculiar. Congress had never legislated directly on the subject, but by the act of 1801 had ordained that existing laws of all kinds were to continue in force till altered. Those existing laws included an elaborate slave code, which in the course of years was outgrown by the humanitarian spirit of Maryland, and therefore was modified by state statutes, but remained unamended in the District. Besides a system of Black Laws, like that of Ohio, there were also fierce punishments for slave offenses, such as hanging and quartering; and stray negroes taken up and unable to give a good account of themselves might be jailed for inquiry, and then sold for their jail fees. In 1828 humanitarian petitioners had for some years been pressing Congress to prohibit slavery in the District, and Chase was drawn into the agitation in a manner which he describes as follows: "One day a respectable Quaker, a mechanic, I think, called on me with a paper, or some scraps of paper containing the leading ideas for a petition to Congress for the gradual abolition of slavery in the District, and requested me to make out from them the draft of a petition for circulation. I complied cheerfully with his request. The petition was drawn and put in circulation, whether exactly as I drew it or after being modified by other hands I cannot say, and received over a thousand signatures from nearly all the leading men of the District of every station and occupation and was presented to Congress, I think in 1828."

Biographers and panegyrists of Chase have attempted to prove by this incident a moral interest which Chase never claimed for it; he acted simply as a clerk, and during the next seven years he gave no evidence that in his judgment the slavery question was vital. In 1829, after reading a speech delivered in the Virginia Constitutional Convention, which asserted that the laborers of the free States were no more intelligent than the slaves, and ought to have no more political privileges, he noted in his diary that such a sentiment was "utterly abhorrent to many people of equal rights." In 1830, in his article on Henry Brougham, he praises him as "the advocate of human liberty" and as "the able champion of the injured and downtrodden children of Africa;" and he even quotes with approval Brougham's appeal to "a law above all the enactments of human codes; . . . and by that law . . . they shall reject the wild and guilty fantasy that man can hold property in man." But Chase does not here put himself forward as an "advocate of liberty," and in June, 1831, he even critically discusses the Ordinance of 1787, with no word of praise for its anti-slavery clause. In his "History of Ohio," published in 1833, he again considers the Ordinance, but carefully avoids any controversy.

This is all the positive evidence that Chase had convictions on slavery earlier than 1836. In his diaries, his letter-books, and the many letters sent to him, not a word appears which shows that he had so much as heard of Garrison; the Lane Seminary episode passes unnoticed; the convention of 1835, the Oberlin contentions, the new state society, Birney's attempts to found the "Philanthropist," — all these were less important in his eyes than obtaining the use of public school rooms for Sunday-schools, or "brother William's debts."

Like thousands of other anti-slavery men, like John Quincy Adams, like Wendell Phillips, Chase was aroused not by the wrongs of the slave but by the dangers to free white men. He did not hear the cries at the Covington whipping-post across the river, but he could not mistake the shouts of the mob which destroyed Birney's property and sought his life; his earliest act as an anti-slavery man was to stand for the every-day right of a fellow resident of Cincinnati to express his mind. An autobiographical fragment, found among his papers, describes his conversion to positive anti-slavery.

"At this time I had come to regard the Slavery

question as among the most important questions of the day; and I was not long in discovering it to be the most important. I heard with disgust and horror the mob violence directed against the Anti-Slavery Press and Anti-Slavery men of Cincinnati in 1836. My own sister was the wife of one of the most worthy and respectable of these Anti-Slavery men, Dr. Isaac Colby. Through them I had become personally acquainted with most of them, though I did not at this time know Mr. Birney, the Editor of the Paper. I knew them to be as pure, upright, and worthy citizens as Cincinnati contained. Yet against these men and their families the fury of a mob, stirred up by politicians and by emissaries from slave States, was directed. My own sister left her house and took refuge in mine. I was opposed at this time to the views of the abolitionists, but I now recognized the slave power as the great enemy of freedom of speech freedom of the press and freedom of the person. I took an open part against the mob. Of the prominent citizens very few stood decidedly on that side. Charles Hammond, a man who had some faults and many virtues, among which last were true greatness of soul and intense horror of cowardice and meanness, was chief among these few. I drafted and he with others signed a call for a meeting of those opposed to mobs. He and I drafted the resolutions intended to be presented in the meeting: but when the hour came and we repaired to the Court House we found the mob there and a meeting organized. A committee was appointed and I was named upon it. In the Committee I read the resolutions we had prepared, but they were voted down, and others reported in their place which, under the circumstances, were justly regarded as approving rather than censuring the mob. Shortly after the meeting adjourned I was for a time in a good deal of personal danger in consequence of a declaration that I would sooner give ten thousand dollars than see the press destroyed by a mob. But my assailants contented themselves with denunciation, without proceeding to a personal attack. On the night of one of these days a mob gathered around the door of the Franklin House, determined to enter and make search for Mr. Birney. I stood in the doorway, and told them, calmly but resolutely, no one could pass. They paused. One of them asked who I was? I gave my name. One, who seemed a ringleader, said I should answer for this. I told him I could be found at any time. The mob did not choose to attack me in my position, and after a while, to my great relief, the Mayor, who had been in the House, came out and declared to the mob that Mr. Birney was not there, upon which they drew off.

"From this time on, although not technically an abolitionist, I became a decided opponent of Slavery and the Slave Power: and if any chose to call me an abolitionist on that account, I was at no trouble to disclaim the name. I differed from Mr. Garrison and others as to the means by which the Slave Power could be best overthrown and

Slavery most safely and fitly abolished under our American Constitution; not in the conviction that these objects were of paramount importance.

"In 1837 I first publicly declared my views in respect to Legislation under the Constitution for the Extradition of Fugitives from Service."

Chase's narrative plainly refers to the second Birney mob, of July 30–31, 1836, in which the office of the "Philanthropist" was sacked, and some negro houses were attacked. General William Birney, in his published life of his father and in personal conference with the writer, declares that Chase, together with his partner Eels, had visited James Birney in the previous year, 1835, and had even examined a title for him; and that his father by elaborate argument prepared Chase's mind to accept anti-slavery doctrine. That Chase had already known Birney is disproved by his own positive remembrance that he had no acquaintance with Birney before the mob. Nevertheless there can be no doubt that Birney's genial personality, conviction, and lucidity of statement, were the strongest, most direct, and most effective influences in bringing Chase to place himself decisively among the few score abolitionists of Cincinnati. That Chase would in the end have taken up the anti-slavery cause is probable; but from Birney proceeded the spark which kindled Chase's soul. General William Birney cannot be mistaken in his recollections of the long conferences in his father's library; Chase was Birney's counsel in the Matilda case in

1837, and thus publicly associated himself with the reformer; and a close examination shows that the constitutional arguments with which Chase smote the Amalekites were founded on Birney's theses, thought over in Chase's mind till he gave them his own stamp. Should other evidence be insufficient, a letter of June 5, 1837, from Birney to Chase, written before Chase had ever made any public profession of anti-slavery, shows how complete was the understanding between them. Birney writes confidentially, in accordance with a promise made to Chase to inform him of the anti-slavery outlook in the East. He tells of a visit to Newport and of Dr. Channing's agreement to join in the agitation; of his two hours' conversation with John Quincy Adams, who desired the support of the abolitionists in his protest against the annexation of Texas; and he urges Chase to stir up all the Cincinnati newspapers against that project. It is the cry of one soldier calling to another on the battlefield.

The instrument of Chase's conversion to anti-slavery was still not the ultimate cause. There must have been some deeper reason why Chase, just established in a pro-slavery community, should turn his back on his own apparent interests to take up a cause inexpressibly distasteful to most of the refined and educated people there — his acquaintances; and it is still more remarkable that he should have put himself out of relation with both the political cohorts which were about to become national political parties. The testimony of those who came closest to him is that he took up the anti-slavery cause because he felt it to be a religious duty, because he believed slavery to be a dreadful moral wrong. Ten years later, indeed, he was much concerned at the apathy shown toward slavery by the Episcopal church, of which he was a member; and all his writings and speeches throughout his life are permeated with the prime conviction that slavery can have no legal justification, not only because it is contrary to the laws of nature, but because it offends and outrages the laws of God.

CHAPTER IV

THE POLITICAL ABOLITIONIST

When a moral conviction was once established in Chase's mind, it never could be removed; but he was a man whose convictions grew upon him as time went on, and it was several years before he had worked out in his own mind the argument against slavery which should carry his principles into other minds. Once enlisted in the anti-slavery cause, he gave to it most of the twenty-four years of his life from 1837 to 1861.

Yet Chase never held himself to be an "abolitionist," but always insisted that he was an "anti-slavery man." In 1834 the Cincinnati "Gazette" said that he was "one of the most distinguished lawyers of the State and . . . not an abolitionist." In 1840 he declined to sign a call to an anti-slavery convention. In 1843 he "discussed with Mr. H. the principles of Liberty men as distinguished from abolitionists." In 1851 he said in the Senate: "I am aware there are some abolitionists or anti-slavery men who regard the Constitution as at war with moral obligations and the supreme law. I am not of them." His last speech on the Kansas-Nebraska Bill, in 1854, and his public utterances in 1855, indignantly disavowed any sympathy with the disunion sentiments of Garrison, a compliment which the "Liberator" and Edmund Quincy repaid in 1859, when they called him a "political huckster, who hopes to carry his principles to the presidential market." Gideon Welles, Chase's colleague in Lincoln's cabinet, says that Chase was sensitive at being considered a political abolitionist; and in a letter of 1863 Chase himself says of his attitude: "I never was an abolitionist of that school which taught that there could never be a human duty superior to that of the instant and unconditional abolition of slavery."

The distinction which Chase made had a logical ground and much political importance, so far as it related to that Garrisonian abolition which then as now was too often accepted as the type of abolition in general. It was a distinction perfectly clear-cut in the East, where John Quincy Adams always refused to be called an abolitionist, though for years the national champion against the slave power. If Garrison and Wendell Phillips were the typical genuine abolitionists, Chase was never an abolitionist: Garrison was for an aggressive warfare on slavery in the slave States; Chase was for warfare everywhere except in the slave States: Garrison kept himself and his followers out of politics; Chase was the great organizer of political anti-slavery: Garrison was for disunion so as to get relief from responsibility for slavery; Chase was for making the Union free so as to destroy the disease altogether.

On the great question of the immediate purpose of the abolition movement Chase was also at odds with the Garrisonians; and he thus expressed his dissent in a letter to Theodore Parker in 1856: "I adopt your motto very cheerfully and heartily, 'No slavery anywhere in America. No slavery anywhere on earth!' The latter is, you say, the 'topmost' idea. The first, then, is not topmost. My sentence, 'No slavery outside of the slave States,' also is not 'topmost.' But it is, to an earnest man, anxious to get to the top, quite as important. It is fundamental. The general government has power to prohibit slavery everywhere outside of slave States. A great majority of the people now accept this idea. Comparatively few adopt the suggestion that Congress can legislate abolition within slave States. . . . I say, then, take the conceded proposition and make it practical. Make it a living, active reality. Then you have taken a great step. Slavery is denationalized."

With the Ohio abolitionists, however, Chase sympathized and consorted; for they had a very practical knowledge of what slavery was, frequent occasion to exercise their abolition principles in aid of fugitives, and, above all, the robust intention of making their principles felt through the ballot-box. The Western abolitionists dealt less in invective than did their Eastern brethren, and more in expostulation, both because so many of them had been born on slave soil, and hence could appeal as repentant brothers to Southerners still out of a state of grace, and also because they knew better than did the New England agitators the real hopelessness of getting the South to act against its apparent economic interest. The Western men knew what they wanted as well as their Eastern friends, and seemed to know better how to get it: in their aims they were abolitionists like Charles Sumner; in their methods they were anti-slavery men like John Quincy Adams. But Joshua R. Giddings, their special representative in Congress, found himself the friend, associate, and ally of both Sumner and Adams; and in like manner Chase worked with out-and-out abolition leaders, like Birney and Samuel Lewis and Dr. Bailey and Levi Coffin, because they all had in view the same ends; and at the same time he stirred and organized many moderate anti-slavery men who never would go into an anti-slavery society, but who were willing to vote in a way to help the friends of liberty.

However Chase may have deprecated the term "abolitionist," his views on slavery were so advanced as to cost him friends and clients in Cincinnati. Several times he was assailed with stones or more fragile missiles when he spoke in Cincinnati, and in 1855 he was unable to carry Hamilton County in his campaign for the governorship. On the other hand, Chase's activity made him acquainted throughout the State with men who were later very serviceable to him, and his fugitive-slave arguments soon gave him a national reputation. His was a case where honesty proved the best policy, where a man deliberately chose an unpopular and unpromising cause, and by his very courage and willingness to sacrifice his interests was launched upon a more splendid career than he could ever have reached by letting himself go with the current.

From 1841 Chase was a favorite speaker at antislavery meetings and conventions throughout Ohio, as well as in neighboring States, and even in the East. He was neither an orator nor a good stump-speaker; indeed, a nervous hesitancy so affected his speech that he used to say: "My tongue is too large for my mouth;" hence he used habitually a clear, moderate utterance, which gave him time to shape his ideas as they came. For that reason his speeches were easy to report, and read well. Since he never could use the buffoonery which sets a great crowd in a roar, and which made his neighbor Tom Corwin a favorite speaker, he must appeal to reason, to the moral sense, at least to enlightened self-interest, not to the coarser passions. Chase's principal deficiency as a public speaker was his lack of a sense of humor. He could not discharge such a barbed arrow of satire as Wade's famous criticism on the proposed annexation of Cuba: "It is not a question of giving lands to the landless, but of giving niggers to the niggerless." Yet he was a very effective speaker, always well grounded, prepared to confront objections if not too unexpectedly put, calm, cool, dignified, an impersonation of reason inspired with righteous indignation. He had great endurance, and knew how to make many speeches on the same theme without too much repetition. His favorite topic was the illegality of slavery, but he knew also how to deliver good hearty blows against his political opponents, how to detect and bring home their inconsistencies.

Chase's *forte*, however, lay in the preparation of formal addresses and platforms, because there he had more room and more opportunity to marshal his thoughts. Such tasks were often intrusted to him by the Liberty and Free-Soil men from 1841 to 1848. He wrote the national Liberty Platform of 1843, the stirring Liberty Address of 1845, the resolutions of the People's Convention of 1847, and the Free-Soil Platform of 1848. The "Address of the Southern and Western Liberty Convention," of June 12, 1845, is perhaps the best work that fell from Chase's pen during this period; a short extract from it will illustrate better than could any criticism his style, principles, and method of attack.

"WHAT WE MEAN TO DO.

"Against this influence, against these infractions of the Constitution, against these departures from the national policy originally adopted, against these violations of the national faith originally pledged, we solemnly protest. Nor do we propose only to protest. We recognize the obligations which rest upon us as descendants of the men of the revolution, as inheritors of the institutions which they established, as partakers of the blessings which they so dearly purchased, to carry forward and perfect their work. We mean to do it, wisely and prudently, but with energy and decision. We have the example of our fathers on our side. We have the Constitution of their adoption on our side. It is our duty, and our purpose, to rescue the government from the control of the slave-holders; to harmonize its practical administration with the provisions of the Constitution, and to secure to all, without exception, and without partiality, the rights which the Constitution guarantees. We believe that slaveholding in the United States is the source of numberless evils, moral, social, and political; that it hinders social progress; that it embitters public and private intercourse; that it degrades us as individuals, as States, and as a nation; that it holds back our country from a splendid career of greatness and glory. We are, therefore, resolutely, inflexibly, at all times, and under all circumstances, hostile to its longer continuance in our land. We believe that its removal can be effected peacefully, constitutionally, without real injury to any, with the greatest benefit to all.

"HOW WE MEAN TO DO IT.

"We propose to effect this by repealing all legislation, and discontinuing all action, in favor of slavery, at home and abroad; by prohibiting the practice of slaveholding in all places of exclusive national jurisdiction, in the District of Columbia, in American vessels upon the seas, in forts, arsenals, navy yards; by forbidding the employment of slaves upon any public work; by adopting resolutions in Congress, declaring that slaveholding, in all States created out of national territories, is unconstitutional, and recommending to the others the immediate adoption of measures for its extinction within their respective limits; and by electing and appointing to public station such men, and only such men as openly avow our principles, and will honestly carry out our measures."

Another agency which Chase valued and cultivated was the anti-slavery press. There were three kinds of anti-slavery periodicals: the radical, aggressive abolition organs, especially Garrison's "Liberator;" the political anti-slavery journal, of which the "National Era" was the chief; and the local Liberty and Free-Soil papers. The "Liberator" furnished plenty of ammunition for abolitionists, but was hopelessly out of touch with the practical politics of Ohio. The "National Era," published in Washington, and edited by Dr. Bailey, formerly of Cincinnati, an intimate personal friend of Chase, was a good newspaper, and had a large influence throughout the country. The local papers were sometimes started for no other purpose than to defend abolition, or, more frequently, to defend the Liberty or Free-Soil party, and they found it a hard task to pay printers' bills. Chase subscribed for many of these papers, and raised, lent, or gave outright, money to keep some of the more important of them afloat; indeed, he confessed in 1852 that people expected too much of him in the way of financial support of these enterprises.

Chase had a keen sense of the influence of newspaper editors and of their inside knowledge of the currents of public opinion. Dozens of them corresponded with him, among them J. W. Taylor of the "Sandusky Register," one of Chase's former law students; Orren Follett of the "Ohio State Journal;" and especially E. S. Hamlin, editor of the "Standard" at Columbus, and political lieutenant to Chase. He also had relations with some of the great dailies in Ohio and outside, — with Molitur, the Cincinnati German, Bartlett of the Cincinnati "Gazette," Horace Greeley of the New York "Tribune," Bigelow of the "Evening Post," and Dr. Leavitt of the "Independent;" but it was always a serious drawback to Chase's political hopes in Ohio that he had not the friendship of any of the influential Cleveland papers. He knew how to set an item afloat in the press, and how to prepare the way for a discharge of journalistic guns simultaneously all along the line; he kept scrap-books of newspaper extracts; he sometimes wrote leading articles; perhaps he overestimated the effect of the press in creating public opinion.

Chase's powers of statement made him a welcome ally of the Ohio anti-slavery men, but he became their leader, in the period from 1837 to 1849, through services which deserve a careful description. In the first place, he framed a convenient constitutional argument against the legality of slavery; next, he applied his principles in a series of slavery cases, which drew upon him the attention of the whole country; and then he showed his friends how to build up an effective political organization.

The great safeguard of slavery was its foundation in vested property rights, protected by what seemed an impregnable legality; the great weakness of slavery was its total opposition to the system of democracy which existed alike in free States, slave States, and the federal government. So far as slavery within the States was concerned, the South might simply ask the abolitionists, "What are you going to do about it?" Right or wrong, dangerous or favorable, slavery existed, slavery was lawful, and slavery was protected by public sentiment. When it came to the powers of the national government, however, the status of slavery was not so clear; but still the slavocracy had a right to assert that the Convention of 1787 was aware of slavery, and had showed no purpose of interfering with it by its handiwork; that the Constitution, in the clauses on the federal ratio, the slave trade, and fugitive slaves, recognized slavery; and that Congress, through successive statutes, supposed to be constitutional, had authorized slavery in the District of Columbia, in some of the Territories, and (through the Fugitive Slave Act of 1793) even in the free States.

If the discussion could have been kept down to

questions of laws and constitutions, the South had the advantage of a title by undisputed possession. Hence the Garrisonian abolitionists forced the issue upon the other point: they denounced slavery as wasteful, cruel, aristocratic, demoralizing, murderous, and soul-destroying. To a sensitive people like the Southerners, who sincerely believed that they enjoyed the flower of human civilization, these attacks were unendurable; and for the sake of their own reputation before mankind they felt compelled to argue that slavery was economical, kind, democratic, civilizing, and beneficent to both blacks and whites.

After this exchange of war cries, it would have been the true policy of the South to assume that the advantages of slavery would prove themselves to impartial men, and to rest behind the protection of undeniable state rights. At the beginning of the active controversy, about 1830, there were no Territories in dispute, and all that was needed by slaveholders was to stand on the right of every State to exclusive legislation on its "domestic institutions," and to make such laws as seemed good to them for the punishment of abolitionists or critics within their own borders. They came out of their own intrenchments when they demanded that the free States should throttle the abolition agitation, and when they took the ground that a free discussion of slavery anywhere in the United States was so dangerous to slavery that it must be stopped at any sacrifice of the principles of free speech or even of the Union.

The Garrisonian abolitionists rid themselves of all the constitutional and state-rights arguments by declaring that the Constitution was "a league with death and a covenant with hell," and that they were willing to accept the logical consequence, — a division of the Union. This position, however consistent, fortunately was contrary to the instinct of the masses of the people, who felt that in the Union was their salvation. The Western abolitionists took up a more practical and more convincing line of argument, by pressing home the inexpediency and degradation of slavery, and at the same time by crossing the line to attack the South in its stronghold of legality.

An extreme position was that of Joshua R. Giddings, who held that the Declaration of Independence had destroyed slavery when it declared that "all men are born equal" and "endowed with certain inalienable rights, among which are life, liberty, and the pursuit of happiness;" he insisted also that the Constitution was "an anti-slavery document." The more practical minds of Chase and his friends refused to accept Giddings's dogma; they admitted without hesitation all that the South claimed regarding the legal right of a State to establish slavery, but treated it as simply a technical right to organize a status of brute force; from the right of a State to make a slave they deduced the principle that no other political organization could create a slave, and therefore they made a strenuous fight against any sanction or protection for slavery in the federal Constitution or through the federal government.

This line of argument was suggested by Birney as early as December, 1836; it was worked into logical form by Lysander Spooner in 1845; it was a stock argument in Western anti-slavery meetings and newspapers, but Chase was the man who stated it most clearly and effectively. To us, who have lived through a civil war, when people managed to get on for years without a constitution, the whole discussion seems forced; why dispute over the phrases of a document framed half a century earlier? Because to the minds of men of that time, both North and South, an appeal to the Constitution had the same kind of force as the equally common appeal to the Bible: they were both codes of law, — "what I have written, I have written." To be sure, the South did not maintain slavery simply because it thought the system constitutional or biblical, and the North did not move upon slavery because so bidden by the Constitution or the Bible; but since the issue was a difference of moral and political standards in the two sections, each sought to avail itself of the conservative forces of society by showing that it was trying to protect a sound form of government and a God-ordained institution. If Chase could make out even a plausible case for the statement that the Constitution was neither anti-slavery nor pro-slavery, but neutral, and that neutrality under American free government always meant freedom, he would give relief and encouragement to thousands of men who were attacking slavery on other than constitutional grounds.

Nothing in Chase's life so well shows his logical powers, his moral sense, and the cause of his political success as his argument on slavery. It must of course be remembered that he took a brief *in re servi*, and made it his business to state every point which could possibly help his client; and it was no part of his function to prepare his opponent's case, or to call attention to decisions which bore against him. It must also be remembered that Chase had to meet an exaggerated argument that the Constitution invariably recognized and protected slavery wherever it was not clearly prohibited; to which he replied that the federal government "could no more make a slave than make a king;" and from that he plunged into declamation almost as exaggerated as that of the other side.

Chase's view of slavery, as a question of moral and political right, grew out of the fact that he was by nature and education a democrat. In addressing colored men in 1845, he said: "The moment the law excludes a portion of the community from its equal regard, it divides the community into higher and lower classes and introduces all the evils of the aristocratic principle." He was really a Jeffersonian, although he appealed to the great Democrat only as an opponent of slavery in the Territories and not as his political master. He was moreover by nature a strict constructionist.

"The old theory of our fathers," said he, "is the true theory. Let us have a poor government and a rich people, — light taxes and abundant individual enterprise, economical expenditure and steady prosperity, — a general government strictly limited to its sphere, and state governments respected and honored because competent and ready to protect the rights and guard the interests of the people."

How was the doctrine of democratic government and strict limitation of national power to be applied to slavery? By what Chase in many addresses and speeches called the "denationalization of slavery." First of all he maintained that history showed that the fathers of the Constitution publicly discouraged slavery, and that there was an understanding that there should be no slavery in any unorganized or new Territory. "Our national government," said Chase, "therefore went into operation upon the principle of no slavery outside of slave States, upon the principle that slavery is local, not national;" and he declared that the later doctrine of "equality" between freedom and slavery was, "morally speaking, a base forgery," that there had not been an early purpose to keep up a balance of free and slave States.

To Chase's mind, moreover, the attitude of the Constitution toward slavery was shown not only by its silence but by its language, especially in the amendment by which "no person shall be deprived of life, liberty, or property except by due process of law," which, he said, added a positive injunction and cut off any implication of a power to establish slavery by national authority.

So far as the text of the Constitution and the purpose of its framers went, Chase was arguing against indisputable facts, and hence he could not convince slaveholders nor strengthen anti-slavery men. The actual legislation from 1789 to 1830 was a continuous refutation of his position, for in 1790 slavery was deliberately permitted by Congress in the territory south of the Ohio River, and three slave States were admitted between 1812 and 1819. There can be no historical doubt that the framers of the Constitution perfectly understood the inconveniences of the "house divided against itself," but preferred union to consistency. Nobody could deny Chase's most effective point, — the desire and hope of the fathers that slavery might disappear; but that argument was set aside in the fifties by the growing Southern opinion that the fathers knew less than their children about what was good for the South, and for mankind.

Behind the constitutional argument, Chase took up a second line of defense, — an absolute denial of any power in Congress to establish slavery anywhere by any process. Here again he was combating the facts of history, for he was obliged to admit that laws had been framed to support slavery in the District of Columbia, in the Territories, and — so far as fugitives were concerned — in free States; but he declared all such laws to be outside of the constitutional powers of Congress. Later in his career this position rather embarrassed him, for it was dangerously like Douglas's doctrine of non-intervention and the principles of the Dred Scott decision. The difference, indeed, was chiefly one of motive. Chase denied the power of Congress to aid slavery, and the Supreme Court disavowed legislative power to limit slavery; the South invoked almost at the same moment congressional action and judicial limitation.

Chase's dialectics were ingeniously applied in the many discussions from 1835 to 1862 on slavery in the District of Columbia. To deny to Congress all power to adopt the previous laws of Maryland and Virginia was farther than Chase dared go, since the land titles of the District rested on just such laws. He therefore set up a very subtle and technical distinction, to the effect that the old laws of Maryland ceased to have effect in the District when it was ceded, although "private rights" continued; and that, since slavery was contrary to the Constitution, Congress could not reënact it. How hard put to it Chase was in this discussion is shown by his appeal to the clause in the preamble of the Constitution professing "to secure the blessings of liberty to our posterity." Such far-fetched arguments were of no service to the cause. A better line of attack would have been to urge that Congress had powers in the premises and should exercise them by emancipating the slaves in the District; but Chase accepted the contradiction of declaring that the Acts of Congress establishing slavery in the District were void, and yet that Congress had power to repeal them.

The Fugitive Slave Act of 1793 furnished a better opportunity for thorough and effective constitutional objections to slavery, and against it Chase appealed literally to earth and heaven. He held it to be contrary to the Ordinance of 1787, which provided for recovery only from "the original States;" opposed to the intention of the fathers; and incompatible with the constitutional form of federal government. "When a slave leaves the jurisdiction of the State," said he, "he ceases to be a slave, because he continues to be a man and leaves behind him the law of force which made him a slave." The statute, argued Chase, makes no distinction between apprentices and slaves, and hence slaves have all the immunities of apprentices; the details of the act are contrary to the letter and spirit of the Constitution, in denying "due process of law" and authorizing "unreasonable searches and seizures;" the expectation of the Constitution was that States and not Congress should be responsible for the apprehension of fugitives; and, finally, "the legislature cannot authorize injustice by law, it cannot repeal the laws of nature, cannot create any obligation to do wrong, or neglect duty. No court is bound to enforce unjust laws."

The appeal to fundamental principles of right and wrong, which could not be superseded by laws, however little it might convince a court, was the most effective of all the anti-slavery arguments, because it brought back the discussion to the absolute incongruity of democracy and slavery, and emphasized both the question of moral right and the social expediency of upholding the moral law. As Chase put it, slavery was nothing but a forcible denial of inborn and God-given rights, and hence it could not have even a legal status except by positive, unmistakable laws; when these laws ceased, slavery ended. Yet in general Chase dwelt less on the wickedness of slavery in the sight of God, than on the iniquity of riveting it upon a free Constitution, meant for a free people; and he made little use in his early arguments of the demoralizing effect of slavery on freemen, though he wrote to O'Connell in 1843: "We find also and we feel in our bitter experience that free labor is dishonored and its wages rendered insecure throughout the whole land by a system which exacts labor without wages and degrades the laborer to the level of the beast."

Taking Chase's chain of arguments as a whole, it is easy to see defects: he was working on a theory not grounded on fact; he argued that slavery could not possibly be covered by the Constitution, chiefly because it ought not to exist; he assumed the moral wrong, without taking the trouble to prove it by a reference to the facts of slavery; and he almost ignored the evil consequences of slavery to the slaveholder and to the white laborer. Yet of all the anti-slavery leaders Chase was perhaps the most practical in making his principles tell in concrete cases, in taking advantage of slips by the enemy, in unwearying effort to keep the question of slavery before the minds of his countrymen. Hundreds of men on both sides liked to make the Constitution a partner in their speeches; hardly any other rendered such services as Chase in defending the victims of slavery who got across the line into the free States. Indeed, his skill, courage, and power of constitutional argument made it possible for him to render the second of his great services, — the defense of fugitive slaves. It was his courage as counsel in those cases, his use of all possible legal technicalities and expedients in behalf of his client, and his fearless and widely circulated speeches, which have made him best known as an anti-slavery man.

In March, 1837, Chase was called in as counsel for an alleged fugitive, Matilda, the daughter and slave of a Missouri planter named Lawrence. She was so light in color that she easily passed for white, and her owner treated her as a favored personal attendant. She became clamorous for her freedom, and in May, 1836, while traveling down the Ohio on a steamer with him, she went ashore — with or without his knowledge — when the boat touched at Cincinnati. She speedily got employment as a servant in the house of the Birneys, who looked on her as a white woman; but in March, 1837, she was seized by one Riley, in behalf of Lawrence, and brought before a magistrate for his certificate that she was a fugitive. Chase, already the intimate friend of Birney, interposed with *habeas corpus* proceedings before a state court, and argued that she was a free person because she had been brought to the State of Ohio by her master, and therefore could not be "a person held to service or labor in one State, under the laws thereof, escaping into another." The judge decided against the claim of Matilda, and she was remanded into slavery. The poor girl was turned over to her captors, carried across the Ohio, and "sold down the river."

To the pro-slavery men of Cincinnati this seemed an occasion to teach the abolitionists a lesson, and accordingly Birney was indicted for "harboring a slave." He had indeed known a few days before the capture that Matilda had been a bondwoman; but Chase, as his counsel, again made the issue that a person brought to the State by a master thereby ceased to be a slave. Again the judge decided against Chase's contention; but Birney appealed, and the State Supreme Court reversed the decision. Unfortunately, its action was based on a technicality which Chase had carefully avoided raising, and not on the bold principle of freedom under the laws of Ohio. Nevertheless, the court took the unusual step of directing that Chase's argument be printed, apparently in order to bring his point to the attention of the profession.

By far the most famous of the Ohio fugitive-slave cases was that of Van Zandt, for here was raised the question of punishing a rescuer. John Van Zandt, a Kentuckian turned abolitionist, had a small farm near Cincinnati, and was known to keep a station of the Underground Railroad. April 22, 1842, a party of nine slaves, the property of Wharton Jones of Kentucky, landed on the Ohio side of the river; and very early the next morning, as Van Zandt started from Walnut Hills to drive home, he found the party of negroes on the road. The testimony did not bring out just what influence led the fugitives from the river bank to a place which a known abolitionist was to pass; at any rate, Van Zandt took the whole party into his covered wagon and proposed to carry them out of danger, and one of the slaves, Andrew, sat on the box and drove. About fifteen miles out of Cincinnati, they were stopped by persons whom Chase designated as "two bold villains," who, although they had no authority from the master or from any one else, simply carried off eight of the slaves and returned them to Kentucky; the ninth, Andrew the driver, ran away, and never was seen again by his pursuers. Here again is an unexplained mystery, on which light might be shed by some conductor of the Underground Railroad. The first legal result of the affair was the prosecution of the "two bold villains" for abduction; but the public prosecutor showed little interest; and according to Chase they were "acquitted, more by the public sentiment than by the jury who rendered the verdict of acquittal."

The period was prolific in slavery suits. In 1838 and 1839 came extradition proceedings, in which Governor Kent of Maine and Governor Seward of New York refused to surrender "slave stealers;" in 1842 the Supreme Court decided the Prigg case, involving the seizure of a fugitive in Pennsylvania without recourse to the courts; and in the same year Wharton Jones, owner of the runaway slave Andrew, brought civil suit in the federal courts against Van Zandt, first to recover the value of Andrew and the expense of recapturing the others; and, secondly, to recover the penalty of $500 allowed by the act of 1793 against a person who "after due notice harbored and concealed" a fugitive. Jones's first suit was defended by Chase and Thomas Morris with great zeal and skill; but in the first trial, in July, 1842, Judge McLean held that Van Zandt's evident knowledge of the character of the negroes was "due notice," and gave damages in $1200, which eventually had to be paid. The other suit for $500 penalty was also decided against Van Zandt, and appealed to the Supreme Court. William H. Seward was now associated with Chase, — both serving without fee, — and in 1847 they submitted their arguments. The court sustained the decision of the lower court, and Van Zandt was mulcted $1700 and legal expenses for the offense of showing kindness to persons whom "he must have known" to be fugitives.

None of Chase's legal arguments ever had such vogue as that presented in this case to the Supreme Court, but never orally delivered. Notwithstanding the careful courtesy of its language toward the Supreme Court, it is evident that he had not the slightest expectation of winning his case: what he aimed at was simply to put before the country a solemn protest against making the free States share in slavery. Justice Story said of his argument, "It is a triumph of freedom;" and the "Law Reporter" ventured to predict that "his points will seriously influence the public mind and perhaps the politics of the country."

After an introduction, in which he ventures to remind the judges that several of them are themselves slaveholders and therefore interested parties, Chase first attacks the averment against Van Zandt in its minutest specifications, but he speedily advances beyond technicalities, by claiming that the act of 1793 is defective and does not cover such a case as Van Zandt's; and that it must be strictly construed as it stands. "Shall it be said," he argues, "that public security is a less important end, than the right of a master to his slave? . . . Will this court by construction attempt to supply these defects?" He now calls into his service the Ordinance of 1787, in his hands a kind of stage property which could do duty on all sorts of occasions. This time he makes it supersede the Federal Constitution, as an unamendable pre-agreement which provides only for the return of fugitives from "the original States," and relieves Ohio from any later fugitive slave law.

Thus far Chase shows agility rather than wisdom; but he now proceeds to weave a fabric of constitutional objections to the statute under which his client was prosecuted, namely, the Fugitive Slave Act of 1793. Here he is arguing against a stone wall; for the Supreme Court had recently decided in *Prigg* v. *Pennsylvania* that the act was for the most part constitutional, although the clauses requiring state magistrates to hold proceedings were void. Chase, however, has the confidence to assure the court that this decision was not unanimous, and was a dictum; and then he uses his favorite argument that the Constitution has nothing to do with slavery, except in States where it is established by state law, and that hence of course there is no constitutional authority possible for a fugitive slave act.

The advocate now becomes more definite, and argues specifically that Congress can under no circumstances legislate on the return of fugitives; that what the clause of the Constitution establishes both for fugitive slaves and fugitive criminals is only "a treaty obligation — a covenant or compact." Elsewhere in the argument Chase goes even further, by the bold assertion that there can be no possible way of giving to one of the parties in a controversy the right to seize the other and to claim a decision on *ex parte* evidence. "What is that," says he, "but to legalize assault and battery and private imprisonment? I say fearlessly that such acts of legislation as this are subversive of the fundamental principles on which all civil society rests."

Chase closes with a calm but eloquent prediction, which might have given pause to a court then on the road to the Dred Scott decision: "Upon questions such as some of these involved in this case, which partakes largely of a moral and political nature, the judgment, even of this court, must necessarily be rejudged at the tribunal of public opinion, the opinion, not of the American people only, but of the civilized world."

The importance of the whole argument does not lie in its constitutional cogency or in its effect on the government. Chase ventured to refer to few decisions, for both law and practice were against him; his doctrine was unacceptable to the Supreme Court, and was rudely ignored by Congress three years later, when a more obnoxious fugitive slave law replaced that of which Chase complained. The real significance of the Van Zandt argument is the passionate protest against making free men and free States responsible for slavery, even though the Constitution, statutes, and practice so bound them. The moral reasons which Chase put forward applied not only to the fugitive slave law, but also to legislation for the District of Columbia and to the organization of new Territories acquired in 1846; and in the struggle over the Wilmot Proviso such arguments as he used nerved the abolitionists to fight to the bitter end against slavery in the Territories.

Between 1845 and 1849 Chase was involved in several other fugitive cases. A slave named Samuel Watson, in January, 1845, went on shore from a steamer lying at the landing in Cincinnati. By *habeas corpus* Chase brought the case before the Ohio Supreme Court, laying stress on the point that, as the escape was made within the low-water mark, it was undoubtedly in Ohio territory. Judge Read, however, decided that a steamer navigating the waters of the Ohio was, so far as slavery was concerned, within the jurisdiction of the southern shore, though he showed a deference to rising public sentiment by saying: "Slavery is a wrong inflicted by force and supported alone by the municipal power of the State or Territory where it exists; . . . . the master must lose his slave if he brings him into a free State." Nevertheless the abolitionists remembered only that Judge Read had returned Watson to slavery, and in 1849 used their balance of power to drop him from the court.

Another case in 1845 was that of Francis D. Parish of Sandusky, charged with "harboring and concealing" a slave woman and her child, and also with "obstructing" the legal owners of a slave by refusing to permit the arrest of the two negroes under a power of attorney from the alleged owner. In spite of Chase's efforts as counsel, Parish was convicted and had to pay a fine of a thousand dollars. One of the jurymen afterward wrote to Chase: "I pray God to hasten the day when law such as we as a jury are called upon to apply may be repealed."

Although Chase was defeated in every one of the slave cases in which he appeared for the defense, a natural result of his zealous efforts was to make him the friend and counselor of distressed colored people both in Cincinnati and far and wide throughout the country. A few examples of the strange relations into which his reputation brought him will throw light on the whole institution of slavery. In 1840 one John Martin, a Georgia planter, writes pathetically in behalf of three mulatto children whom he has sent to Ohio to be emancipated, — the too familiar case of a father seeking to get his own flesh and blood out of bondage. "You will confer a great favor on an unfortunate man to select good homes for them," he says; and he begs that one of the girls may be taken by Mrs. Chase as a house servant. In March, 1841, Mary Townsend writes in a beautiful hand from Oberlin, asking Chase to learn what her former master will take for free papers for herself, and for three boys left in Kentucky. In September, 1841, R. G. Corwin submits the case of Daniel Washington, slave of Amos Kendall, who was sent South to be sold to pay some of Kendall's debts, but came ashore from a steamer lying at Cincinnati. Corwin declares that "there can be no doubt that he is as free as the God who made him," and proposes to send him to Canada. In 1844 Benjamin Stanton writes from Iowa: "I think I heard thee express a desire to get a case to test the constitutionality of slavery," and gives details of such a case.

In July, 1845, Chase's legal advice is asked in the case of "*The State of Ohio for the use of the Poor of Washington Township, Preble County, on complaint of George Wagoner* v. *H. Monfort.*" Monfort had been fined for employing a negro woman, who had not given bond that she would not become a public charge. In March, 1846, Chase is called upon in behalf of Jerry Finney, who had been kidnapped at Columbus. "I know," writes his correspondent, "I need not invoke your aid in this matter, always being found ready to assist and protect the poor African." In April, 1848, a gentleman from Vicksburg asks Chase how manumission may be obtained in a free State for a family for which the negro mother has purchased freedom at an expense of over five thousand dollars. In view of these and other instances, it is no wonder that Chase was called the "attorney-general of fugitive slaves."

The colored people of Cincinnati showed their gratitude for his defense of Watson in 1845 by presenting to him a silver pitcher; his enemies made much capital out of this selection as the special friend of "the nigger," and more out of his speech to the donors, in which he boldly stated the extremest abolition doctrine of negro suffrage twenty years before any political party would take it up. "I regard," said he, "the exclusion of the colored people as a body from the elective franchise as incompatible with true democratic principles." The pitcher had an interesting history. Later, when Chase was governor of Ohio, he used it as a kind of official punch-bowl for lemonade, to the wrath of extreme Democrats and moderate drinkers; and eventually it became an heirloom, treasured for its associations with his anti-slavery career.

Of more importance to Chase's political future was his position as a kind of Western anti-slavery oracle. During the period from 1840 to 1849 he was in correspondence with most of the Western and Southern abolitionists. W. Aldam, Jr., an Englishman, furnished him material on slavery in the West Indies; students of Lane Seminary in 1843 thanked him for his statement to them of his views on slavery; John Jay began a correspondence which lasted for many years. In 1844 John G. Fee and Edgar Needham of Kentucky wrote to him describing their anti-slavery efforts, and from time to time thereafter they reported to him. Fee was a minister, the son of a slaveholder, and one of the sturdy native abolitionists who held their ground in their own State; later he founded Berea College, a kind of Kentucky Oberlin, where blacks and whites since the Civil War have been educated together. That Chase, the cold New Englander, should be the friend, adviser, and confidant of such men as Birney, Fee, and Needham, shows the confidence which had been inspired by his fearless efforts to give the negro his legal rights and to defend the friends of the slave. From this time to the Civil War, he was one of the men upon whom the abolition fraternity called for advice and assistance.

With all his reputation and all his friends, Chase was in many respects a lonely man in Cincinnati. His fugitive slave cases brought fame, but no fees and no paying clients; and when Birney and Bailey left Cincinnati he had no abolitionist intimate of strength and character in whom he confided. It is easy to look back through his life and see what advantages at last came to him through his steadfastness in this dark period; but at the time he was doing an unpopular service to humanity.

From 1840 to 1849 Chase led a kind of triple life: he had his private and professional interests; he had his anti-slavery pursuits; and he had also the great political task of organizing the Liberty and Free-Soil parties. Anti-slavery now began to play a part in Ohio politics; long before 1840 a few men in important offices had not been afraid to be known as anti-slavery men; such were Leicester King, president of the Ohio Anti-slavery Society, in the state Senate from 1833 to 1838; Benjamin F. Wade, a Whig, also in the state Senate from 1835 to 1839; Joshua R. Giddings, at first a Whig, then abolitionist member of the national House of Representatives from 1838 to 1861; and

Thomas Morris, United States senator from 1833 to 1839.

For the formation of a distinct anti-slavery party in Ohio, and for the first national organization, two men are chiefly responsible, James G. Birney and Salmon P. Chase. The Garrisonian principle of non-participation never had much influence in Ohio, where all the abolitionist leaders continued to vote at every election and had a keen sense of what might be done by a proper concentration of ballots; but they were not always agreed as to which to choose out of three possible courses: whether to vote only for candidates who were of their regular party, but were against slavery; to throw their votes from one side to the other, according as this or that party put up an anti-slavery man; or to form a third party.

The first of these methods was suggested by Birney in the Ohio anti-slavery convention of 1835, when he wanted the "elevated principles of holiness" applied to politics, and proposed a pledge that abolitionists should vote for no candidate who was not against the Black Laws. Nevertheless, even such decided abolitionists as the Oberlin people continued to vote the Whig ticket at election after election.

Birney could not stand still in his conception of political abolitionism. In September, 1836, his paper, the "Philanthropist," urged abolitionists not to unite with either of the great parties. The local anti-slavery societies began to take up the idea in their conventions, and in 1837 the state society voted: "That it is time for the abolitionists of Ohio to relinquish all party attachments, and act with a single view to the supremacy of the law, the inviolability of constitutional privileges, and the rights of all." For a time the anti-slavery men contented themselves with questioning candidates as to their principles on slavery; but this method broke down in 1838, when the abolitionists destroyed the Whig supremacy in the legislature by voting for pledged Democrats, only to see the pledges ignored and to witness the passage of a scandalous state fugitive slave act.

The natural result was a general movement toward a third-party organization, and in 1839 one member of the legislature was elected as an avowed separatist from both parties. Meanwhile similar movements were taking place in other States; and in 1840 the political abolitionists in the American Anti-slavery Society broke away from the Garrisonians, and through an informal national organization nominated James G. Birney for the presidency, as the candidate of the Liberty party.

Up to 1840 Chase had little to do with politics, though a delegate to the National Republican convention which nominated Clay in 1832. When the election of 1836 drew on, he was a Whig, and urged the nomination of Judge McLean; but he knew General Harrison, who lived near Cincinnati, and finally, with some qualms, voted for him. In

1840 he showed no sympathy when his friend Birney, as the head of the new Liberty party, called out the political anti-slavery forces. He remained a regular Whig, and a second time supported Harrison in the hope that his candidate would look more kindly than Van Buren on the efforts against slavery in the District of Columbia. The result of the campaign was the election of Harrison, while the Liberty movement proved pitifully weak; out of 1,500,000 votes Birney got only 7000, in his own State of Ohio polling only 903 out of a total of 274,000.

Thus in November, 1840, Chase was still a Whig; but in May, 1841, he took an active part in the county convention of the Liberty men in Cincinnati. Since this was the first political crisis in his life, his motives deserve critical examination. Schuckers, who got a strong impression from Chase himself, accounts for the change simply by saying that the Birney movement "did express a conviction that some form of organization against slavery had become a political necessity," and "in that conviction Mr. Chase now joined;" but Schuckers also intimates that Chase looked to see an anti-slavery Democratic president in 1844, and hence he leaves unexplained the union with the Liberty men. Pierce, in his unpublished memoir (inspired by Chase), lays Chase's change of front to his studies into the aggressions of slavery, and to his dissatisfaction with the obtuseness of Harrison and Tyler; but Chase had as yet not worked out his constitutional theory, and in 1840–41 showed little dissatisfaction with Harrison. Hoadly, in his memorial address, says: "I learn from Hon. Rufus King, who was then a law student in his office, that Mr. Chase was a candidate for the Whig nomination for state senator, and was defeated in the nominating convention principally at the instigation of his brother-in-law, H. H. Southgate, upon the avowed and open ground that he was an abolitionist. How notice could have been more distinctly given to Chase that there was no place in the Whig party of Ohio for him or his principles, I fail to see." This theory might have accounted for a bolt in 1840, but hardly for one in 1841, after the election of Chase's candidate for the presidency.

Chase himself has left several different statements of his motives. In a letter to Charles Sumner of March 9, 1849, he says: "In 1840 I supported General Harrison, though I then favored the sub-treasury system rather than a bank of the United States. I supported him because I imagined that his administration would be less proslavery than Mr. Van Buren's. As soon as I discovered my mistake, I was ready to concur in an independent movement, and was one of the first who took an active part in organizing the Liberty party in Ohio." Much later, in 1868, he wrote: "I was not a life-long Whig, but a sort of independent Whig, with Democratic ideas, from 1830 to 1841. Sometimes I voted for a Democrat, but more generally for Whigs." These explanations are doubtless sincere, but they do not cover the whole ground; for when Tyler succeeded to the presidency in 1841, nobody dreamed that he was about to disrupt the Whig party. Moreover the anti-slavery Whigs in Ohio at that time were by far the largest body of anti-slavery men in the State; in leaving them, Chase went into a small and feeble party.

The real reason for Chase's change of front may safely be inferred from some scattered and apparently disconnected facts. During the campaign of 1840 Harrison said that "he would as soon appoint an abolitionist to office as anybody else, if qualified," and he chose Chase to go to Bailey, editor of the "Philanthropist," and expostulate with him for his criticisms. Numbers of office-seekers supposed Chase to be deep in Harrison's confidence and asked his indorsement. Early in 1841 Chase took part in a meeting at Cincinnati which urged Harrison to discountenance slavery in the District of Columbia, and he felt himself in a position to justify a letter to Harrison two weeks before his inauguration, urging him not to favor slavery in his inaugural. Harrison wrote civilly in reply, but his inaugural took ground against any interference with slavery, and the slender hopes based upon him were shattered by his death, in April, 1841. A month later Chase had forever left the Whig party, and had cast in his lot with Birney and Bailey, with the Oberlin abolitionists, with the Western Reserve supporters of Giddings.

It is plain that Chase held to the Whig party up to 1841 on the chance of being able to exert a personal influence over Harrison. So far as the Whig "principles" were concerned, Chase had come to see that the old Jacksonian issues of the bank and the tariff were moribund, and hence his natural sympathies were with the Democrats; but that party in Ohio in 1840 enacted a state fugitive slave law at the demand of the government of Kentucky. As a member of either regular party Chase must vote for and with active pro-slavery men, and hence he sought other alliances. His change of party was a distinct sacrifice of his material interests, for most of the respectable people in Cincinnati were Whigs, and the Liberty party was very feeble and discouraged. Chase reluctantly followed his convictions by throwing in his lot with an unpopular set of men engaged in what seemed a hopeless crusade.

From this time to the election of 1860, Chase preserved an undying distrust and hatred of the Whig party, and often of Whigs as individuals. "It is a party of expediency and compromise," he said in 1843; "every vote for a Whig is a vote against abolition." Seward in 1845 sent him a letter of protest at his bitterness against his former associates, but in 1850 Chase still made the confident assertion that the Whigs were really pro-slavery. On the other hand, he always believed that by a proper pressure the Democratic party might be brought to take up the anti-slavery cause.

The accession of Chase was a great joy to the Liberty men, for hitherto they had been weak in the southern part of the State, and had lacked tacticians. At once he was seized upon for tasks in which he showed great skill: he could write inspiring addresses; he could organize conventions and get them to do their work in his way; it was his vigor and snap which made the Ohio Liberty party the most efficient of the political abolitionist organizations in the whole country during the next six years. Issues were plenty: the Ohio Black Laws, which had so far stood against all attacks; the right of petition to Congress; slavery in the District of Columbia; the slave trade; fugitive slaves and kidnapping; after 1842 the Texas question; and after 1846 the territorial question and the Wilmot Proviso.

Within a year after his conversion Chase had become practically the leader of the Liberty party in Ohio, and for eight years he continued his work of organizing conventions, preparing party addresses, bolstering up the Liberty press, and comforting distressed brethren, with the result that the party had an encouraging growth within its small limits. In the state Liberty convention of 1841 Chase was very active, writing at this time the first of his remarkable "Addresses." It was a preliminary statement of the doctrine afterward worked out in the Van Zandt arguments of 1847, namely, the absolute disassociation of the Constitution from slavery except as States might create the system; and it led up to a climax in the often quoted sentence: "The honor, the welfare, the safety of our country imperiously require the absolute and unqualified divorce of the government from slavery."

By 1842 the question of the attitude of the Liberty men in the presidential election of 1844 came up, and Chase saw opening before him an attractive field of influence in the choice of a national Liberty candidate. Nearly three years before the election Birney wrote to Chase, protesting against the suggested nomination of Governor Seward until he should become "an abolitionist in name," or of John Quincy Adams, "who," says Birney, "looks on the doctrine of immediate emancipation as held by our friends as ridiculous." In the national Liberty convention at Buffalo in 1843, Birney was again nominated for the presidency; but the convention was carried away by one of those cyclones of radicalism which gave such delight to the enemies of the abolitionists, and against Chase's protest it was voted that the fugitive slave clause of the Constitution might be excepted by a mental reservation in taking oath to the Constitution.

The paramount issue in the campaign of 1844 was the annexation of Texas. Van Buren was replaced as the Democratic candidate by Polk, an ardent annexationist, on an annexation platform. Clay received the Whig nomination, but under the pressure of the campaign wrote letters to reassure the Southern wing of the party, thereby alienating some thousands of anti-slavery Whigs. This was the opportunity of the Liberty men, who alone stood for uncompromising opposition to the admission of slave territory, and they joyfully received the bolting Whigs. Nevertheless, Birney's total vote was but 62,000.

Certain charges against Birney no doubt much cut down the Liberty vote in Ohio, which had risen from 900 in 1840 to 2800 in 1841, to 5400 in 1842, and to 7000 in 1843; but which, in all the excitement of the presidential year, 1844, was but 8000. In the pivotal State of New York, however, the Liberty vote, chiefly withdrawn from the Whig party, was more than enough to turn the scale against Clay; and the result was the transfer of that State, and thus of the electoral majority, from the Whig to the Democratic column.

Then and since, this use of the balance of power has been laid against the Liberty men as a great error of judgment, on the ground that within four months after the election Texas was annexed. But it was never the political object of the third-party men to put into office men or parties moderately favorable to themselves: what they desired was to impress the country with their determination to accept nothing but the "denationalization of slavery." Of the Polk Democracy most of them were hopeless: they saw that the party could not be inclined to their cause whether they voted with it or against it. The Clay Whigs, on the other hand, were supposed to be more friendly to anti-slavery, and for that very reason might perhaps be coerced into the principles of the Liberty party, if otherwise they must be beaten. Such was the argument of the Liberty men, and it took ten years to convince them that neither of the great national parties would ever take ground which involved the loss of all its Southern following.

The opportunity for a political anti-slavery party seemed at last to have come; in 1845 Texas was annexed; in 1846 the Wilmot Proviso came up; in 1847 was the culmination of the Mexican war; yet the vitality of the Liberty party in Ohio was so nearly exhausted that in 1845 its vote fell to 7000, and though in 1846, on the local issue of the repeal of the Black Laws, it ran up to 11,000, yet in 1847 there was not even a state convention, and only about 4000 votes were polled. Chase himself was profoundly discouraged, and wrote to John P. Hale in April, 1847: "I see no prospect of greater future progress, but rather of less. As fast as we can bring public sentiment right, the other parties will approach our ground. To build up a new party is by no means so easy as to compel old parties to do a particular work. . . . If we can once get the Democratic party in motion, regarding the overthrow of slavery as a legitimate and necessary result of its principles, I would have no apprehensions at all of the work being laid aside until accomplished."

During 1847 the Liberty men took the field for the campaign of 1848, on the old straight issue. Birney was now out of public life, through the effects of a physical accident, and Chase's correspondence is full of a manager's talk about candidates. In January he sounds Judge McLean on accepting a nomination; in March a New York abolitionist suggests Seward; in May Chase proposes Judge John C. Wright of Ohio; in June the chairman of the New York Liberty state committee suggests "Gerrit Smith and Salmon P. Chase" as the ticket, and Chase replies that he would vote for Smith; in August H. B. Stanton reports that a committee has waited on John P. Hale of New Hampshire, and that "he is with the Liberty party in principles, reasons, and feelings."

Out of all the candidates suggested, Hale was the most available. In 1846 he was elected to the Senate as an independent anti-slavery man, though of Democratic antecedents; he was distinguished for his keen and caustic rhetoric and absolute fearlessness. Chase, however, was more alive than his associates to the signs of the times: the question of slavery in the annexed territory must come before the next Congress, and he had strong hopes that the Democratic party would take such ground as would enable the Liberty men to unite with them. He therefore urged the postponement of the Liberty convention to the spring of 1848, but he was overruled, and the convention met at Buffalo in October, 1847. Chase was a delegate, and declined a nomination as vice-president on the ticket with John P. Hale, the nominee of the convention.

The division of feeling among Liberty men was ominous. In the spring of 1848, Chase took the responsibility of setting a back fire against his own party by manipulating a shrewd call, signed by three thousand disaffected Whigs and Democrats, for an "Ohio Mass Free-Territory Convention," to meet after the nominating conventions of the two regular parties. Meanwhile he was writing right and left to urge the suppression of the national Liberty ticket, even personally urging Hale to withdraw, on the chance of being nominated again.

When the Whig national convention in May nominated Taylor, a slaveholder on a no-platform platform, and the Democratic convention in June nominated Cass, a Northern dough-face, especially hateful to the Liberty men, many Whig and Democratic politicians and newspapers could stand neither nomination. In New York the anti-slavery wing of the Democrats — the Barnburners — bolted solidly under the leadership of their chieftain, ex-President Van Buren; and it was evident that a union of all anti-slavery men would again hold the balance of power in the campaign and might carry some States.

In forming such a union no man had a more arduous or a more honorable part than Chase. The apparently spontaneous Ohio mass convention of June 21, 1848, was really skillfully engineered by him and his friends; a thousand delegates enthusiastically attended; Chase spoke; Chase wrote the admirable resolutions; Chase prepared the addresses; Chase secured the call for a national Free-Soil convention; yet Chase as a Liberty leader kept in the background. On the same day and at the same place the Ohio Liberty convention met and formally dissolved the party by accepting the proposed Buffalo Convention.

For seven years Chase had been the leading manager of the Liberty party in the Northwest; he knew the men; he prepared the official addresses; he kept in touch with the newspapers. For the second time in his life he had left his party, though it had a nominee before the country. In his own mind, and in fact, his principles were unchanged, but he had found a new way of expressing them: he was working now to establish a new kind of organization, an "anti-slavery league," in which all the anti-slavery men in the country should refuse to vote for pro-slavery men. He had no confidence in the Whig party, and in June, 1847, had expressed the belief that the Democracy would "be compelled to take substantially the ground of the Liberty party." It is plain that in the Barnburner bolt he welcomed what he considered the evidence of the long-desired purifying of the Democratic conscience. He would, however, have left the Liberty organization even if the Barnburners had remained with the Democrats, for he saw no hope in third-party methods; a reorganization of the friends of freedom, and a widening of their basis of action, seemed to him essential.

With the call of the Buffalo Convention the name "Liberty party" disappeared and was never renewed. The term "Free-Soil" implied a narrower issue, for it meant at the moment no more than the Wilmot Proviso, and thousands of Liberty men hesitated to give up their full principles and their identity in order to go into a new organization. But the foundations of the great deep were breaking up; the public sentiment of the North seemed now overwhelmingly in favor of the Wilmot Proviso, though it had been repudiated by both the regular parties; and the obvious course was to give the popular protest an opportunity to crystallize in votes.

During July, 1848, delegates to the Buffalo Convention were elected in all the Northern States, and in Delaware, Virginia, and Maryland; and in the six available weeks men from all over the country asked Chase's counsel as to the platform and the candidates. As an old Whig, long a Liberty man, inclined to a free Democracy, Chase formed a centre for the Western delegates. He was also the friend and correspondent of many of the New York and Eastern men, especially of H. B. Stanton and Charles Sumner, and he was certain to be a power in the convention. He had for months suggested Judge McLean, uncle of the wife whom he had recently married; but he avoided committing himself to any candidate, and expressed a willingness to accept Hale if the convention nominated him.

No national political convention in the United States ever seemed so spontaneous and so unfettered as the assemblage at Buffalo on August 9–10, 1848. An immense concourse of voluntary delegates appeared; as the long-suffering reporter said, "men seemed to think that because they were Free-Soilers and had 'left home to come up here,' they had a perfect right to take possession of any position, place, or seat they might choose." Within this unwieldy mass of attendants was a large number of accredited delegates irregularly sent from sixteen States; out of these a so-called "Committee of Conference" was organized, made up of 465 members, and this was the real nominating convention; within this body again was a "Committee of Resolutions" of 48 members. While the "Conference" balloted, the large so-called "Convention" amused itself with stump speeches made by all sorts of people, from Joshua R. Giddings to "Mr. Bibb, a colored fugitive." The life and energy of the gathering are set forth in recent reminiscences of Dr. Albert Gaillard Hart, a delegate from Ohio.

"I can hardly recall any public gathering where the enthusiasm was so universal and unbounded. Every reference to the determination to stop the aggressiveness of slavery, and to move steadily forward to its overthrow, was met by the loudest response which thousands of throats could offer. On the second day in the afternoon the nomination convention, of which I was a member, met in a Universalist church, not far from the convention. Here Judge Chase presided. I recall perfectly his dignified and impressive bearing, his candor and fairness in presiding. Benjamin F. Butler of New York State, regarded as Mr. Van Buren's first lieutenant, made an adroit and eloquent speech in favor of the nomination of Van Buren. Knowing full well the determination of the North that slavery should be abolished in the District of Columbia, and as well that Van Buren had repeatedly declared that it could not be done without the consent of the South, he in that part of his speech exclaimed, 'and if the South refuses to consent to the abolishment of slavery in the District of Columbia, then we will remove the seat of government to the bright banks of the Ohio.' The anti-slavery men could easily carry the nomination. But here was a host of young, eager, enthusiastic men, ready and anxious to enlist under our banners. We might make the platform, only let them bring with them their old and beloved leader, who, though seventy-four years of age, had much of the fire of youth, and would in time come up to our standards. We knew perfectly that he and the 'Barnburners' were only anxious to 'beat Cass' and the Baltimore Convention, and that they had no hearty hatred of slavery. John P. Hale was the logical candidate of the old guard. But enough delegates thought it best to act upon the hope that once with us they would continue to be our allies in the future, and so Van Buren was nominated. At the ratification meeting of the general convention held that night, one of the speakers, a Barnburner, quoted: —

> "'Now is the winter of our discontent
> Made glorious summer by this sun of York,
> And all the clouds that lour'd upon our house
> In the deep bosom of the ocean buried.'

"Free-Soilers and Barnburners, — few after fifty years survive. But of those still living none can fail to recall the fiery wave of enthusiasm and the roar of cheering voices when the Committee on Resolutions read last: 'That we inscribe on our banner "Free Soil, Free Speech, Free Labor, and Free Men," and under it will fight on and fight ever until a triumphant victory shall reward our exertions.'"

In all the work of the Buffalo Convention Chase was the leading spirit; he drafted the strong resolutions, the spirit of which was summed up in the phrase, "No more slave States and no more slave territory;" and he added planks advocating national improvements, homestead land grants, and a tariff for revenue. To Chase's influence also is due the choice of Van Buren as a candidate; for he early came to an understanding with the New York men that they might name the candidate if the Liberty party might frame the platform. Chase probably was no more confident than any one else of Van Buren's change of heart, but he had made a practical combination, which he pressed forward in a strong canvass. Hale withdrew, and most of the state Liberty organizations were dropped; but old Whigs, who had fought Van Buren from 1828 to 1844, found it hard to vote for him. Chase did not speak outside of the Ohio districts, but for the first time an effort was made to reach the Germans, through documents and speeches in their language. The election showed only 300,000 votes for Van Buren, and of these 120,000 were in New York. The Free-Soil vote in Ohio was 35,000, the high-water mark of the third-party movement up to 1853. Perhaps because of this vote Cass carried Ohio, and nothing but the Barnburner defection caused him to lose New York; the third party had apparently succeeded only in electing a slave-holder. In the very close state election in Ohio, however, the Free-Soilers had eleven members of the state legislature, and enjoyed the balance of power for the choice of a United States senator. Perhaps Chase had this result in mind when he wrote to Charles Sumner in November, 1848, apropos of the Buffalo platform: "I should not be greatly surprised if the coming winter should witness a union between the old Democracy and the Free Democracy in our legislature upon the principles of that platform."

CHAPTER V

THE ANTI-SLAVERY SENATOR

As the smoke cleared away from the field of 1848, it became possible to see how changed was the status of the anti-slavery movement. The old abolition societies and press had been losing vitality ever since 1841. Their great mission had been to compel the American people to think about slavery; and all the assaults upon them had only brought out more clearly the fact that slavery and free speech could not exist in the same communities, and hardly in the same federation. They could not stave off the annexation of Texas, a question which presented an issue far short of abolition, but at the same time created anti-slavery allies for the time being among Northern legislators and party agents. Since 1820 not a foot of land had been redeemed from the curse of slavery; while a small fraction of the present Missouri and all of Texas had come under it. The fierce contest over the Wilmot Proviso, from 1846 to 1850, showed that anti-slavery was put on the defensive, and that, so far from "securing immediate abolition" in the slave-holding States, the system of slavery was extending into additional regions formerly free. Even the political abolitionists had in 1848 given up the sweeping Liberty platform, and had accepted the issue of Free-Soil as the utmost for which they would at that moment contend.

Chase was one of the leaders who saw most distinctly that the slave power was advancing, and one of his objects in furthering a coalition with the Barnburners was to put a pressure upon Congress to stand by the Wilmot Proviso; and the plain and predominant purpose of the Free-Soil coalition was, in his mind, to alarm the Democratic party. He supposed also that the Barnburners would stand out till their faction had forced the Democratic party to come over to its ground and thus to become the party of liberty.

The union of Free-Soilers and Democrats had elected no President. Could it be effective in other contests, — for example, in the choice of a senator from Ohio to succeed William Allen? That contest included many complications, but came down to this result: Chase's friends voted to admit to the legislature two contested Democrats, on conditions that the Black Laws be repealed; and by the aid of those two votes Chase was elected senator. Chase's part in this episode has been a subject of much controversy; and the senatorial election of 1849 must therefore be studied in its details.

The first element in the struggle was the "Hamilton County election." A Whig partisan apportionment act of 1848 had for the first time in the history of the State divided a county into electoral districts; the object being to secure two of the five Hamilton County (Cincinnati) delegates, who had hitherto been all Democrats.

In the election of 1848 the Democrats in Hamilton County refused to recognize the statute, though all the other districts in the State had availed themselves of it. Instead they nominated and voted for five candidates as before, all of whom were declared elected by the Democratic county clerk. But the Whigs in their new district had a majority for two candidates, who contested the seats of Pugh and Pierce, Democrats. It fell out that the state election was very close; the Whig candidate for governor had 148,666 votes against 148,321 for his opponent, and the legislature was not controlled by either regular party; while to organize the House the two disputed votes from Hamilton County were necessary. In the House of 72 members the returns were as follows: Straight Democrats, 32; straight Whigs, 30; Free-Soilers, 8; contested seats, 2; but when it came to the delicate questions of organization and the choice of a senator, the Free-Soilers broke up into 5 Whig Free-Soilers, 1 Democratic Free-Soiler (who eventually voted with his Whig brethren against Chase), and 2 Independent Free-Soilers (Townshend and Morse). The Whigs, with the Whig Free-Soilers and their 2 Hamilton County contestants, could make the 37 necessary for a quorum; but the straight Democrats, even with Pugh and Pierce and the Democratic Free-Soiler, were at the start 2 short of the quorum of 37.

In the confused state of the membership, nobody could predict who would form a combination capable of organizing the House and of passing on the contested seats. The Democrats, therefore, formed and executed the bold plan of "rushing" the lower House, by coming together unexpectedly just before the regular time of meeting, and hastily swearing in Pugh and Pierce and three straw contestants, thus making 37 members; they then proceeded to elect officers. The Whigs swarmed in a few moments later, swore in their two contestants from Hamilton County, and organized a House in like irregular fashion on the other side of the room. Day after day, from December 4 to December 26, the two bodies harangued and voted and skirmished side by side. When the contest was all over, Chase wrote to Charles Sumner the following account of the breaking of the deadlock and its results: —

"These opposing claims, and the bitterness growing out of the great question, led to scenes which marked the opening of the session, and I do not doubt would have occasioned the dissolution of the legislature and perhaps bloodshed, had not the Free-Soilers intervened as pacificators, Messrs. Townshend and Morse having been nominated by a convention entirely independent of both the old political parties and elected in opposition to the candidates of both were in a position which gave confidence to the Democrats that their claims would be fairly heard and decided without adverse prepossessions.

"The legislature was therefore organized and the claim of the contestants for the seats of Hamilton County was referred substantially to the umpirage of these two gentlemen, for it so happened that all the other members were regarded as committed to one side or the other and were equally divided. Upon the question of the *prima facie* right of the Democratic claimants, and on their certificates, assuming at this stage by common consent the constitutionality of the division, these gentlemen themselves divided, and the Democratic claimants were excluded by a tie vote. The Whig claimants, whose *prima facie* evidence was regarded as still more defective, were excluded by a majority of six. Upon the final question of absolute right to seats, which depended upon the constitutionality of the law, these gentlemen declared in favor of the Democratic claimant, who was consequently admitted by a majority of one. The first demand of the Independent Free-Soilers (for so these gentlemen were distinguished in contradistinction to the Democratic Free-Soilers on one side and Whig Free-Soilers on the other), was the immediate repeal of the Black Laws. The Democrats, having obtained justice for themselves, were now the more ready to do justice to others. The Black Laws were repealed, the Democratic votes for repeal greatly outnumbering the Whig, and the Whig votes against repeal out numbering the Democratic.

"The real thing was the election of a senator. Here the Independents were again divided. Mr.

Morse preferred Mr. Giddings, being his neighbor and personal friend. Dr. Townshend preferred me. The Democratic Free-Soilers preferred me. Several of the Whig Free-Soilers preferred Mr. Giddings; while the majority of them preferred neither of us, but wanted a man more diluted with Whiggism than either of us. But neither Mr. Giddings's friends nor mine would consent to any third man thus brought forward, and it was finally understood that, if the Whigs would support Mr. Giddings, and the Democrats would not support me, my friends would vote for him, and also for Whig nominees, if fit and capable for Supreme Judges, etc.; and, on the other hand, that if the Democrats would not support me, the Whigs would not support Mr. Giddings, the Whig Free-Soilers would vote for me and for Democratic Supreme Judges, etc. Most of the Whigs were willing to go for Mr. Giddings, but there were some who refused to go for him under any circumstances, and his election, therefore, became hopeless. The Democrats, on the other hand, had long regarded me with favor. I was known to be opposed to the whole Whig action in regard to the apportionment law, and I have little doubt that, had I been a Democrat in regular party standing, I could have been elected over any candidate they had on my own strength. They, therefore, felt comparatively little reluctance in coming up to my support; though they found it hard, not only to go out of the ranks, but to vote for an abolitionist. Finally, I received every Democratic vote, fifty in all; and also the votes of three Democratic Free-Soilers, and of the two Independents, and was elected by a majority of four. I did not receive a single vote from the Whig Free-Soilers. Why they withheld their votes in disregard of the understanding which my friends certainly supposed to exist and which on their part would have been faithfully adhered to had Mr. Giddings received the Whig vote and the Democrats treated me as the Whigs treated him, I do not undertake to explain. Mr. Giddings, I have every reason to believe [is] in no respect responsible for their action."

The above account is accurate and candid so far as it goes, but it minimizes Chase's own part in the struggle, a part for which he was then and afterward assailed with charges of unfair or of corrupt dealing; Douglas, in the heat of the Kansas-Nebraska struggle, twitted Chase with coming to the Senate by "a corrupt bargain or a dishonorable coalition." All the accusations against him touch one or other of three points: whether he changed his opinion on the apportionment act of 1848; whether he made a pretended "deal" in the repeal of the Black Laws; and whether he brought about a corrupt agreement between the Free-Soilers and Democrats. The evidence, when carefully examined, acquits him on all three counts, though it shows that he was the man who secured the admission of Pugh and Pierce, who insisted on the repeal of the Black Laws, and who practically arranged the combination for his own election.

On the question of the Hamilton County election Chase's position was constrained, though not dishonest: he preferred to have the legislature repeal the law, and then call another election on the old apportionment; but throughout the discussion he steadily took the ground that the apportionment of 1848 was unconstitutional and that Pugh and Pierce were legally elected. Townshend and Morse, the only members really independent of party bonds, were both brought — chiefly through Chase's agents — to vote for Pugh and Pierce. The arrangement as to the Black Laws was also due to Chase's agents; Chase himself drafted the repeal bill, but it was carried through by Morse, one of the two Independents, who, before he gave the vote necessary for the admission of Pugh and Pierce, demanded and secured a written pledge signed by those two men and others, that they would vote for the long-delayed repeal of the Black Laws.

These two preliminary measures brought about a total breach in the little Free-Soil contingent. All the eight men in the House came from the Western Reserve, where Whig influence was strong; hence it was plain that in a Free-Soil caucus the five men elected as Free-Soil Whigs would predominate, and that the votes of the whole eight would be thrown for some Whig for senator. After the admission of Pugh and Pierce, the legislature was about equally divided, and the balance of power was again in the hands of Townshend and Morse, as is shown in the following table: —

	Demo-crats.	Whigs.	Free-Soil Whigs.	Inde-pendents.	Total.
Senate.	18	15	3		36
House.	35	29	6	2	72
	53	44	9	2	108

Necessary for a choice, 55.

As early as January 11, Stanley Matthews, Chase's lieutenant, reported that he thought he had arranged terms with the Democratic leader on the following basis: "That it was very important that the reliable Free-Soil members (Townshend and Morse) and the Democrats should coöperate together; that to that end, Pugh and Pierce should be admitted to seats in the contest, to justify which, the Democrats will assist in your election to the U. S. Senate, provided that in other matters of office the Democrats shall have the two supreme judges, the presiding judgeship in Hamilton County and other Democratic counties, the Free-Soil men to have their own selection in the other counties." In the end the Democrats came up to the plan sketched by Matthews and approved by Chase. On January 22 the struggle of nearly three months was ended by the choice of Chase as senator, every Democrat voting with Townshend and Morse to make the necessary majority of 55.

Of few fiercely contested senatorial elections are there such intimate accounts. Besides the reminiscences of Morse, and of A. G. Riddle, the leader of the Free-Soilers, we have the reports of Chase's envoys, Eli Nichols and Stanley Matthews, as well as Chase's private letter-books and diaries. In the whole transaction Chase had nothing to conceal. He began in November, 1848, to work up his candidacy; he was glad to be acceptable to the Democrats through his attitude on the Hamilton County question; but he is fully borne out in his own claim: "I will not say that by the counsels I gave last winter I was uninfluenced by personal considerations; but I can say that I do not believe that I was influenced by such considerations in any extraordinary degree. Certainly I neither modified nor compromised in any way my political principles. I made no pledges, came under no obligations which at all impair my absolute independence of party restraint."

When Chase took his seat in the Senate at Washington, March 6, 1849, he was beginning his first service as a public officer of the State or of the nation. In his own mind he was the representative of the anti-slavery forces of the West, and at the same time was to take a powerful part in reshaping the Democratic party. An early and unwelcome lesson was the evidence of his own insignificance in the eyes of nearly all his fellow members; to his colleagues, with one or two exceptions, he came as a member of a small and very disagreeable third party, elected by an accident, and likely to follow Giddings's exasperating tactics of dragging the slavery question into debate when respectable people were tired of it.

So far as the spread of sound doctrine went, the Senate was the place for a man of Chase's convictions and ability of statement; and Sumner predicted that he would "trouble Calhoun on the slavery question more than any others." Chase took an early opportunity to arouse the Southern members by a direct attack; his maiden effort in debate, in January, 1850, was, as he said, "intended only as a first attempt on a small scale by way of feeling my way. It stirred up the Southerners wonderfully." He was quickly cooled and disarmed by the lack of sympathy among his colleagues. To a confidant he wrote: "You . . . know how much we need men in Congress. There is not one in the Senate who is willing to adopt and carry out a systematic plan of operations against the slave power except myself. Hale is a first-rate guerrillist. Seward is a Whig partisan, though perfectly reliable on any vote where our questions are concerned, and, independent of his Whiggism, a noble fellow. Hale has no love for the Democracy. I alone sympathize with the Democrats on general questions and push out my Democratic principles to their anti-slavery application. If I had four more men who held the same relation to the Democratic party in the Senate, the days of doughfacery would be numbered."

In the course of his term Chase and Hale were reinforced by two other anti-slavery men: Wade came from Ohio in 1851, as an anti-slavery Whig, but the two senators always felt that their State was not large enough to hold both of them; Sumner came also in 1851 by a Free-Soil Democratic combination; already a warm friend and frequent correspondent of Chase, he became his most intimate coadjutor, but never an aid in his parliamentary struggles. It was not until the great conflict over Kansas-Nebraska that other Whigs and Democrats — Hamlin, Fessenden, Seward, Everett, — came forward and joined in the onslaught on slavery. In the House during 1849–51 there were less than a dozen Free-Soilers. Chase enumerated Wilmot and Howe of Pennsylvania, King of New York, Allen of Massachusetts, Booth of Connecticut, Tuck of New Hampshire, Durkee of Wisconsin, Root of Ohio, and, last but first, Giddings.

The parliamentary side of Chase's senatorial career was a painful disappointment to him. When the time came for forming the committees, in December, 1849, his case was duly considered by the Democratic caucus, and nearly all the Northern senators proposed to recognize him as one of themselves by giving him a chairmanship of a good committee; but Southern men objected; and when the "slate" was made known, out of the one hundred and twenty-two committee places there were none for Chase and none for Hale. A little later Chase was put on the insignificant Committee on Revolutionary Claims. In 1851, although he enrolled himself in the official list as a "Democrat," he had only one committee appointment; and in 1852 neither Chase, Seward, nor Hale had any committee places, except as later they were called to fill vacancies. By the next year, however, Chase had won a position for himself, and in the appointments for 1853–55 he had three places.

This cavalier treatment showed a radical difference of opinion between the regular Democrats and Chase as to his political status. In his own mind he had created a "Free Democracy," or "Free-Soil Democracy," or "Independent Democracy," in which the great principles of the old party were acknowledged, such as the sub-treasury and free trade; and, in addition, he expected soon to see the principle of anti-slavery accepted by the regular Democracy. Hence he said in July, 1849:

"I am a Democrat, and I feel earnestly solicitous for the success of the Democratic organization and the triumph of its principles. The doctrines of the Democracy on the subjects of trade, currency, and special privileges command the entire assent of my judgment. But I cannot, while boldly asserting their principles in reference to those subjects, shrink from their just application to slavery." He did not blink the probable effect of the new policy on the party. "Let it be so," he said. "The compensation will be found in the concentration, unanimity, and the invincibility of the united Democracy in the free States. Triumphant in the free States, and strong in the strength of their principles even in the slave States, the Democracy can elect all its national candidates, under such circumstances, in despite of all opposition."

Throughout his term Chase was a busy and conscientious senator, with a strong sense of interest in his constituents and of duty to his State, but also with an energy to see the public business done, and a watchfulness to protect the public treasury. In the conduct of public business Chase showed a lofty impatience with delays, with extravagance, and with secrecy. He had a strong sense of urbanity in debate, and held himself well against the numerous attacks made upon him; he had also a timely feeling of the prerogatives of his station, and insisted that the Senate had a right to originate money bills; but he came out strongly against the private sessions of the Senate, and in 1853 got fourteen votes (including that of Douglas) for opening the doors during executive sessions.

For his Ohio constituents Chase was a pushing and a successful representative; he felt the dignity of standing for a great State and expressing its will on public questions; he also felt that his constituents were entitled to share in the favors of the federal government. Hence he urged and secured an elaborate custom-house building, a marine hospital for Cincinnati, and a canal around the Portland Falls at Louisville, one of the few river improvements which have proved of large benefit to commerce.

The most serious questions on which Chase had to take ground, aside from the issue of slavery, were those arising out of the public lands. From the beginning, immense areas had been granted, first for bounties, then for state purposes, and finally, since about 1830, to States, to be used for building canals. Since so much was given, sales of course fell off; hence about 1850 a new idea came to the front, — that of offering public lands as gifts to people who would settle them for five years. Both Chase and Wade were among the most ardent supporters of some kind of land grants, and the Ohio legislature instructed them to push the Homestead Bill. "I regard the public lands," said Chase, "as the estate of the people, and Congress merely as a trustee." In July, 1854, the Homestead question was well debated, and the most serious objection against it was the incitement to immigration. Though the Know-Nothing movement had now begun, and many prudent men hedged on the question of inviting in more foreigners, Chase boldly favored the admission of immigrants, and the bestowal upon them of the privileges of the act; and he also moved to strike out the limitation to "white" persons.

The railroad land-grant system, which began in 1850, with a gift to the Illinois Central, was contrary to the extreme Democratic principle of withholding governmental support of States or people; but when so ardent a Democrat as Douglas took the lead, Chase could do no more than try to reduce the acreages granted and the privileges given to the railroad companies. The rapid development of California caused an agitation for a railroad to the Pacific, which took form in a bill debated in 1852–53. At the very beginning of the discussion, Chase pointed out the political importance of the question as to whether the eastern terminus should be placed North or South, and he secured what he afterwards called "the first practical measure looking to the organization of a Pacific railroad, which received the sanction of Congress;" this was an appropriation for surveys to be made previous to any selection of the route. In 1855 he interested himself in the passage of a bill for the construction of the Pacific railroad, but it failed in the House and went over until 1862.

As a member of a committee on pensions or claims during most of his term, Chase was impressed by the readiness of the Senate to approve undeserved claims, and to tack upon appropriation bills items against which committees had reported. Hence he heartily supported the Court of Claims, proposed in 1850 and finally created in 1855. In the annals of the Senate Chase appears almost always as a critic of appropriation bills and as a mover of amendments to strike out doubtful clauses. He patiently watched and repeatedly exposed certain perennial jobs, especially one involving a sum of $350,000, inserted year after year, for "Creek depredations;" he also blocked an attempt to secure the L'Amistad claim, against which the Supreme Court had indirectly decided in 1842. Indeed, Chase pushed his watch-dog character so far that he opposed a new treasury building, and succeeded in striking out a clause for official residences for the Vice-President and heads of departments, two propositions which would have been very serviceable to him eight years later. He even spoke against new water-works for Washington, and decidedly opposed raising the salary of the district judge of New Hampshire from $1000 to $1400, on the ground that the State paid only $1200 to its supreme judges. No man can be perfect in economy, however, and Chase had his pet extravagance: he strongly urged an appropriation of $30,000 for a statue of America by Hiram Powers, notwithstanding the objection of a fellow senator, who bluntly affirmed, "I do not believe in buying any more female figures on trust." His ideas of the functions of government in general are summed up in a speech of December, 1852, in which he refers to "these principles of economy, prudence, loyalty, and reform which distinguish genuine from false Democracy."

On most of the great questions which came before the Senate, Chase rarely made a formal speech. He had his principles and he expressed them; but he felt that his energies belonged to the cause of anti-slavery, of which he became the national champion in the Senate, as Giddings was in the House. Hale was a free lance, and it was not in his caustic nature to convince anybody; Sumner was not a tactician; Wade was no man to lay out a line of argument and carry it through a long debate;

Seward was, as Chase said, "first for the Whig party." The watchman on the wall was Chase; the debater who could confute Douglas was Chase; and Chase was the man whose speeches summed up the calm argument of the unflinching anti-slavery men and spread it through the country in the crises of 1850 and of 1854.

His first parliamentary experience was in the furnace heat of the Compromise of 1850. We now know that the purpose of the Mexican war had been to secure California, and thus to extend a slave belt across from the Gulf to the Pacific; therefore the slaveholders felt deprived by the California free constitution, and tricked by President Taylor, especially when he refused to turn over any part of New Mexico to Texas, and tried to make New Mexico also a free State. Indeed, there was good constitutional reason for believing that in New Mexico and California slavery had already disappeared under Mexican law. The question gave to Chase a new chance to present his favorite constitutional arguments on slavery.

To the men of the South, however, the issue was not one to be settled on narrow arguments of constitutionality, or through the application of Mexican law, or by hostile majorities in Congress. The doctrine that slavery was to be regulated exclusively by States had served very well in the early days of the republic, when slavery was an institution of local concern, like land tenure or primogeniture or the whipping-post. Ever since 1820, however, slavery had become consciously a system, in the maintenance of which slaveholders in every State and Territory were interested, for they were all put on the defensive by the humanitarian progress of the world, which had left the South behind.

Those writers who charge upon the abolitionists the responsibility of arousing the South and compelling it to take the offensive-defensive, forget that there must have been numerous and aggressive abolitionists, unless the Northern States were to remain just where they had been in 1750. In colonial times the two sections had the same standards of treatment of inferior and dependent beings: they were both brutal to apprentices, indentured servants, debtors, prisoners, paupers, insane people, and slaves. During the half century from 1775 to 1825, the frank, undisguised, unashamed cruelty of the eighteenth century gave way in the North; but it still continued in the South. The jails and penitentiaries had been Gehennas everywhere in 1790, and were such still in most of the Southern States in 1850; but the Pennsylvania state prison was a model for the world. Hence the cruelty of slavery, which was the stock in trade of the abolitionists, was to the Southern men of 1850 still a disagreeable necessity; they even invited Northern friends to come down and view the institution, just as Russian officials have welcomed travelers to see the Siberian prisons, supposing them to be a normal kind of prison. But while intelligent

Northern men admitted the heartlessness of their slaveholding fathers, the South positively denied that slavery had ever been cruel, and treated her own reformers as public enemies.

Furthermore, the Southerners had grievances which to them seemed to come of simple Northern hypocrisy. The abolition efforts to prohibit slavery in the District of Columbia had in their eyes no other purpose than to degrade them by setting a national disapprobation on a practice which had lasted in Washington half a century. The open defiance of the fugitive slave laws seemed to them not only a refusal to carry out a constitutional obligation, but also an annulment of regulations without which the fields could not be tilled, or food prepared for the family. Hence when the South was asked to fulfill its constitutional obligations by proper treatment of free negroes from the North and from abroad, it answered simply that the presence of slaves in free States was not a menace to the lives of the people, but that strange free negroes in the South might be inciting insurrection, and they could not be allowed to go at large.

Even had it been true, as Calhoun and his followers alleged, that slavery was "a positive good," the zeal of the South to extend it into other regions was not a benevolent desire to extend the positive good. It was the instinctive feeling that slavery could not stand in the face of the disapprobation of the federal government, and that to prevent such disapprobation they must have more slave

States, and more senators and representatives, and more electoral votes. Hence the absolute determination of the South never to admit the principle crystallized in the Wilmot Proviso, the principle that freedom was the normal condition of annexed territory.

Against the compact forces of slavery, with their perfect understanding, was opposed, in the Congress of 1849–50, a disorganized and temporary coalition of anti-slavery Whigs and Democrats who hated and distrusted each other and could not stand side by side, while many Northern Democrats and some Northern Whigs were ready to vote with the South. Into this controversy came Chase, then forty-one years old, an able speaker and abler reasoner, and full of the force of conviction. On January 10, 1850, he took occasion to say that no menace of disunion could move the anti-slavery men from their path; he declared that the true Democratic principles were those of the Ordinance of 1787, which included the prohibition of slavery in the Territories. Butler of South Carolina had already prepared himself to crush the upstart, and now read one of Chase's letters, which was plainly a prophecy that the Democratic party must eventually shake off its Southern membership and become sectional. Chase made no reply; and two weeks later Butler accused him of drafting the resolution of 1843, described above, approving "mental reservations" in an oath to the Constitution. Chase absolutely denied authorship of, or adhesion to, the resolution, but was evidently timid of measuring strength with Butler.

These were skirmishes preliminary to the great debate on the Compromise. February 2 Chase wrote to a friend: "You have seen Clay's Compromise resolutions — sentiment for the North, substance for the South — just like the Missouri Compromise — all that is in issue given up by the non-slaveholders — unsubstantial concessions of matters not in issue by the slaveholders. The great discussion is evidently near at hand, and I must speak. Well, I have broken the ice, though all circumstances have conspired to prevent any adequate preparation on my part. I will speak. Perhaps the sling and the five stones from the brook will again avail against Goliath."

It was impossible for Chase to understand that the Compromise was already decided, since the agreement of Clay and Webster meant the effective coalition of the Southern Whigs and Northern "Cotton Whigs." Even Webster's "Seventh of March speech," to which Chase listened with an indignation set forth in a letter of that date to Sumner, was virtually an announcement that the Senate would vote for the Compromise, and that there was no combination of anti-slavery men in the House which could stand out.

The two great speeches against the Compromise were Seward's and Chase's. The two men had now been for some months associated, but there seems to have been little sympathy between them.

In December, 1850, Chase wrote: "I don't know what Seward will do. I have never been able to establish much sympathy between us. He is too much of a politician for me." When, in January, 1851, Seward asked Chase's support for an anti-slavery Whig in Ohio, Chase replied: "So far as I could judge from the tone of his friends in New York towards me, I could not think that I appeared to them in any very agreeable light, for they, especially the 'Tribune,' were in the habit of abusing me without any stint." Indeed, there was a strong contrast between the two senators, each in his first term: Seward, fresh from the prestige of service as Governor of New York, leader in a powerful party, protected by the devices of Thurlow Weed, the confidant of the President; Chase, an accidental senator, with but one sympathetic colleague, fighting in an unpopular cause. Yet of the two men Chase was the stronger assailant of the proposed Compromise.

The senator from Ohio was at the time in great anxiety over the dangerous illness of his wife, but his speech of March 26–27, 1850, is the best piece of work which he had as yet done. With a modest allusion to his own lack of experience in debate, he states at once his formidable position: "We have no power to legislate on the subject of slavery in the States. We have power to prevent its extension, and to prohibit its existence within the sphere of the exclusive jurisdiction of the general government. Our duty, therefore, is to abstain from interference with it in the States. It is also our duty to prohibit its extension into national territories, and its continuance where we are constitutionally responsible for its existence." By a long historical argument he aims to show that the fathers of the Constitution, so far as they could, legislated against slavery; and then he points out how the slave power has possessed itself of the federal government, noting, by way of illustration, that the South has always had a majority of the judges of the Supreme Court, and that "no Northern man has filled the office of chief justice during this century."

The second half of the speech goes directly to the merits of the various branches of the proposed Compromise: he objects to the "Omnibus Committee," and insists that the California question has already been settled by the California constitution; he proposes to leave the question of the Texan boundary for later settlement, and denies any obligation to erect new States out of Texas; and he firmly insists on the recognition of New Mexico without slavery. Regarding the District of Columbia, he denies that Maryland has a right to require the continuance of slavery there, and he affirms the power of Congress to regulate the interstate slave trade. As to fugitive slaves, he finds not the slightest power in Congress to legislate concerning them. On every point, except the slave trade in the District of Columbia, he traverses the Compromise resolutions, and on every point he surpasses every speaker on his side in clear and cogent statement of the constitutional reasons for his convictions, in insight into the real purposes of the slave power, and in a firm stand against disunion.

At the time this speech was delivered the serious questions before the Senate had narrowed down to two, — a new fugitive slave law, and the status of slavery in New Mexico, including the Texan boundary. To these two questions Chase addressed himself in his highest strain. He cited the historical precedents for the power of Congress to prohibit slavery in the Territories; he called to witness the state legislatures which had instructed nearly half the senators to vote for the Wilmot Proviso; and he relentlessly followed out, point by point, Webster's declaration "that he would not take pains to reaffirm an ordinance of Nature, nor to reënact the will of God." "Sir," exclaimed Chase, "I should like to know what laws we are to reënact if we are not to reënact the will of God — the rights of human nature are not derived from human law. Men are 'created equal,' they are 'endowed by their Creator with inalienable rights.' Aggressions upon these rights are crimes." As to the national exclusion of slavery from the Territory, Chase took ground which was abundantly justified by the experience of the next ten years: "So long as a powerful and active political interest is concerned in the extension of slavery into new Territories," said he, "it is vain to look for its exclusion from them except by positive law." Furthermore, he drew from Southern senators the statement that in their view a master had the same right to take slaves into a Territory as to take any other property thither, and that the federal government was bound to protect such slave property.

In the light of later history, Chase's argument is sound and convincing; but he recognized that the question was not wholly one of constitutional right, and that there was a possibility of Southern action contrary to law or reason. Webster had made a splendid apostrophe to union, much dulled by his opinion that the Union was in no danger. Chase took higher ground: "The South will dissolve the Union! This cry, Mr. President, neither astonishes nor alarms me. Shall we yield to the outcry? For one, I say, Never! In my judgment, it is time to pause. We have yielded point after point; we have crowded concession on concession, until duty, heroism, patriotism, shame, demand that we should stop. . . . We of the West are in the habit of looking upon the Union as we look upon the arch of Heaven, without a thought that it can ever decay or fall."

Upon the critical question of slavery in New Mexico, the radical men on both sides demanded some explicit statement. On June 3 Jefferson Davis raised the direct issue by moving, "That nothing herein contained shall be construed to prevent said territorial legislature passing such laws as may be necessary for the protection of the rights of property of any kind which may have been, or may be hereafter, conformably to the Constitution and laws of the United States, held in or introduced into said Territory." Then Chase proposed the searching amendment, "that nothing herein contained shall be construed as authorizing or permitting the introduction of slavery or the holding of persons as property within said Territory." The issue thus presented obliged Cass and Douglas to explain themselves as to their theories regarding the right of the people of the Territories to govern themselves; and the fierce debate led to a test vote on Chase's amendment showing 21 affirmatives (including both Chase and Douglas) and 36 negatives (including Cass). Although hopelessly beaten by this vote of the Senate on the main question of territorial slavery, Chase continued to offer amendments intended either to modify or to annul offensive clauses.

The death of Taylor made it possible to utilize the majorities in favor of the Compromise, and from August 9 to September 14, the six successive compromise bills passed the Senate. Chase stood out to the last, and on September 18 introduced a bill to prohibit slavery in the Territories, as an indication of his desire to reopen the controversy just settled. But the solid business men of the North, whose influence brought statesmen like Webster to support the Compromise, were satisfied; and, indeed, a large majority of the voters, both North, and South, were glad to be at peace. The actual question of slavery in New Mexico seemed and indeed proved insignificant; but the organization of the two Territories of Utah and New Mexico with clauses "extending" the Constitution and laws, and promising to admit them as States "with or without slavery as their constitution may prescribe" was a virtual admission of the two dangerous principles, that the South was entitled to a share of annexed territory, and that in all its portion of such territory it was at liberty to introduce slavery, if circumstances permitted. Chase wrote to Sumner, September 8, 1850: "Clouds and darkness are upon us at present. The slaveholders have succeeded beyond their wildest hopes twelve months ago. True, some have demanded even more than they have attained; but this extreme demand was necessary to receive the immense concession which has been made to them. Without it executive influence and bribery would, perhaps, have availed nothing. 'Well, what now?' I say with blind Milton, glorious child of Freedom, though blind,—

> 'Bate no jot
> Of heart or hope, but still bear up and steer
> Right onward.'"

The violent rescue of the fugitive Shadrach in Boston, in February, 1851, gave Chase an opportunity to point out how impossible it was to put an end to discussions on slavery; indeed, he prophesied that the Fugitive Slave Law would "produce more agitation than any other which has ever been enacted by Congress," and that it would never be effectively executed. This summary of the facts of the case drew upon Chase the wrath of Douglas, whose bold misstatements were too much for Chase's debating skill. It also led Clay to taunt Chase with being an abolitionist. Chase replied with spirit, denying any connection with disunionists, but asserting his fellowship with those "who, within the limits of constitutional obligation, seek to rescue this government from all connection with slavery."

The greater part of Chase's energy during 1851 and 1852 was directed to a vain attempt to build up what he called the "Free Democracy." He made efforts to support and encourage newspapers favorable to his plan, and especially to stem the tide which was drawing Free-Soil Democrats back to their party. On May 30, 1851, in a speech at Toledo before a Democratic mass-meeting, he declared: "I was elected as a Democrat, recognizing and well known to recognize the duty of carrying out Democratic principles in their practical application to every subject of legislation." But though he might be a good Democrat, the other good Democrats would have nothing to do with Chase's Free-Soil friends, and the tide ran steadily against him. In 1850 the Ohio Democrats refused to accept anti-slavery doctrines; yet Chase gave formal notice that he should support the Democratic state ticket against his old Liberty friend, Samuel Lewis.

At no time in his life was Chase so far separated from his anti-slavery friends as during the two years, 1851 and 1852; and though he afterward regained their confidence, he never got back the feeling of hearty friendship which would have been so valuable for his own later political hopes. In the campaign of 1852 he was virtually compelled by the nomination of Pierce on a "finality" platform to join his old Free-Soil allies.

In the election of 1852 the fortunes of the Free Democracy seemed to be at as low an ebb as those of Chase himself; they could not strike a responsive note in the popular mind, and the Whigs, from whom more was to be expected than from the Democrats, were routed. Pierce was triumphantly elected, and Hale got only 157,000 votes, about half the Free-Soil vote of 1848. The new Democratic President at once surrounded himself by ultra pro-slavery influences, and made Jefferson Davis a member of his cabinet. Nevertheless the election of 1852 showed the third party in excellent fighting trim, especially in the Northwest. In 1853 it made a strong canvass in the state elections; and in Ohio, where Chase took an active part in the campaign, it raised its vote from 32,000 to 50,000. A few far-sighted men saw that the great Whig party was about to resolve itself into its elements, and that the field was open for a new political aggregation founded on the slavery issue.

In an open "Letter to Hon. A. P. Edgerton," dated November 14, 1853, Chase showed his growing despair of the national Democracy, which adhered to the Compromise of 1850 and especially to the Fugitive Slave Law, and was trying to cry down the discussion of slavery everywhere. After that letter there could be no place and no hope for Chase in the Democratic party. In the Ohio state election of 1853 the legislature which would elect his successor to the Senate showed a clear Democratic majority, and in due time elected George E. Pugh; and Chase's six years' effort to influence the Democratic party was at an end.

The Nebraska Bill, introduced by Douglas in 1854, was simply an attempt to make good to the South the expected advantages which had not accrued from the Compromise of 1820; that is, to give to the slave power the strip west of Missouri, at least as far as California, in compensation for the barrenness of New Mexico; and it came about at just this time because the great electoral majority of 1852 made the Democratic leaders think that no excess could deprive them of their power. The proposal to set aside the Missouri Compromise came as a surprise to the Southerners, who had not supposed that the deficiency of which they were beginning to be conscious could be made up without another annexation; but it was just the kind of aggressive measure which Chase and other abolitionists had long predicted. Yet Chase was as much taken aback as others not in the secret. On December 31, 1852, he thought that the administration "would worry along without any marked defeats henceforth;" but on January 22, 1854, the conflict had begun and he writes: "Douglas, I suppose eager to compel the South to come to him, has out-southernized the South; and has dragged the timid and irresolute administration along with him."

Chase's greatest opportunity had at last come to him; for in the Kansas-Nebraska debate he was able to concentrate all the previous experience of his life. A fair parliamentarian, held back by no party allegiance, already cut loose from his constituency in Ohio, standing for the free Northwest against the Northwestern champion Douglas, strong in constitutional exposition, matured by five years of conflict in the Senate, known far and wide as a fearless political abolitionist, above all inspired by seventeen years of conscientious hatred of slavery and the slave power, Chase showed himself not only a bold, sagacious, high-minded man, but also a skillful leader of the unorganized anti-slavery forces, a formulator of great principles, a herald of freedom to his countrymen, and one of the founders of a new national party. His part in the Kansas-Nebraska contest is attested by his chief adversary, for Douglas later said of him: "In opposition Seward's and Sumner's speeches were essays against slavery. Chase of Ohio was the leader."

The questions included in the contest may be briefly stated. The prime object was to give to the South a slave State north of Texas; but the Missouri Compromise stood in the way. To repeal that statute would be an act so aggressive that Douglas invented the ingenious romance that it had already been "superseded" by the Compromise of 1850. The South demanded something more definite; Douglas introduced a clause setting forth that the Act of 1820 had been "repealed" by the Act of 1850, and he took his stand on the "principle of non-intervention," by which, he said, the people of a Territory were left free to deal with the question of slavery for themselves. The early stages of the Nebraska Bill, therefore, indicate Douglas's attempt to shape his measure so as to command the support of Northern Democrats by its principle of the freedom of territorial voters, and to satisfy Southern Democrats by its principle of the slavery of the territorial negro.

On January 4, 1854, Douglas reported his bill in its first form, as a simple proposition for the organization of the Territory of Nebraska; on slavery the bill simply repeated the uncertain clause of the Compromise of 1850. In a second form, dated January 10, the bill declared that all questions relating to slavery should be settled by the people themselves through their appropriate representatives. The third form, reported January 23, divided the region into two Territories, and in express terms declared the Missouri Compromise "inoperative," in that it was "superseded" by the legislation of 1850. In its final form the bill contained what Benton called "a stump speech injected into the belly of the bill,"—a long declaration that the power over slavery in the Territories resided not in Congress, but in the people of the Territories.

At every step there was constitutional, political, and moral reason for opposing this bill in any of its protean forms. It was unnecessary; it was illogical; it was inconsistent; it was founded on a falsehood; it broke faith which had been kept a third of a century; it brought on a sectional conflict. Nevertheless it had elements of strength, and was from the outset likely to pass. In the first place, some act organizing the Territory was necessary, and this was the bill reported by the regular Committee on Territories. In the second place, Douglas was a terribly hard fighter. He was counted the most dangerous debater in public life, because he had great power of bold and satirical statement, and that advantage which the madman has over men cautious for their own lives, for he could and would say anything that was likely to be damaging to an adversary, without stopping to ask if it were true; and because he had amazing address in explaining away any previous utterances that might embarrass him; or, if he were cornered, he would plaintively assert that he had explained these things so many times that it was insulting to the intelligence to repeat his argument. In the third place, Douglas had by instinct seized upon a principle which was certain to be popular. The frontier Territories were really colonies on their way to become States; their legislatures, counties, towns, and school districts did actually manage nearly all the affairs of their communities; it was therefore a taking proposition to say that they were as competent to settle the question of slavery as were the States. In the fourth place, Douglas early got the adhesion of Pierce, and thus secured a good part of the Northern Democrats. The Southern Democrats could of course be depended upon to support a party measure introduced for their benefit, and Douglas confidently and with good reason counted on the Southern Whigs to aid him. In the fifth place, Douglas never in his whole life understood why men like Chase and Lincoln were opposed to slavery; he represented southern Illinois, and imbibed the sentiment of its early settlers from the border slave States, — the sentiment that slavery was a fact, like fire or rain or human nature, with good and bad sides, but fixed and unquestionable.

Most of the points favorable to the bill were early seen by Chase. January 29, 1854, he wrote: "I am fully advised that the Aments [amendments] as they now stand were concocted in consultation with Pierce, and that the administration, with a good deal of trepidation, has resolved to risk its future on the bill as it now stands. Many of its warm friends say that they are sure to go down upon it. There is certainly great alarm and misgiving. Cass told me to-day that he was not consulted and was decidedly against the renewal of the agitation; but he will vote with the prevailing side. A personal and near friend of the President's called on me to-night and told me that Cass was excluded from consultation. They want to drag him along. Even New Hampshire wavers about respecting the bill. All Rhode Island, except, perhaps, Jones, is against it. Every Northern Whig without exception is against it. Houston and Benton are against it."

To concentrate the elements of opposition and to lead the attack on Douglas and his combination of forces, was Chase's task. Among the most significant incidents in the history of the measure are Chase's "Appeal of the Independent Democrats," Chase's personal controversy with Douglas, and Chase's amendments. The great danger was that the Nebraska Bill might be rushed through both Houses before the public sentiment of the country could be brought to bear or an opposition organized in Congress. On January 25, two weeks after the second report of Douglas's committee, which disclosed the project to make "squatter sovereignty" the basis for the new Territories, there appeared in the press an "Appeal of the Independent Democrats in Congress to the People of the United States." This document, probably suggested by John Quincy Adams's "Appeal against the Annexation of Texas," in 1842, and based on a draft by Giddings, was written by Chase, who a few months later claimed it "as the most valuable of my works." He had aimed at first to get the signatures of Ohio members of all parties, and to address it to Ohio; but it had taken a wider range, and was signed by Chase, Sumner, Giddings, and Edward Wade of Ohio,

Gerrit Smith of New York, and De Witt of Massachusetts. The change of purpose had delayed it so long that, though dated January 19, it did not appear until the 25th and 26th. The appeal was at once taken up as the statement of the free North. In terse, brief, vigorous form it revealed the real blackness of the bill, its violation of the compact of the Missouri Compromise, unquestioned for thirty years, its effect on free laborers, its invasion of human rights. A few extracts will better show its spirit than can any analysis.

"We arraign this bill as a gross violation of a sacred pledge; as a criminal betrayal of precious rights; as part and parcel of an atrocious plot to exclude from a vast unoccupied region immigrants from the Old World and free laborers from our own States, and convert it into a dreary region of despotism, inhabited by masters and slaves. . . .

"The pretenses, therefore, that the territory covered by the positive prohibition of 1820 sustains a similar relation to slavery with that acquired from Mexico, covered by no prohibition except that of disputed constitutional or Mexican law, and that the Compromises of 1850 require the incorporation of the pro-slavery clauses of the Utah and New Mexico Bill in the Nebraska act, are mere inventions, designed to cover up from public reprehension meditated bad faith. Were he living now, no one would be more forward, more eloquent, or more indignant in his denunciation of that bad faith than Henry Clay, the foremost champion of both compromises. . . . The interests of freedom and the Union are in imminent peril. Demagogues may tell you that the Union can be maintained only by submitting to the demands of slavery. We tell you that the Union can only be maintained by the full recognition of the just claims of freedom and man. The Union was formed to establish justice and secure the blessings of liberty. When it fails to accomplish these ends it will be worthless, and when it becomes worthless it cannot long endure.

"We entreat you to be mindful of that fundamental maxim of Democracy — EQUAL RIGHTS AND EXACT JUSTICE FOR ALL MEN. Do not submit to become agents in extending legalized oppression and systematized injustice over a vast territory yet exempt from these terrible evils.

"We implore Christians and Christian ministers to interpose. Their divine religion requires them to behold in every man a brother, and to labor for the advancement and regeneration of the human race. . . .

"Whatever apologies may be offered for the toleration of slavery in the States, none can be offered for its extension into territories where it does not exist, and where that extension involves the repeal of ancient law and the violation of solemn compact. Let all protest, earnestly and emphatically, by correspondence, through the press, by memorials, by resolutions of public meetings and legislative bodies, and in whatever other mode may seem expedient, against this enormous crime.

"For ourselves, we shall resist it by speech and vote, and with all the abilities which God has given us. Even if overcome in the impending struggle, we shall not submit. We shall go home to our constituents, erect anew the standard of freedom, and call on the people to come to the rescue of the country from the domination of slavery. We will not despair; for the cause of human freedom is the cause of God."

Although in form the address was directed against the slave power in general, its spirit was a denunciation of the men who were responsible for it; indeed, the third report of Douglas's committee, January 23, had caused Chase to wait a day in order that he might add a hasty postscript, in which he used such harsh language as the occasion justified. The "superseding" clause he called "a manifest falsification of the truths of history — Mr. Douglas himself never advanced such a pretense until this session. . . . Will the people permit their dearest interests thus to be made the mere hazards of a presidential game, and destroyed by false facts and false influences?"

That Douglas was the one responsible force in bringing forward this bill no one doubted, least of all Douglas himself. Four years later he said to his autobiographer, Cutts: "I refer you to my speeches in the Senate for the whole argument on the Kansas-Nebraska Act. I passed the Kansas-Nebraska Act myself. I had the authority and power of a dictator throughout the whole controversy in both houses. The speeches were nothing. It was the marshaling and directing of men and guarding from attacks and with a ceaseless vigilance preventing surprise." Hence Douglas must have expected hard knocks, and was prepared to defend himself by one of his usual savage attacks.

January 30, Douglas came into the Senate in a reckless fury, crying: "Our motives are arraigned and our characters calumniated — coarse epithets are applied to me by name. . . . This was done on the Sabbath day and by a set of politicians, to advance their own political purposes, in the name of our holy religion." He declared that Chase had "violated all the rules of courtesy and propriety;" and when Chase disclaimed offense, Douglas added: "It may be that I shall be able to nail that denial, as I have the statements which are over his own signature, as a bare falsehood." With his usual hawk-like keenness, Douglas fixed upon Chase, as an evidence of bad faith, an erroneous statement made by some New York papers; though at the same time he did not hesitate to interpolate words into his own quotations from the "Appeal."

This study of legislative billingsgate is necessary, because it was the first time that Chase's honesty had been questioned in the Senate, and because behind the vituperation of Douglas was a method, — an attempt to transfer the discussion from the objections against the bill to the objectors themselves, and thus to terrorize his opponents. No man living enjoyed debating against Douglas.

Lincoln, four years later, was barely able to drive him into a corner; and Chase would have been glad to avoid the controversy. "I know the gigantic stature of the senator," said he, "I know the weight and importance which he possesses in the country — and I know also the great disadvantages under which I enter into any controversy which he provokes." Afterward, indeed, Chase made a rather weak attempt to disclaim having had Douglas especially in his mind. "We spoke of the bill," said he, "and spoke of its character. We said nothing about the individuals who were its authors." But the most powerful argument against the bill was its bad faith; and who but Douglas had made bad faith its principle? The next day the controversy was renewed, and Chase was nettled into saying: "I expect no courtesy and desire none from the senator from Illinois." Douglas later recovered his temper and made overtures of peace, but the proud Ohio statesman could not forget the assault upon him.

Issue was at once joined in both Senate and House on the merits of the Kansas-Nebraska Bill, and for many weeks the attention of the whole country was given to the debate. By amendments offered February 3 and supported by a long and able speech, Chase singled out two minor yet vital questions; namely, whether the Compromise of 1850 did in fact "supersede" the Compromise of 1820, and whether the territorial legislature was really expected to have full control over slavery.

To the first point Douglas directed all his formidable powers, for it was his policy to avoid the rôle of a disturber of the peace. The second point was distinctly brought out by Chase in the clause usually called "the Chase amendment," "under which the people of the Territories, through their appropriate representatives, may, if they see fit, prohibit the existence of slavery therein." This was a direct test of the sincerity of Douglas's doctrine of popular sovereignty. Without such a clause, as Chase showed, the legislature was left subject to a governor's veto and to the construction of judges appointed by the President. Douglas could not be brought to meet this question squarely. He was satisfied to leave to the territorial government powers "subject only to the Constitution of the United States;" for he knew as well as Chase that a favorite Southern doctrine was that under the Constitution neither Congress nor a territorial legislature could interfere with any master who chose to take his slave into a Territory. Chase's amendment was therefore voted down, 10 to 36; and in like manner was treated every one of his amendments intended to make the territorial government more popular, — such as his proposals to let the people elect their territorial officers, to create only one Territory instead of two, and to extend the suffrage to aliens who had declared their intention of becoming citizens.

So far as the Senate was concerned, the result was from the first predetermined, for Douglas must have known, on January 24, that he had more than a majority. But the country had become aroused, and by the time the Senate came to a vote, on March 3, Chase was at the head of a compact body of strong men, Whigs and Democrats. Hale was now out of the Senate; but Chase's colleague, B. F. Wade, stimulated by the overwhelming sentiment of Ohio, came to his aid with a coarse but effective rhetoric, resembling that of Douglas. Seward also entered the lists against Douglas, carefully confining himself to the repeal of the Compromise of 1820; and Walker and Dodge of Wisconsin, and Fessenden of Maine took valiant part in the debate. For two days, March 2 and 3, there was a running fight, in which Douglas showed his immense powers, silencing his opponents right and left, and returning with the most furious language to his attack on Chase, unblushingly twisting his own record, and insisting over and over again that the Compromise of 1850, though in its terms applying to New Mexico and Utah, was intended to repeal the Missouri Compromise, which applied to the Louisiana purchase. Chase was no match in debate for this extraordinary man, and on the test vote, March 3, the bill passed the Senate by 37 to 14.

The fate of the measure now depended on the House, in which Chase's counsels and magazine of arguments were useful; but he had no such influence as that of Douglas, who carried half the Democrats with him, lobbied on the floor of the

House, and passed the bill by a majority of 108 to 100. On its return to the Senate, Chase made his last speech on the subject, presenting a calm view of the real purpose of the bill, — the perpetuation of the slave power, — and predicting that so far as the new Territory was concerned the South would lose in the end, because this Territory would be colonized by men from the free States.

Wade truly said: "The humiliation of the North is complete and overwhelming. No Southern enemy of hers can wish her deeper degradation." In 1846 most of the Northern States had favored a prohibition by Congress of slavery in every Territory in the Union except in the Indian Territory; in 1854 Northern Democrats opened to slavery every Territory then existing or to be annexed. Slavery, instead of decaying by the slow process of emancipation, for which many slaveholders had once hoped, had resisted every attempt made to check it by national action, and was now advancing into free regions.

The North was beaten, but it was aroused. From the "Appeal of the Independent Democrats" in January to the passage of the act in May, there had been a succession of public meetings which threatened political ruin to Northern members of Congress who should side with Douglas, and which sent out addresses, protests, and memorials. For example, John Jay wrote to Chase on February 7: "*We accept the gauntlet thus thrown down to the free States.* I am ready for the fight between

Slavery and Freedom. . . . We swear for ourselves, and will teach the oath to our children, never again to enter into a truce with such an accursed and faithless power, — but to fight on and to fight ever, until Congress has gone to the *farthest limit of its power* for the extinction of slavery and the slave trade — and the Constitution has been so amended as to leave us free from all responsibility for the devilish system."

Jay and the thousands of anti-slavery men like him, both old abolitionists and recent converts, had to be organized before their importance could be felt in Congress and in the state administrations. In the last hours of the final debate Chase pointed out, and Douglas anathematized, the inevitable political result of the Kansas-Nebraska Act. Chase declared that the Whig party was rent in twain, and that the Northern wing was about to unite with the Independent Democrats in a new party. Douglas replied in his fiercest vein, declaring that such a coalition meant "civil war, servile war, and disunion. I do not hesitate," he exclaimed, "here in the presence of its leaders and confederates, to denounce the scheme as involving treason in its most revolting form. I accept your challenge; raise your black flag; call up your forces on the Constitution, as you have threatened it here. We will be ready to meet all your allied forces." With that challenge and reply the discussion of the Kansas-Nebraska Bill ended in the Senate, and the Republican party began.

To Chase the end of his term as senator, in

March, 1855, was a disappointment. In his six years he had gradually become a power in that conservative body, and, notwithstanding his antislavery principles, he appears to have carried away with him the respect of all his colleagues except Douglas; even Soulé, most ardent of the fire-eaters, had a personal regard for him. Though Chase never could learn the quickness and adroitness which made Seward and Hale such formidable debaters, he knew how to argue, and especially how to state great principles in a popular form. The "New York Evening Post" said of him, at the end of his term: "We always counted on his opposition to a corrupt or extravagant expenditure or appropriation; and we could always depend on his coöperation to restrain action of the federal government within its proper sphere." On all the phases of the slavery question he was the senator who cared most about it, and who therefore never yielded or compromised. When he left the Senate there was no one to take his place, for Seward and Wade and the other leaders of the new Republican party had the caution of chieftains, showing a willingness to yield a part of their platform if they could get the rest. In his career in the Senate Chase showed that lack of imagination in things political which was a characteristic throughout his life. What seemed to him reasonable he thought must have equal weight in other minds; but he also showed his other dominant characteristic, — a consciousness of moral responsibility in his political service.

CHAPTER VI

THE REPUBLICAN GOVERNOR

THE reason for the existence of the political abolitionists was that slavery was a political question, was a vital question, and must eventually become the basis of a division into national parties. The new economic conditions of the country so far caused the disappearance of old party issues that the low revenue tariff of 1846 was in the fifties accepted by the whole country, the Bank was no longer urged by anybody of influence, and though people squabbled over land grants, internal improvements, and homestead laws, none of these questions were tenets of party faith. Ever since the debates on the annexation of Texas, however, the issues which really interested voters and occupied party leaders brought in some phase of the slavery question. The Liberty men seized upon a live issue, took definite ground upon it, and had reason to expect that large numbers would come out from the old parties to join them. Hence the new life and the elasticity shown in the elections of 1853, when the Free Democrats became aware that the Whig party was at last moribund.

Among the Whigs some strong anti-slavery men,

like Seward, were always allowed to remain in regular standing with their party; but the Democrats deliberately crushed out that element in their party by the Kansas-Nebraska Bill. Douglas probably expected to see the loss of voters through the secession of Northern Democrats made good by the adhesion of Southern Whigs; and though he was shrewd enough to foresee a combination of the bolting Democrats with the Northern Whigs and the handful of organized Free Democrats, he relied on branding such a coalition as a "sectional party;" and his inability to understand the moral indignation against slavery caused him to underestimate the number of Democrats who would not accept any further extension of slavery.

The Kansas-Nebraska Bill was therefore the shock which started a new process of party crystallization. While the debate was in progress, conventions of "Anti-Nebraska" men began in the Northern States; and the passage of the act, May 30, 1854, increased the excitement, and stimulated a formal organization of political anti-slavery men. In various Northern States, members of Congress and men at home united in calling local conventions to nominate state and congressional candidates for the elections of 1854. The Michigan convention, held at Detroit, July 6, 1854, took upon itself the name of the Republican party, already several times used by local gatherings. The new title was assumed by the Ohio anti-Nebraska convention of July 13, and during the campaign Republican organizations were formed in all the other Northern States. In this great movement Chase had a large part, perhaps larger than that of any other one man. He describes his action in his own State as follows: "Immediately after the passage of the Nebraska Bill I prepared a call for a convention in Ohio to organize a 'Democracy of the people' in opposition to the servile Democracy. Wade joined me in a letter inviting signatures, and the letter and call were sent to . . . Ohio; but a movement for a similar convention, less definite in object, . . . superseded that which we proposed."

This movement at once proved its popularity. Though Pierce had 13,000 majority in Ohio in 1852, the election of 1854 showed a Republican majority of 80,000; the congressional delegation of 1853 was 12 Democrats, 6 Whigs, and 3 third-party men, but every member elected in 1854 was an anti-Nebraska man. Some States, including Massachusetts, elected Anti-Nebraska state officers; and in the congressional election nearly all the Northern Douglas Democrats in the House lost their seats, and a clear anti-Nebraska majority was chosen for the national House, which would assemble in 1855. Such was the reply of the country to Douglas's principle of squatter sovereignty.

From Chase's own statements it is plain that during 1854 he had not yet rid himself of the belief that a purified Democracy was the party of the future; he could not understand, and never did clearly understand, the importance of choosing a new name and making a new party in which Whigs, Democrats, and Free Democrats might all join without feeling that they were accepting the designation or the principles of former political enemies. In December, 1854, he still calls himself an "Independent Democrat," and says: "In the recent election in Ohio I entered heartily into the People's movement, which was nothing more or less than a coöperation of Liberal Democrats, Independent Democrats, and Whigs, for the election of reliable slavery prohibitionists to the next Congress and of rebuking the pro-slavery action of the administration party." By coöperation Chase meant temporary fusion rather than a consolidated party.

Three influences combined to waken Chase from the delusion that there could be a Democratic anti-slavery party: these were the rise and fall of the Native American, or Know-Nothing party, his nomination for governor of Ohio in 1855, and the Kansas troubles. The Know-Nothings began to come up as the Whigs disintegrated; they formed a convenient rallying point for Northern and Southern Whigs, who liked to act together and were willing to take common ground against the foreigner; and as their success in the state elections of 1854 and early 1855 seemed to promise them continuance as a national party, thousands of ardent anti-slavery men went into their organization. Chase, however, by nature and education was opposed to distinctions founded merely on race or birthplace, and in dignified and spirited, although cautious, terms expressed his lack of sympathy with the movement in a private letter to Dr. Paul, December 28, 1854.

"For one," he says, "I wish to see this People's movement go on in the liberal spirit which has thus far characterized it. But if it is to be understood that the Know-Nothings who participated in it will henceforth ignore the anti-slavery element or support no candidates who are not members of their order, or whose nominations are not dictated by them, those who regard the slavery question as of paramount importance and whose principles will not allow them to become members of Know-Nothing associations, must of necessity assume an antagonistic position. If this conflict shall arise, it is plain that the People's movement cannot go on or must go on without the Know-Nothing coöperation. It becomes the friends of Liberty to be prepared for every event. . . . I cannot take upon myself any secret political obligations. I cannot proscribe men on account of their birth. I cannot make religious faith a political test." . . .

February 21, 1855, Chase expressed himself with more freedom: "There is not in my opinion the slightest reason to believe that the ultra-Nativism and anti-Catholicism imputed to the Know-Nothings will be permanent characteristics of any great political party. Just as little reason is there to think that secrecy can be maintained as a vital element of political organizations. I do not therefore share the apprehension which some of the best friends of Liberty sustain in respect to the Know-Nothing movement."

Chase's power of political organization, narrowly successful in the senatorial election of 1849, now brought to him a new dignity. In July, 1855, he was nominated by the Anti-Nebraska Republican convention for the governorship of Ohio. Among the "Come-Outers," Chase still stood as a Democrat, and among the old Whigs he was still looked upon as a renegade; hence the decision in both nomination and election lay with the Know-Nothings, who gave him to understand that he might have their nomination only by joining their order. For several months negotiations went on, with a view to securing both Know-Nothing and Republican support; and the letter to Dr. Paul, of December, 1854, was published in June, 1855, to show the kindly feeling of Chase toward good Know-Nothings who were opposed to slavery, and at the same time to make clear to the Germans that he had not bowed the knee to the anti-foreign Baal.[1]

[1] A letter of J. M. Ashley, under date of May 9, urges Chase to omit a paragraph and otherwise to revise the letter; with these changes, he says, "there can be no doubt in our minds of its placing you far in the ascendency of Seward or any other man in the United States." Ashley said that the changes would not affect the principles of the letter. There is no evidence to show that Chase consented thus to appear to have said what he did not

In spite of all these efforts, the Independent Democrats and Republicans called separate conventions. The old Whigs offered Chase the nomination as state supreme judge, but he insisted on an anti-slavery platform and a fair division of the ticket as the condition of fusion with the Know-Nothings. The critical date was July 13, when a "People's Convention," in part made up of Know-Nothings, assembled at Columbus and nominated Chase for governor. The old Whigs nominated Trimble, a Know-Nothing; and the old Democrats nominated Joseph Medill.

Chase looked upon his nomination as a public protest against the repeal of the Missouri Compromise, and in the campaign which followed he made one of his most arduous and effective tours of stump-speaking. In this triangular campaign, the attitude of the Germans became a matter of great importance; they had usually preferred the Democratic party in the Northwest, especially after the forced emigration of some of the ablest and most liberal of their countrymen, in 1848, for acting as democrats in Germany. Hence it was a delicate matter for Chase to hold both the native American and the German vote. On election day the vote was as follows: Chase, 146,000, Medill, 131,000, Trimble, 24,000. Ford, candidate for lieutenant-governor, got 13,000 more votes than

say; but as this is the only approach to untruthfulness discovered in Chase's political life, it has seemed desirable to state the facts upon it.

Chase on the same ticket; yet there can be no doubt that Chase was the strong element in the political combination. The effects of this election were far-reaching: in 1855 the anti-Nebraska movement seemed to lose elasticity, and State after State went back to the Democracy; it was Chase who stemmed the tide, held the third State in the Union, strengthened the national party for the election of 1856, and retained his place as one of the official leaders of the Republican party.

When he was inaugurated as governor of Ohio, in January, 1856, the State was no longer the frontier community of the earlier days, for which a canal-boat was thought to be a proper emblem on the great seal of the commonwealth. Coal-mining, long important, had become a large industry since 1845, when bituminous coal was first used in Ohio for smelting iron; the State was now bound together, east and west, north and south, by lines of railroad; Cincinnati and Cleveland had become manufacturing cities; and the population had been much altered by Irish and German immigration. In national affairs Ohio was beginning to assume a position as a central and pivotal State; indeed, one Northwestern president, Harrison, had been an Ohio man, and Ewing, Corwin, and Lewis Campbell were leaders in Congress.

The chief magistrate of Ohio, however, might still be described by a phrase which Chase had used twenty-five years earlier in his History of Ohio, —

"The governor is a name almost without meaning." Without a veto power, with very small powers of appointment, with little official ceremony or prestige, the ablest governors had few opportunities to affect the destiny of their State, and many chances to make blunders. The governor could not control other state officers elected on the same ticket with himself, and yet was certain to be held responsible for their faults.

Chase was not cut out for a popular governor. While in the Senate he had been accused of coldness, aloofness, and lack of human instincts, although his sense of his own uprightness and his belief in his clearness of judgment had been much chastened by his first four years in that body. Now, as a renowned champion of freedom, for the first time in his life chosen to an important office by popular vote, one of the defenders of the cause in Kansas, a sage in his own party, Chase found himself almost in a new atmosphere, and had already begun to muse upon that picture of "President Chase" which came back to his mind every year during the rest of his life.

The lack of "personal magnetism" did not prevent him from making an excellent governor. His small patronage was skillfully fostered, and the Germans had full recognition. Of his policy in state affairs he says later: "I at once addressed myself to the duties of my new position. I sought to promote all practicable reforms; encouraged, by all the means in my power, the interests of education; endeavored to reorganize the military system of the State; and omitted no opportunity of making the voice of Ohio heard on the side of freedom and justice. At the same time, I endeavored, as far as practicable, to conciliate opposition founded on misapprehension, and succeeded finally in organizing a compact and powerful party, based on the great principles of freedom and free labor."

There was plenty of opportunity for a man to make his influence felt in such matters. He reformed the militia system, which was in such a condition that a refusal to issue arms to other than uniformed companies was regarded as an innovation; he took much interest in securing a geological survey of the State; he advocated a bureau of statistics; he urged better opportunities for the state university and for common schools; and he busied himself in founding a railroad commission. This last suggestion came from an early foresight as to the power likely to be acquired by great corporations through the control of all the transportation upon a large area. Chase was one of the earliest statesmen to see this danger and to try to provide against it.

Hardly had the new governor begun his service when the election of 1856 again called out his greatest energy. The national Native American party, of which Horace Greeley had said that "you might as well talk of a national anti-potato-rot party," broke up in February, 1856, by the secession of the anti-slavery Know-Nothings. With their aid and that of the bolting Democrats the Republicans had a fair hope of outrunning, in the Northern States, both the regular Democrats and the old Whigs. This is the secret of the near approach to the choice of a president by the Republicans in 1856; for they proved to have pluralities in every Northern State except New Jersey, Pennsylvania, Indiana, and Illinois.

How far a man may, with good taste and uprightness, enter into a personal canvass for a nomination to the presidency is a difficult question of ethics. To Chase it seemed simple; he believed sincerely that he had the qualities of a president; he believed that the principles for which he stood were those to which the Republican party must commit itself if it was to be honest; he believed that he had a large popular support throughout the country; and he believed that proper organization and means of making himself known would bring about his nomination. He had no experienced lieutenants like Thurlow Weed in New York, political moles to prepare the ground for him unseen; Hamlin and Ashley and Hoadly were energetic young men, but of little public reputation; and though Chase possessed and cultivated an acquaintance in New York and New England, he had no workers in the East who could secure delegates or make combinations for him. The feeling of leadership, the desire to be President, were right and natural, and it does not appear that Chase used any but straightforward means to secure a nomination. It was his fault to overestimate other people's inclination toward him, and his weakness not to be on cordial terms of equal friendship with any of the other Republican leaders.

During the first half of 1856 Chase and his few friends were hard at work. The preliminary Pittsburg convention of 1856, the first national Republican gathering, gave an opportunity for comparing the respective strength of candidates, and one of Chase's friends who was present was sure that he would have been nominated had the convention undertaken to present a candidate. By this time the possible nominees had all come forward. Bailey wrote, February 21, that Seward would not risk seeking a nomination, and that the leading candidates were Preston King, Colonel Frémont (brought forward by Frank J. Blair), and John McLean. Just at this time Banks was chosen speaker of the House of Representatives, and he also loomed up as a candidate. In his intimate correspondence with Edward L. Pierce, Chase revealed his own hopes and fears; he inveighed against "the feeling, which some men seem to have fallen into, of taking up an untried man for President;" he complained that Hiram Barney, his lieutenant in New York, was "a little disposed sometimes to forbear working, in fear that nothing can be done." But Pierce felt compelled to write a cooling letter, in which he predicted the inevitable nomination of Frémont.

Even with a solid Ohio delegation and the prestige of his governorship, Chase could hardly have been successful against the combination formed in favor of Frémont; but he was now to learn the strength of his home opponents and enemies. Of the Ohio delegation he could count on only thirty-five, while thirty-four were for either McLean or Frémont. "My friends did not act," said he, "with the skill and decision which was required." In addition to these thirty-five faithful ones, about sixty delegates to the Philadelphia Convention from other States were for Chase; though it was a sore point with him that he could not secure the New Hampshire delegation. Yet he was still confident. "It seems to me," said he, "that if the most cherished wishes of the people could prevail, I should be nominated." Nevertheless, he gave to Hoadly a letter of withdrawal, to be used if necessary. Hoadly saw nothing else to do, Chase's name was withdrawn, and Frémont was nominated. It was well that Chase did not succeed in risking his reputation in that campaign, for no out-and-out anti-slavery man could have polled a larger vote than the neutral and unknown Frémont, and yet he was defeated by James Buchanan.

Though no man was himself more incorruptible in office, Chase could not help knowing that the state Republican administration, of which he was the titular head, was very corrupt, and that the state treasurer, Gibson, had refused to show his books; and Ashley wrote: "There has been a very large number of these blood-sucking Republicans by name, who have shown that they would ruin not only the party but their nearest friends." Yet it seems to have been an unexpected blow to Chase when in June, 1857, Gibson brazenly and defiantly admitted that $500,000 was missing from the state treasury. Chase when roused showed much resolution, and even invented a new method of removal from office; for when Gibson refused to resign in order that a successor might be appointed, the governor brought him to terms by threatening to make a vacancy by instituting legal proceedings against him. Still it seemed hard for Chase to admit that embezzlement had been going on among his friends, and he spoke of Gibson as "reckless" and "infatuated," rather than criminal.

The incident was very dangerous for a party about to enter on a campaign; hence when pressure was put upon Chase to accept a renomination and head the fight, he could not resist, though he knew that he was taking in his hand his chances for the presidency in 1860. The campaign was more than arduous, it was anxious. Payne of Cleveland, Chase's opponent, tried hard to hold the governor responsible for the Gibson fraud, and is reported to have freely bought votes with money assessed on Buchanan's federal office-holders. The Whigs and Know-Nothings were now completely broken up, and the struggle lay between Republicans and Democrats. Chase was successful by a scanty plurality of 1500 in a total vote of 330,000; but the New York "Evening Post" said of the result: "It is the most complete political victory that the governor has ever achieved." Chase's reëlection was a triumph because it set the seal of his own State on his place as a Republican leader. During the next three years, in the State and out of it, he occupied in the Republican party much the same position of general political counselor that he had held in the Liberty party ten years earlier. Even in state affairs he was thinking of national issues, and his second inaugural address was a kind of apostrophe to liberty. He felt himself in a stronger position with the legislature than heretofore. There were no new treasury scandals, and the credit and repute of his State increased; but a new crop of slavery questions now came up and caused him great trouble.

On the fugitive slave question the Compromise of 1850 had from the first been a failure: it could not prevent a slave from taking to his heels; it simply stimulated the Underground Railroad to do more business; and it played into the hands of the abolitionists by furnishing, in nearly all the Northern States, object lessons as to the necessary violence and cruelty of slavery. By taking the execution of the law entirely out of the hands of state officers, the Act of 1850 had only suggested a new batch of "personal liberty laws," passed by Northern States to compel the federal government to do all the work of pursuing the fugitives and securing them in its own buildings. The spectacle of a master laying his hand upon a shaking fugitive and taking him before a United States commissioner was unpleasant; and it was still more hateful to the people of the North to see a negro seized by a professional slave-catcher, whom he had never seen before, armed with a power of attorney or a bill of sale; besides, many people liked the excitement of leading the deputy marshals and their assistants astray, or of defying federal authority.

Another self-destructive element in the Fugitive Slave Law was its plain and necessary violation of the ordinary principles of human justice. Under the act, the question whether a man was or was not the fugitive described in the allegation was decided by "summary proceedings," without a jury. If a slave, he was legally subject to the process and had no right to complain; but if he was a free man, he was entitled to the ordinary protection of life and liberty, which this law denied him. A jury trial was what the anti-slavery people continually demanded; but everybody knew that in a free State it was next to impossible to impanel a jury in which twelve members would unite in holding any particular negro to be a fugitive or any rescuer to be a criminal; one might as well expect a Georgia jury to acquit a slave-stealer. In some States personal liberty bills prescribed a jury trial in defiance of the Act of 1850, or even required state attorneys to defend the negroes claimed.

On the other side, the Act of 1850 had laid new and severe penalties for interference with capture by "harboring or concealing" the fugitive, or by resisting the pursuer; in 1852 an attempt was even made, in the Castner Hanway case in Philadelphia, to hold resistance to slave-catchers to be constructive treason, so as to fix upon the crime a death penalty. State governments grew restive over the status of both black and white citizens or residents who were thus swept within the authority of the federal courts on charges growing out of the Fugitive Slave Law. A favorite method of raising the question as to the rival jurisdictions of State and nation was to get a *habeas corpus* from a state court, so as to examine the status of alleged fugitives or their rescuers; and in 1858, in the famous case of *Ableman* v. *Booth*, the Wisconsin Supreme Court hewed through the difficulty of rival jurisdiction by roundly declaring the Act of 1850 unconstitutional, and therefore no bar to state proceedings, and no cause for national interference.

In this exciting controversy Chase was one of the great figures, though by his moderation of conduct he gave much offense to the ultra-abolitionists. Late in March, 1855, he was called as counsel for Rosetta, a colored girl of sixteen, who had been taken from the control of her master, while traveling by rail through Ohio, and declared free by a state court. She was, however, seized by a United States deputy marshal, and from his custody rescued by a writ of *habeas corpus*, argued before a state court by R. B. Hayes. A second time the marshal seized her. On Chase's advice a test case was made, by asking for proceedings for contempt against the marshal; he was, however, discharged by Justice McLean of the United States court, on the ground that the process authorized by the Fugitive Slave Law was not subject to interference by a state court. To-day it is clear that the federal authorities, in their insistence on the superiority of federal law, were on the side of orderly national life. The Fugitive Slave Law was simply one of the instances in which a proper discretion must include the power to do injustice.

About two weeks after Chase's inauguration as governor, a slave family named Garner escaped to Cincinnati; the next day United States Marshal Robinson came to capture them, but the slaves resisted, and in a frenzy of excitement Margaret Garner seized a butcher's knife and killed her little daughter. The capture of the fugitives was at once traversed by an indictment of the Garners in a state court for murder; nevertheless they were given into the custody of the marshal by *habeas corpus* proceedings before a United States court, and by him taken before Commissioner Pendery, who held them to be fugitives; thereupon they were forthwith carried to Kentucky and delivered to their master.

These legal proceedings had dragged on for four weeks. The proposed state trial was of course simply a means of holding the negroes out of the master's hands, and was likely to keep up the general excitement over slavery; for everybody knew that under such circumstances no Ohio jury would convict a slave mother or her accomplices of murder. The case put Governor Chase into a cruel perplexity. At the beginning he had promised to sanction the process of the state courts "by the whole power at the command of the executive;" but the final delivery of the fugitives had been hasty and unexpected, and nobody could claim for the negroes that they were not legal slaves. As a last resource, on March 4 he sent a requisition to the governor of Kentucky for the return of the "murderess," arguing with much force that slaves could not be permitted to cross the river into Ohio and there commit crimes with impunity. Governor Morehead of Kentucky granted the request; but the master had by this time carried the slaves out of his State, and the confidential agent whom Chase sent to buy them reported that Margaret Garner had been sent "down the river." The Kentucky authorities had no wish to examine into the matter again, and no further proceedings could be had.

In 1864, when the question was again raised by the furious attacks of Wendell Phillips, Chase wrote that Cincinnati was at that time hostile to him, that he was taken by surprise, and that he was in Columbus at the critical moment. The real reason probably lies somewhat deeper; the governor of a State is bound to exercise more caution than a private man. Chase had formerly been attorney for fugitives; he was now governor of the whole State, and hence attorney for all its people. In a similar case, that of the fugitive Anderson, in 1857, the part which Governor Chase took in the controversy was thus described by himself some years later: —

"Judge Leavitt, at Cincinnati, then issued a writ of *habeas corpus* directed to the sheriff, requiring him to produce his prisoners. The writ was obeyed, and application was made to me to have the State represented upon the hearing. I at once directed the attorney-general to appear, who did so, and argued the questions arising in the case with great ability. Mr. Pugh and Mr. Vallandigham appeared on the side of the slave-catchers. The result was what was indeed foreseen — an order by Judge Leavitt discharging the prisoners.

"The leading administration paper denounced my action as a declaration of war on the part of Chase and his abolition crew against the United States. I was indifferent to it."

The matter had grown so serious that in July the governor went to Washington to settle the controversy. Cass, Secretary of State, had retained a feeling of admiration for Chase from their senatorial days, and he now brought about a meeting with President Buchanan, in which it was agreed that the suits should be dropped on both sides. A few months later, however, Chase, in the canvass for his reëlection, took a more belligerent tone. "We have a right," said he, "to have our state laws obeyed. We don't mean to resist federal authority. Just or unjust laws properly administered will be respected. If dissatisfied we will go to the ballot-box and redress our wrongs. But we have rights which the federal government must not invade, rights superior to its power, on which our sovereignty depends; and we do mean to assert these rights against all tyrannical assumption of authority. I know not what will be done in Champaign County. The courts will determine that. But I do know that if the marshals who violate our laws are indicted and the writs for their arrest are placed in the hands of our state officers they shall be executed. And we expect the federal government to submit."

The next year the validity of state process when opposed to national was put to another test. In September, 1858, a fugitive slave, John Price, was rescued out of the hands of his claimants by an armed mob of Oberlin people. The proceedings dragged on till the summer of 1859, when two of the rescuers were convicted. Meantime application had been brought before the Ohio Supreme Court to grant a *habeas corpus* to inquire into the status of the two convicted men, a step which would practically mean raising the question of the constitutionality of the Fugitive Slave Law. May 24, 1859, a mass meeting was held at Cleveland to protest against the convictions. Governor Chase came, and threw the weight of his official influence against violence, and also against the Fugitive Slave Law. His first words, "Citizens of Cleveland! law-abiding citizens of Cleveland!" struck a responsive chord in the meeting, and made it easy for him to add: "I will only say what I have frequently said before, that as long as the State of Ohio remains a sovereignty, and as long as I am her chief executive, the process of her courts shall be executed. The process of the United States courts must not be slighted or resisted; but as long as I represent the sovereignty of our State, I will see that the process of our state courts shall not be interfered with or resisted, but shall be fully enforced."

The state Supreme Court stood three to two against interfering; whereupon the next Republican convention punished one of the three, Judge Swan, by refusing him a renomination. Meanwhile one of the counsel for the prisoners, A. G. Riddle, had made an effective use of state process: the capturers of John Price had been indicted for kidnapping, and as their man was gone they could not prove that he was the person described in their papers. They would be tried in the same county in which Oberlin lay, and they might count on a unanimous and hostile jury. The administration now showed its interest in the whole controversy by sending Attorney-General Black to look into the cases; and when Riddle proposed to him to abandon the kidnapping suits, if all the suits against the rescuers were discontinued, the astute Philadelphia lawyer saw nothing else for it. This result was summed up by an administration organ in the caustic words: "So the government has been beaten at last, with law, justice, and facts all on its side, and Oberlin, with its relentless, higher-law creed, is triumphant."

The period of Chase's governorship was also a period of great influence and usefulness in national questions of slavery, especially on "Bleeding Kansas." Douglas's moral obtuseness had played him a trick when he brought forward the repeal of the Missouri Compromise. He not only failed to foresee the indignation of the North, but he also left out of his calculations the probability that Kansas, the southern of the two new Territories, might be controlled by free-state men. When the Southerners saw the danger of its slipping out of their grasp, they naturally held Douglas responsible; and he, in his wrath at the practical workings of popular sovereignty, could only reply that "the whole trouble in Kansas was due to the Emigrant Aid Societies." In November, 1854, the first territorial election showed 2000 votes from a community with only 1200 voters, and in March, 1855, a territorial legislature was chosen by the most shameless intimidation and fraud. Throughout 1855 and 1856 Chase was in communication with the men in Kansas who were trying to undo this wrong, — writing letters of counsel and comfort, rousing energy, promising "good rifles," and in public speeches denouncing the policy of the successive presidents, Pierce and Buchanan.

Fortunately for Kansas and for the country, the national House of Representatives from 1855 to 1857 had a majority of anti-Nebraska men, who could and did restrain any action by Congress in favor of the pro-slavery domination of Kansas. When, in July, 1856, a local civil war broke out in Kansas, Governor Chase wrote, in the fiercest indignation, to Governor Grimes of Iowa: "We must not sit still while our brethren in Kansas are in such imminent peril. You are nearest of all the free-state governors to the theatre of action. . . . It seems to me that no time should be lost and no efforts spared in sending out men fully provided, who will remain in the Territory as actual settlers . . . should the pro-slavery men of western Missouri and other States again invade Kansas . . . every sentiment of honor and every obligation of duty requires us to give our outraged brethren . . . prompt and efficient succor, without reference to settlement."

This was not the only suggestion of civil war made by Chase. When Charles Robinson, titular free-state governor of Kansas, called on some of the Eastern governors for support, Chase took the responsibility of sending to the Ohio legislature a stirring message, in which he recounted the wrongs of the Ohio men in Kansas, and rose to the emphatic declaration: "These representations cannot be properly disregarded. As an equal member of the confederacy, Ohio is entitled to demand for her citizens, emigrating to the Territories, free ingress and egress by the ordinary routes and complete protection from invasion, from usurpation, and from lawless violence. If the general government refuse this protection, I cannot doubt the right or the duty of the State to intervene."

One of the purposes of the Dred Scott decision of March, 1857, was to tie the hands of the free-state men in Kansas, and of their adherents everywhere. But Chase, the future chief justice, had long entertained and several times expounded his want of confidence in the Supreme Court. In May, 1847, he wrote to Hale in protest at the pro-slavery construction of the Constitution: "The people will overthrow it if they have to overthrow the courts too." In his Syracuse speech of August, 1853, he pointed out how there came to be a permanent majority of pro-slavery justices, adding, "I take it upon myself to question, and with some degree of boldness, the decision of the court upon the subject of the Fugitive Slave Act;" and in many public utterances of 1858 and 1859 he repeated his dissent from the doctrine that slavery must go into the Territories, and his intention to disregard the decrees of the Supreme Court.

On the question of the Lecompton constitution, in 1858 Chase, like most of his friends, was befogged; and he wrote a letter advising the Kansas men to accept it, and then take possession of the new state government and amend their constitution at their leisure. For this counsel Chase was less blamable, because the Republicans in Congress failed to comprehend that the issue was one of principle, and that the Republicans could not vote to admit a slave State at any time, whatever the prospect of its changing its status later, without undermining the foundation of their party. Douglas's opposition to the Lecompton outrage even deceived many good Republicans into supposing that he was about to take their ground, and Horace Greeley urged the Illinois Republicans to drop Lincoln and let Douglas go back to the Senate. But in December, 1857, Chase wrote: "I expect little from the Douglas demonstration. He has no solid base in him. He may bluster, but he will not grapple with the slave power;" and again in November, 1859, "The great error in respect to Douglas was that of . . . giving him the lead in the anti-Lecompton fight, leaving the Republican senators and representatives only a secondary place, and giving to the country the impression that they were about ready to adopt his doctrine that slavery is as good as freedom, if a majority of qualified voters say so."

One of the greatest characters in the anti-slavery struggle now appears in direct relations with Chase. In December, 1856, Chase indorsed a recommendation of Charles Robinson, commending Captain John Brown to the confidence of the friends of Kansas. In 1857 he subscribed twenty-five dollars for Brown's use, and later he received the following very characteristic letter, sent from Tabor, Iowa, under date of September 10, 1857.

"Enclosed please find First number of a series of Tracts which have lately been gotten up here. Your frank opinion of it is respectfully asked (not *for any kind of publication*). My principle object in again troubling you, is to say that *I am in immediate want* of from Five Hundred to One Thousand Dollars for *Secret service and no questions asked.* I want the friends of Freedom to '*prove me now herewith.*' WILL YOU exert your influence to have it made up: in your own hands, subject to my order: or placed in the hands of any suitable, and responsible man you may name?

"Please write me or *have some person* write me, directing Envelope to Jonas Jones Esqr of this place.

"Very Respectfully Your Friend,

"JOHN BROWN.

"Friend J. Jr. will inclose this *anew* to destination at once."

Like others of John Brown's correspondents, East and West, Chase had shut his eyes to the use that might be made of his subscription, and he was startled by the news of the Harper's Ferry raid in October, 1859. The New York "Herald" accused him of being a party to the conspiracy, a charge which Chase always denied; but he was drawn into the controversy by a letter of Governor Wise of Virginia, complaining that armed expeditions were forming in Ohio (presumably for the rescue of Brown), and warning him, "If another invasion should assail the State of Virginia, I shall pursue the invaders into any territory, and punish them wherever they can be reached by arms." Chase quietly replied that Ohio could not "consent to the invasion of her territory by armed bodies from other States;" and with this exchange of defiances the matter was dropped.

From the above account of Chase's four years as governor, it appears that his chief activity and his interests were, as they had been for the twenty years previous, in the anti-slavery cause. His most important addresses and messages to the Ohio legislature turned on slavery and on national questions arising out of slavery; the most stirring events within his State were phases of slavery; his place as a national leader was due to his eminence as an anti-slavery man; his warmest personal friends and correspondents were anti-slavery men, and many of them abolitionists. While Seward said strong things and then tempered them, while men like Henry Wilson sought to find other issues for the Republican party, while Douglas was reëlected senator from Illinois on the programme of not caring whether slavery was voted down or voted up, Chase stood out unswervingly as a political abolitionist.

It is true that while governor he smoothed down his utterances, and avoided making the issue with the general government which his radical friends desired; but to his mind the great question before the people of the United States was the extension of slavery beyond the limits of the existing slave States, and his influence, voice, and purse were unwaveringly against the taking of fugitives, or the introduction of slavery into the Territories. Sumner and Giddings may have had more violent convictions, but neither of them held so prominent a station as Chase. Seward, Cameron, and Thurlow Weed had more influence in determining the policy of the Republican party, but there was not in the whole country in 1860 any man who had so high a reputation as Chase for long, unceasing opposition to the powers of slavery, through political means. If the Republican party intended in the campaign of 1860 to nominate a man whose name was a platform, he was the man.

CHAPTER VII

THE ELECTION OF 1860

CHASE'S reëlection in 1857 showed greater Republican vitality in Ohio than in some other States, for the party in general lost ground that year. In the congressional elections of 1858, however, the Republicans for the first time secured a working majority in the House of Representatives, the House which was to sit from 1859 to 1861; and Buchanan took so crushing a rebuke in his own State of Pennsylvania that he himself dolefully said of it: "Our defeat is so complete as to be absurd." As 1860 came in, therefore, the Republicans were alert and confident: with an available candidate, a safe platform, and prudent management of the campaign, they ought to hold and even increase their vote, especially since their opponents were so disunited that Jefferson Davis, as representative of the Southern wing, had refused fellowship to Douglas.

Manœuvres for the Republican nominations began very early, and Chase conducted in his own behalf a long and anxious preliminary canvass, which throws much interesting light on the methods of bringing a presidential candidate before the public. For example, in April, 1857, he chides a correspondent for speaking too well of Frémont, and bids him remember that "there is no hope for our cause in the future unless there is a clear manifestation of confidence in our principles and in the men whom the common voice declares to be the true representatives of them." By September, 1857, scattered correspondents begin to announce that they will support him for the presidency; and in November, just after his reëlection as governor, Chase himself says: "At present it looks to me as if I might secure it."

From this time on, though busy as governor, frequent in counsels on national affairs, and stunned like all his countrymen by the din of the Lecompton controversy, Chase sets himself steadily to inspirit his friends and to impress the public. He revives a plan for a campaign life of himself, which had been projected in 1856; he asks his followers to say "good words in correspondence, by the pen, and in conversation till the time shall call for a public movement;" he stirs up his old friends the newspaper men; he goes to Commencement at Dartmouth College for the first time in thirty-two years, and is gratified by the cordial feeling in his favor which he thinks he finds in New Hampshire; he eats a "complimentary dinner to Governor Chase" at the Parker House in Boston, and keeps the bill of fare. In Ohio everything seems to his satisfaction; old rivals take the field for him with enthusiasm; and he learns that the Republican congressmen from Ohio are for him. In other parts of the country, West and East, he renews correspondence and finds friends. "Governor" Charles Robinson writes favorably from Kansas; in Pennsylvania, Joshua Hanna, a Pittsburg banker, and a warm personal friend, works steadily; since Sumner has been disabled by Brooks, no man in New England has much interest in him except Pierce, who does intelligent work, and writes candid and discouraging letters about the prospect; New York is Seward's stronghold, but Chase has there a devoted lieutenant in James H. Briggs, whom he has appointed to the valuable office of financial agent of Ohio. Nevertheless, Chase appears to be the only really energetic supporter of Chase; at the end of the year he can count up more intrigues of rivals than new supporters.

During 1858 Chase became interested in the contest in Illinois, and stumped the State for the Republican state ticket, but neither he nor his correspondents mention the local politician who was contesting the Illinois senatorship against Douglas, or appear to have recognized any rivalry from that quarter. Like many other Republicans, however, Chase did discover that there was an intrigue, in which Schuyler Colfax had a leading part, to make Douglas the Republican candidate in 1860. As to Seward, Chase's friends thought, as was the case, that he had injured himself by his "irrepressible conflict" speech at Rochester; and the "New York

Tribune" and the "Independent" were supposed to be against him. Thus far the Ohio man was at least holding his own as a candidate.

During 1859 it became important to Chase to keep his standing as a man in public life by showing his strength in Ohio after the expiration of his governorship. He was therefore much gratified when, on February 3, 1860, he was elected senator of the United States for the term beginning March 4, 1861. By this time the elements of the presidential contest were more clearly revealed, and a new and very troublesome question arose, — that of Chase's opinions on the tariff. From Rhode Island, from New York, and from Pennsylvania came reports that he was considered unsound on protection. This objection was one of the unavoidable results of his candid belief in the Democratic doctrine of "as little government as possible." He had approved the tariff policy of 1846; in many public utterances he had expressed his adherence to the Democratic doctrines as to trade; and probably he still believed them to be the best; so that he was hard put to it to know what to say or do. In the Northwest, which was recognized as a weak spot for Chase, a few of his friends were trying to work up a sentiment for him, and reported hopefully.

The rival candidates now began to come out more distinctly: Banks, in Massachusetts, already almost overborne by his adhesion to remnants of Know-Nothingism; Cameron, in Pennsylvania; F.

P. Blair, patron of Frémont in 1856, had deserted his candidate, and was now pushing hard for Bates of Missouri, who was advertised as able to carry the border States along with the North. Chase's lively counselor, James M. Ashley, proposed to head off this wicked plot against a Western candidate's chances by "letting our friends in Illinois put Lincoln on the track;" but an Illinois editor wrote that his own ticket was "Chase and Lincoln," for there seemed to be an impression that, whoever headed the ticket, Lincoln was likely to be vice-president.

In his own State Chase had not the warm support of any of the recognized party leaders or great newspapers; but he counted on the good will of the Germans, and felt sure of a unanimous delegation to the national convention. One of his correspondents felt so much confidence in the future that he asked to be made minister to Persia; and another so far overestimated Chase's influence on the incoming national House of Representatives, in which there was a Republican majority, as to cry: "I just ache to have the position of clerk, with 20 or 30 subs of my own appointment." All that can be said of Chase's chances at the end of 1859 is that he was a man of presidential timber and a founder of the Republican party, who nevertheless was looked upon as a stranger by the leaders of his own party, and seemed to have a poorer chance than any one of half a dozen lesser men.

In the spring of 1860 came the real struggle.

Looking back forty years, we speak of "the Republican party of 1860," as we might speak of the "Federal party of 1800," or the "Whig party of 1840." In reality there was as yet hardly more than a coalition; in 1854–55 a common term had been "Fusion party;" in 1856 the Native Americans were almost as important as the Republicans; in 1860 the former Whigs, former Democrats, and former Know-Nothings, now united as Republicans, had no tradition of common principles or common leaders, and were still jealous of each other and often hostile. They came together like Highland clans for a common fight, marching side by side with men who a short time before had dented their shields and hewn at their heads. Every man suggested for the nomination was therefore tested by his power to attract, or his likelihood to repel, Conscience Whigs and Cotton Whigs and Hunker Democrats and old Free-Soilers and ultra-abolitionists, Irish and Germans and Nativists. Hence the strength of a movement for a man like Bates, who hoped to draw the border-state vote because he was an old slaveholder, and to satisfy the abolitionists because he had emancipated his slaves, to carry Pennsylvania because he was a tariff man, and to sweep Vermont because he was an old Whig. Hence the weakness of a man like Seward, who had assaulted the Democrats in Congress and on the stump; and of a man like Chase, who had deprived the Whigs of the Ohio senatorship in 1849. As the months drew on, however, the

Chase men believed that the contest was really narrowing to two candidates, the New York and Ohio champions.

Seward was Chase's most dangerous rival, through both his good and his bad qualities. He was good-natured, companionable, and attractive; he had had long experience in public life, and was known from end to end of the country; he was naturally a warm advocate of freedom, and he had gone further than Chase or any other leading Republican in the phrasing of extreme anti-slavery views, especially in his "higher law" speech of 1850 and in his "irrepressible conflict" speech of 1858. On the other hand, he was not a leader in legislation or in organizing resistance to slavery in Congress; he had a habit of withdrawing or altering his most radical utterances, and he was a very late comer into the Republican party, and might still pass as a radical but reclaimable Whig.

The chief objection to Seward was the atmosphere of political corruption which surrounded him. The outcome of the Chicago Convention of 1860 cannot be understood without knowing something of the frame of mind in which honorable men outside New York, and a small but very determined band of Republicans within the State, looked upon the régime of Thurlow Weed and his management of Seward. Throughout the canvass suggestions were thrown out that Seward was unavailable because of his friends. Thus, Charles Robinson of Kansas wrote February 3, 1860: "He is the spendthrift of the party, politically, I mean, and would take from us all arguments against the former corrupt and extravagant administration, and is supported so far as I can learn chiefly by the spoilsmen, who would destroy the party in four years should they get the government with their candidate at the head." H. B. Stanton, a New York delegate who voted for Seward in the Chicago Convention, wrote in July, 1860: "New York Republicanism has been made a reproach, a by-word, by the rascally conduct of our state legislature, under the lead of Weed." Even cautious Chase, in a letter of May 10, 1860, said: "If Albany is to be transferred to Washington, the party cannot succeed." In a long and careful letter of March 27, 1861, R. Campbell, then a New York state senator, thus described Seward's political manager, the New York boss of that time:—

"You can only faintly imagine the extent and ramification of the machinery of that section of our party which acknowledges Mr. Weed as its leader.

"Pardon me for this personal allusion; I would ignore it if I could, and never mention it, were it not that in so doing I should stultify my convictions and become a party to the speedy downfall of Republicanism in this State. Believe me when I assure you that I have not the least feeling personally against Mr. Weed. He has his good qualities, which I believe I know how to appreciate, and yet is the worst man in our party in this State in the light of influence.

"To explain to you the means which he resorts to, to control the primary meetings throughout the entire State, his system of levying assessments and holding office — to refer to the horde of political pensioners, dependents, and expectants which he has quartered upon our party, and to explain how by these and kindred resorts he has all along controlled state and local conventions, and, in short, defeated every wish of the better portion of our party, would only be elaborating upon what you can anticipate. . . .

"Now, dear Governor, I have no other desire than to retire to private life at the earliest possible period. I never asked or desired office, nor have I anything now to ask of Mr. Barney for myself or a single relative on earth.

"I nevertheless desire to see Mr. Weed's power entirely broken in this State. I desire this, first, because the great majority of the men under his control are mere vassals, and large numbers of them are a disgrace to our party. I desire this because he makes use of favoritism to destroy the political integrity of our entire party. I desire it because I believe in wholesome legislation, in a just, honest, and virtuous administration of public affairs, and because I hate thieving, and utterly abhor an organized system of profligacy and corruption.

"And now let me assure you that I do not believe our ills can be abated by any other means than by keeping these dependents of Mr. Weed just where they would keep all of our friends had they the power, — out of office. I do not believe in proscription, nor would I advise it in any ordinary case. Depend upon it, however, this is no ordinary case. Every one of these dependents and vassals of Weed are so abject in service that they do nothing else than foster faction continually. Whenever appointed to office through his influence, they seem to become his property.

"A great popular movement is on foot to break forever the power of this unscrupulous political tyrant. That movement is sure to prove successful. The breaking of that power would disenthrall our party, and restore to the people their representative rights."

Of the other candidates, the one whom Chase and his friends most feared was Bates, as the only Westerner who was likely to compete with Chase for votes wrested from Seward. Cameron's candidacy none of the Chase men took seriously; they reasoned that if there were any Eastern nominee it would be Seward. Banks they placated, in the hope that when he realized that he was out of the race he would turn his friends to them instead of to Seward. Lincoln Chase never looked upon as a rival until the day of the convention; on the contrary, in March, 1860, his lieutenant, Briggs, reported among other small matters: "Mr. Lincoln of Illinois told me that [he] had a very warm side towards you, for of all the prominent Republicans you were the only one who gave him aid and comfort. I urged him by all means to attend the convention. I was pleased with him, I paid him all the attention I could, went with him to hear Mr. Beecher and Dr. Chapin. Mr. Barney went with him to the 'House of Industry' at the Five Points, and then took him home to tea. He was very much pleased with Mr. Barney." Neither Chase nor Barney suspected that within a year the big, modest, friendless visitor, to whom they had exhibited the splendors of the metropolis, would be in a position to requite this kindness by giving Barney the great prize of the collectorship of New York.

In the early months of 1860 came the choice of delegates, and Chase kept careful watch of the state conventions, preserving a list of delegates elect, on which appear such memoranda as the following: "California — Leland Stanford of Sacramento and Charles Watrous of San Francisco, will have great influence. The first choice of delegates, Seward; second, Chase — in favor of any well-known Republican and opposed to any old fogy;" "New York — George W. Curtis, the author, for Seward first, with a warm side for C." Little comfort, however, was to be had from the choice of delegates. New York sent a solid delegation of Seward men; Pennsylvania, except six delegates, of Cameron men (to leave their candidate when the expected consideration was offered); Illinois, of Lincoln men. In order to have any hope of nomination or any standing in the convention,

Chase must also have a unanimous and interested delegation from Ohio. On March 3 the Ohio Republican convention did indeed vote by 385 to 69 that Salmon P. Chase was the first choice of Ohio, but it relegated the choice of delegates to the local conventions, and thus designedly gave the opportunity for Chase's enemies to send men unpledged, or even opposed to him. Although Chase did not realize it, by this action his last chance was gone, many weeks before the Chicago Convention met.

Through the district conventions several former anti-Chase men got in. Old Judge McLean could neither give up his presidential hopes nor forgive Chase for his part against him in the Free-Soil contest of 1848, and he picked up some delegates in southern Ohio. Senator Wade had his own views as to who was the ablest Republican in Ohio, and his friends got delegates in northern Ohio, especially D. K. Cartter of Cleveland, later chief justice of the District of Columbia. Although Hoadly, one of Chase's nearest friends, had warned him in February that he did not stand the slightest chance, Chase was buoyant, and ten days before the Chicago Convention was sure that the Ohio delegates would vote solidly for him, and that he would be nominated, if his friends "had the means and the activity used by Mr. Seward's."

As the time for the convention approached, Chase found a few friends and stanch delegates from other States; but he got glimpses also of a stratum of intrigue into which he could not descend. The Spragues were said to have bought the Rhode Island state election for $100,000, and some of the Rhode Island delegates were "purchasable;" some delegates from Iowa were "on the trading tack," and in Indiana there was a "floating and marketable vote." A Philadelphia editor wrote to him with unblushing frankness that he had worked for Cameron, but that "if any little sub-contract could be given us which would enable us to realize a little profit, we would endeavor to serve Ohio to the full extent of our ability." But neither Rhode Island, Pennsylvania, Iowa, nor Indiana gave any votes for Chase at Chicago.

The convention which met at Chicago on May 16, 1860, was a tumultuous body, excited by the roars of an unusual number of spectators. The state elections of 1859 and early 1860 made it practically certain that all New England would give its electoral vote for any man nominated in Chicago; the Northwestern States — Michigan, Wisconsin, Iowa, and the recently admitted Minnesota — seemed also safe. Hence the fighting had to be done in the six doubtful States between the ocean and the Mississippi, — New York, New Jersey, Pennsylvania, Ohio, Indiana, and Illinois. Out of these, only New York and Ohio had been Republican in 1856; and Illinois was Douglas's State, and had been carried for him in 1858. Hence the problem before the convention, or rather before the controlling spirits among the delegates, was really, Who can carry all the States of Pennsylvania, Indiana, and Illinois?

The Seward men were confident that their candidate could carry anything, and the New York delegation of 70 was backed up by a great and enthusiastic band of politicians who argued, shouted, and paraded uproariously. Edward L. Pierce, one of the few earnest Chase men in New England, was bottled up in the Massachusetts delegation, and had to vote for Seward. The Seward men could at the outset count up nearly 200 delegates out of the 233 necessary to nominate; but there were two weak elements in their calculations, — the undeserved reputation of their candidate as an extreme anti-slavery man, and the relentless hostility of Greeley and some other New York Republicans.

The next candidate in apparent strength was Chase; the Ohio delegation of 46 was inferior in size only to those of Pennsylvania and New York; coming from a Western State, it could appeal to a growing conviction that a Western man must be found to confront Douglas. The situation had some strength, in case it should be found that Seward could get no majority. Therefore Chase's friends made the most of his integrity of character as compared with Seward's loose financial administration, of his unwavering devotion to anti-slavery as compared with Cameron's recent conversion, and of his proved ability as a public officer as compared with Lincoln's inexperience. Just before the convention George Opdyke of New York urged the nomination of Chase as a former Democrat, and hence likely to draw from Douglas; he was confident that a combination of Chase's friends with the Banks men and the Blairs could control the convention.

But Chase was now to learn the bitter lesson that the approval of a popular vote in Ohio, twice given, did not secure for him the cordial aid of all the Ohio Republicans. The old Whig element had never forgiven him for his combination with the Democrats in the senatorial election twelve years before; his use of his scanty patronage as governor had made some new enemies; and he had not the art of disarming opponents by suavity and tact. Had there been an Ohio manager at this juncture to compel the forces of the State to pull in the same parallel; and above all had Chase ever gained the friendship and confidence of the Republican leaders in other States, — senators, congressmen, governors, and chieftains, — he might perhaps have been nominated, notwithstanding his reputation for abolitionism.

On the very first ballot in the convention, it was seen that Chase was out of the race. The Ohio delegation was divided, Chase receiving only 34 out of 46, and the total Chase vote was only 49 out of 465. On the second ballot, since there was no rallying-point in the Ohio delegation, Chase sank to 42½, and on the third ballot only 15 Ohio men still adhered to him. This danger of a divided Ohio vote had been foreseen; and inasmuch as the favorable recommendation of the Ohio state convention was not accepted as an instruction, Chase had urged his friends to secure a vote of the delegation pledging a unit rule. The Ohio delegation, wrote a correspondent to Chase, "shut themselves up discussing what it was impossible to determine beforehand, — how long they should vote for you as a unit, and what other Ohio man they should vote for as a unit. This continued Tuesday, Wednesday, and part of Thursday. Then when they determined to vote their preferences they worked some. But in the meantime those bent on defeating Seward combined to a great extent on Lincoln."

Delegates who attended these long sessions have revealed the secret of the division in Ohio. Against the proposed unit rule, which was Chase's sole chance, some of Chase's warm adherents voted, because on arrival in Chicago they found that so many men were saying that Chase could not carry the doubtful States, or even Ohio, that they lost heart; and they feared that when Chase was out of the way, Wade with his many friends in the Ohio delegation would sweep the Western delegates. Another element of Chase's ablest supporters, — David Dudley Field, Hiram Barney, and George Opdyke of New York, — when they found his weakness in Ohio, went over to the most promising candidate then available, that is, to Lincoln; and thus Chase suddenly lost support both in and out of his State.

That the danger from Wade was overestimated,

and perhaps imaginary, seems almost certain, as we look back on the affair. Wade was an old Whig, a very violent partisan, of rough and boisterous temper, without the prestige of support by his own state convention. If Chase were really out of the way, Lincoln was the strongest Western candidate and the one most acceptable to Chase; Lincoln was also the second choice of Indiana and Pennsylvania, the two States which really had a right to insist on a nomination which would satisfy them, because their vote was indispensable. Although correspondents assured Chase that nine tenths of the Republican voters in Ohio desired his nomination, an intimate friend in the convention told him that there were "not more than a dozen of the whole delegation earnestly desiring or working for you;" and Brinkerhoff said: "The truth is, the old Whigs of this State are extremely hostile to you; even [John] Sherman, who is as liberal a Whig of the old school as I know of, and has a high regard for you, yet I am satisfied is secretly a Seward man."

The turn of the votes, however, gave Chase's friends a chance to do a service to Lincoln. At the end of the third ballot, when he lacked one and a half votes of a nomination, four votes were suddenly transferred to him by Ohio delegates, for reasons thus frankly explained to Chase by one of the delegation: "The fifteen adhering to you had it in their power to nominate Mr. Lincoln and did it. This places us in good position with the

Illinois delegation, and leaves you right with the incoming administration."

That Lincoln felt amicably was shown a few days later by a remark which he made about Chase to George Opdyke: "I prefer him to myself; for Dr. Branford says Governor Chase combines greater executive, administrative and high statesmanlike ability than any man living." In May, 1861, Chase wrote a cordial note of congratulation to Lincoln, in which, however, he could not forbear saying: "I err greatly in my estimation of your magnanimity if you do not condemn, as I do, the conduct of delegates from whatever State who disregard, while acting as such, the clearly expounded preference of their own state convention."

Chase had come nearer to the coveted dignity than he was ever again to come, for this was the last time that he had any votes in a Republican nominating convention. His very greatness made him a weak candidate; he does not appear to have made the slightest concession or concealment of his principles, further than to recommend a platform of generalities and a candidate "whose name would be a platform." None of his correspondents refer even to the usual promises of cabinet places and other offices as a means of influencing votes. Chase, like Lincoln, had no body of rich and powerful friends to make a campaign for him. His situation and his chances are well summed up in the apothegm of a friend: "If the Republican party is consistent, it will nominate Seward, and if it is not consistent, it won't nominate you."

In the campaign Chase was active, but not conspicuous. His State, by its Republican plurality of 21,000 in October, presaged a triumph in November. When, therefore, on November 6, Lincoln and Hamlin got 180 of the 303 electoral votes, it was found that Ohio gave Lincoln a plurality of 44,000 over Douglas, and a clear majority of 21,000. It has often been said that Lincoln's election was due to the Democratic split and the existence of four tickets. Study of the returns, however, shows that had Lincoln or Chase or any other respectable Republican been the candidate against Douglas alone, or Breckinridge alone, or Bell alone, or any two of these candidates, he would still have been elected by small Republican majorities in the free States; for in every Northern State except New Jersey, California, and Oregon, Lincoln had more votes than his three adversaries combined.

To Chase the result was, notwithstanding his personal disappointment, the crowning of his life work up to that time. The day after the election he wrote to Pierce: "How superb is the Republican triumph! At length the first of the great wishes of my life is accomplished. The slave power is overthrown. When will the other, namely the denationalization of slavery and the consequent initiation of emancipation by state action, be realized?"

John Sherman

W. P. Fessenden

CHAPTER VIII

THE CRITICAL YEAR 1861

"THE very first thing that I settled in my mind," said Lincoln in an account of the result of the election of 1860, "was that these two great leaders of the party should occupy the two first places in my cabinet." The two great leaders were Seward and Chase, and the first places were the State Department and the Treasury; but it was not till after Mr. Lincoln was inaugurated as President, in March, 1861, that he could count unreservedly upon the services of either of the two men. While he "was musing the fire burned;" before he could frame a policy or form a cabinet, the country had begun to shrink, and on the day of his inauguration fourteen seats in the Senate had been vacated. Yet in the midst of the popular excitement and uncertainty, Lincoln struck out a policy of no-compromise, compelled Seward to accept it, inspirited Chase, managed his party in Congress, and drew into his cabinet every man upon whom he had set his heart.

The political problem was appalling. Ever since the introduction of the Kansas-Nebraska Bill, in January, 1854, the country had been divided on the question of territorial slavery; the Republican platform of 1860 was absolutely opposed to the creation of any new slaveholding region, whether by annexation, by territorial laws, or by the admission of a new slave State, while the Southern Democrats in the campaign of 1860 demanded, as the least that they would accept, positive protection to slavery in the Territories by federal statute. To the minds of the Republicans, the whole secession agitation was simply a device to deprive them of what they had gained by electing a President, and to compel them to accept a proslavery policy. Before enlisting his cabinet ministers, therefore, it was necessary for Lincoln to make clear to them the solution of the crisis as he saw it, and to come to an understanding as to the future of an administration which many people asserted could never be formed at all. Hence, for a full month after his election he made no offer of any place in his cabinet.

Meanwhile the status of political affairs changed from week to week, as the secession leaders developed their plans, as the border States became conscious of the difference between their interests and those of the gulf States, and as President Buchanan's do-nothing policy stood revealed. On the day after the presidential election the legislature of South Carolina began to prepare for secession, and from that time on the keenest observers believed that the disunionists were in earnest, and that the crisis could be met only by one or another of three courses, — by accepting secession, by compromise, or by coercion. Though all the three methods were urged at the same time, each had its opportunity in one of three successive periods: peaceable acceptance of secession was put forward especially during November, 1860; compromise was demanded during December to stay the cotton States, and during January and February to placate the border States; and people talked of coercion during March and April.

During the first of these epochs Chase was simply a senator-elect, and for two months he was little consulted by the party leaders, and not at all by Mr. Lincoln. His correspondents kept him informed of the drift of affairs in Washington; and he knew that in a meeting of the Ohio delegation, on December 18, Senator Pugh scoffed at any attempt to retain the seceding States by force, and Representative Vallandigham predicted that by inauguration day Washington would be in the hands of "a foreign government." The belief that the Union was no union was not confined to Breckinridge Democrats, for the Republican journalist and leader, Horace Greeley, was in the clearest tones preaching non-resistance; on November 9, 1860, his New York "Tribune" declared that "if the cotton States shall decide that they can do better out of the Union than in it, we insist on letting them go in peace." Extremists like William Lloyd Garrison of course were delighted at the opportunity to free the Union from its slaveholding contingent; and thousands of Northern Republicans saw no legal or practicable way of resisting secession, however wrong it might be and however disastrous it might prove.

Chase meanwhile seemed to be waiting for something. For many weeks he expressed no public opinion on the crisis; but at last, on November 30, he wrote to his sister-in-law, Mrs. Hunt of New Orleans, a letter apparently intended for publication, in which he said distinctly: "I abhor the very idea of a dissolution of the Union. If I were President I would indeed exhaust every expedient of forbearance consistent with safety. But at all hazards and against all opposition the laws of the Union should be enforced." These sentences in brief form describe Chase's line of policy down to the firing on Fort Sumter, a policy which involved concessions by grace of the new administration, but none by act of Congress.

A new phase of the question was opened up when Congress met in December, 1860; for the responsibility of preserving the Union was then thrown jointly upon President Buchanan and the two Houses at Washington, with neither of which powers Chase had influence at that time. Seward, on the other hand, had been in conference with Lincoln, and on December 8 was notified that the secretaryship of state would be offered him. As a leading senator he played a large part in the first effort for a compromise; an editorial in the Albany "Evening Journal" inspired by his intimate friend and manager, Thurlow Weed, strongly urged compromise and a constitutional convention. During December an attempt was made to find some halfway point which would satisfy South Carolina and the other cotton States. A committee of thirty-three in the House, appointed December 6, undertook the task, and on December 13 voted to recommend "additional and more specific and effective guarantees of the constitutional rights of the South;" but the next day thirty Southern members of Congress united in a public address, stating that in their judgment no compromise would be offered that the South could accept. No delay was effected in South Carolina, where on December 20 a convention declared the State no longer a part of the Union.

The Senate Committee of Thirteen did not meet till December 21, and the only hope of compromise then was to make such an offer to the Southern members of that committee as would recall South Carolina. It fell to Seward to frame the Republican concessions. He agreed to an amendment to the Constitution denying the right of Congress to interfere with slavery in the States, and he was also willing to ask the repeal of the personal liberty bills; but he would go no further, and coupled his proposals with a demand for a jury trial of alleged fugitives, a proposition very unpalatable to the South. The border-state men then proposed the Crittenden compromise, of which the essence was to fix slavery in all the

Territories south of 36° 30′. Though Seward's own judgment tended toward compromise, he refused to accept this plan, and we now know that he was carrying out the expressed wishes of Abraham Lincoln, and gaining his first experience of subordination to the will of that masterful man. The committee broke up without result, and within five weeks six more States had seceded.

In January, 1861, Chase at last found his bearings, for he was then approached by Lincoln upon the subject of taking a cabinet position. That he should expect such an offer was natural; he stood for the principle of aggressive political anti-slavery, which had furnished a large element in the Northern majorities; he had a good reputation for political skill as well as for ability; he was probably the most distinguished of the former Democrats then in the Republican party; and he was one of the few leaders who had shown to Lincoln personal sympathy in his struggle with Douglas in 1858. Letters to three different friends, on November 10, 1860, show that he had gone through the process of not definitely making up his mind to refuse cabinet office, long before Lincoln had come to the point of offering it to him; and he had evidently decided that the secretaryship of state was suited to his powers, and would be a proper recognition of his services. It seems probable that he felt it to be prudent to keep silence during November, till Lincoln had declared himself on secession.

On December 31 Lincoln at last decided to telegraph Chase to visit him. The conference lasted two days, and was embarrassing to both. Lincoln began by asking "whether you will accept the appointment of Secretary of the Treasury, without, however, [my] being exactly prepared to make you that offer." Chase replied with good sense and good temper that, if Seward were to have the State Department, he should not refuse the Treasury for any reason of pique. When they parted, neither man stood committed; but there was a tacit understanding that Mr. Lincoln wanted Chase, and probably could have him if he insisted. Chase later wrote upon the qualified proposition: "Had it been made earlier and with the same promptitude and definiteness as that to Mr. Seward, I should have been inclined to make some sacrifices." What was really accomplished was the bringing of both statesmen to an understanding with the future President; thenceforward Chase felt that he was included in the circle of Lincoln's advisers and probable ministers. A few days after the interview he even took Seward so far into his confidence as to write that they had "a common interest;" and eloquently counseled him and Thaddeus Stevens "to give countenance to no scheme of compromise" and to offer no "concessions of principle."

The question before the country was no longer secession, for by the middle of January disunion was an accomplished fact; it was whether the border States could be kept in the Union. After

January 1 the only hope of finding common ground for border-state loyal Democrats and Northern Republicans was in Crittenden's compromise; but on a test vote of January 16, 1861, the Republicans, who now had a majority in the Senate, refused to support the measure. Three days later, as a last step, the Virginia legislature called a "Peace Conference," to be held in Washington. Meantime Chase had set forth his solution of the difficulty in a phrase which rang throughout the country, "Inauguration first, adjustment afterwards;" and as one of the Ohio commissioners to the Peace Conference, at last he had some opportunity to affect the settlement of the issue. In the Conference, which sat from February 4 to February 27, he was the leader of the non-compromisers. Nevertheless, for some weeks he had hopes of "an agreement on something which, without compromising our course or our party at all, will yet help to an amicable understanding." This "something" was a plan for a general constitutional convention, and its chief advantage was that it would postpone action till the new administration could be seated.

Behind the plan of delay was a purpose eventually to offer a scheme of concession, to be drawn up by the Republican administration as a peace offering; but at no time in his public career did Chase more distinctly set forth the ultimate authority of the national government than in his one long speech in the Conference. "If the President does his duty," said he, "and undertakes to enforce the laws, and secession or revolution results, what then? War! Civil war!" The Conference took the line of concession by recommending to Congress an amendment substantially identical with the Crittenden compromise; it was a third time rejected; and the insoluble problem was turned over to Lincoln's administration.

The two things for which the country now looked with eager interest were the inaugural address, as an earnest of the President's policy, and the list of his cabinet advisers, which would reveal the influences in his administration. The address proved to be steadfast against a constitutional right of secession; and the names of the members of the cabinet showed that the President would have good support in trying to save the Union. During the two months since Chase's interview with Lincoln in Springfield, he had never received a distinct promise of the Treasury, though he was told at second or third hand that Lincoln had decided upon him. Meanwhile the friends of Cameron continued vigorous efforts to set Chase aside, in order that their favorite might have the coveted Treasury portfolio. Chase was described as a free-trader, who could not be trusted to carry out the new Morrill protective tariff; he was assailed as a former Democrat; he was held up as the rival and enemy of Seward. Months afterward a correspondent described how, a few days before the inauguration, on Lincoln's refusal to strike Chase out of his list, Thurlow Weed came away in a rage, declaring that "Mr. Chase had been placed in the cabinet to control the patronage and appointments in the city and State of New York, to prevent Governor Seward from controlling the appointments, and to deprive him [Mr. Weed] of all power and influence."

It may be doubted whether Lincoln insisted upon appointing Chase because he expected him to back up the anti-Seward men in New York; but it is equally unlikely that he discovered in him the qualities of a great financier, or indeed that he felt any need of a great financier. It is more probable that he selected him as a representative of a large body of radical Republicans, as a strong rival for the nomination, and as one of those former Democrats whom he intended to use as a balance to the old Whigs in his cabinet, while at the same time he had a genuine respect for Chase's character and abilities.

To the last moment Chase had no positive assurance that he would be appointed, and he was not consulted about the rest of the cabinet slate; hence he could truthfully say that the sending his nomination to the Senate was a surprise to him. However honorable the secretaryship, his pride was hurt by the long delay; and, like Seward, he hesitated to give up his safe senatorship without some guaranty as to the policy of the President. At any rate, he held off till Lincoln in a personal interview insisted that he should accept, and probably gave him some assurance as to his purposes toward secession. Of the weight of financial responsibilities which he was taking upon himself he seems to have had at the beginning no inkling, and there were many times during the next four years when he wished that he had retained his seat in the Senate.

On the second day of the existence of the new cabinet, Elizur Wright wrote to Chase in praise of the inaugural address: "The whole drift shows that the new President's heart is in the right place, and that, though far in advance of the average North, he knows how to make it follow him." Before the North could follow, however, it was necessary to know who was the leader; and to several of the members of his own cabinet Lincoln seemed inferior to themselves in initiative, in abilities, in experience, in administrative powers, and in public confidence.

For a month or more Seward continued to believe that he was to be the head of the new administration, an attitude which he had unconsciously assumed in the previous congressional discussions on compromise. During the weeks preceding Sumter, while Seward was testing the will of the President, Chase set himself in a business-like fashion to the duties of his office. Many of his friends had predicted that he and Seward could not sit in the same cabinet; but from the first the Secretary of the Treasury sought to establish friendly relations with the Secretary of State, and mutual friends were authorized to express good will. If Chase had any notion of controlling the President, it was not through personal ascendency: the most that he ever sought was to make the cabinet, as a board of advisers, more powerful than the President.

The relation of the President with his seven adjuncts was first distinctly defined in their discussions on the status of Fort Sumter soon after the inauguration. All the government posts in the seceding section had been seized and occupied, except Fort Pickens, Key West and the Dry Tortugas, and Fort Sumter, which last was occupied by a garrison under Major Anderson. The authorities of South Carolina, and later those of the Confederacy, had demanded the surrender of the forts, but had finally been induced to wait for the new administration; and Sumter, which commanded one of the few Southern cities, at once became the turning-point in the whole controversy. To yield it would be practically to acknowledge the success of secession; to reinforce it would begin civil war.

The appearance of three new Confederate commissioners in Washington compelled Lincoln's attention. General Scott was consulted, and on March 11, 1861, he pointed out the military difficulties, and discouraged any attempt to retain the forts. It was in this exigency, on March 15, that the President took the written opinions of his advisers. The question which the President had to settle was really neither constitutional nor military nor political; it was the state of mind of the Northern people; and this no member of the cabinet could ascertain, because the people themselves did not understand their own minds. On the critical question of relieving Fort Sumter, therefore, only one of the seven, Montgomery Blair, expressed the opinion that it was worth while to put to a test the support which the nation might give to bold measures. Seward and Chase were at one in advising that no step should be taken which would lead to hostilities; but Chase drew the deduction that the simple provisioning of a fort ought not to lead, and would not lead, to civil war.

This was one of the few periods of wavering judgment in Chase's life. His best friends were overwhelming him with letters urging him to stand by Fort Sumter; but he preferred another policy, which he expected to be effective in keeping the border States in the Union, and which he thus frankly explained in a letter of April 20, 1861: —

"True it is that before the assault on Fort Sumter, in anticipation of an attempt to provision famishing soldiers of the Union, I was decidedly in favor of a positive policy and against the notion of drifting, — the Micawber-like policy of waiting for something to turn up.

"As a positive policy two alternatives were plainly before us: 1. That of enforcing the laws of the Union by its whole power and through its whole extent; or, 2. That of recognizing the organization of actual government by the seven seceded States as an accomplished revolution, accomplished through the complicity of the late administration, and letting that Confederacy try its experiment of separation, but maintaining the authority of the Union and treating secession as treason everywhere else.

"Knowing that the former of these alternatives involved destructive war and vast expenditure and oppressive debt, and thinking it possible that through the latter these great evils might be avoided, and the Union of the other States preserved unbroken; the return even of the seceded States, after an unsatisfactory experiment of separation secured; and the great cause of freedom and constitutional government peacefully vindicated,—thinking, I say, these things possible, I preferred the latter alternative."

The error of judgment was one from which Lincoln alone, among the great statesmen of the period, was wholly free. He alone saw clearly at that time that secession must bring eventual war, and that the issue might as well be met at once, if only the Northern people could be roused to resistance. Chase's faint heart was speedily strengthened, for on March 29, on another call for opinions, he, as well as Welles and Blair, advised reinforcement at all hazards. Three days later Seward submitted to the President his "Scheme for Foreign Relations," which in effect suggested that the President incite war on England and France, and give up to him the leadership of the administration. Lincoln quietly put aside this proposal that he abrogate his authority, and he made his own decision to try to throw provisions into Fort Sumter. The intention having been communicated to the Confederate government, on the morning of April 12, 1861, fire was opened on Fort Sumter. On the 14th it surrendered, and the dreaded Civil War had begun.

The practical question whether the North would respond to a call to arms was answered once for all by the pouring forth of men in answer to the President's proclamation of April 15. The next problem to be faced was how an efficient army could be organized and brought to bear for the confusion of the Confederacy. The regular army was small, scattered, unfitted for large operations, and weakened by the resignations of Southern officers. The question of financial ways and means was not so clearly critical throughout 1861 as it became later; and hence for many months the new Secretary of the Treasury felt quite as much responsibility for the army as for the Treasury, and put forth his greatest energies outside the boundaries of his own department.

In part this martial activity of the civilian was displayed at his own suggestion, in part it was expected and encouraged by the President, in part it was necessary on account of the President's want of confidence in Cameron. Surely the numbers and organization of the army were within the province of the War Department; but when the President by a proclamation of May 3 called for 42,000 three years' volunteers and for 41,000 regular soldiers and sailors, he turned to Chase and not to the Secretary of War to frame the famous

"Order No. 15" and "Order No. 16," which organized the new troops. When Congress reached the subject it legalized the President's extra-constitutional increase of the army, but it greatly altered and in Chase's opinion diluted the Orders.

In his double labors the Secretary of the Treasury put forth his utmost strength. In May, 1861, he wrote: "In laboring for those objects, I know hardly the least cessation and begin to feel the weight as well as the strain of them. Would my criticisers equal me in labor and zeal, I should most cheerfully listen to their criticism." Cameron showed no resentment, and Chase was careful to cultivate his friendship, and continued to express confidence in him long after the country was clamoring for the removal of the Secretary of War, and Chase's friends were begging him to take no more responsibility for a falling chieftain.

A good reason for giving Chase an unusual responsibility was his recognized status as the representative of the West, and as especially qualified to deal with the Western border States. Though Bates came from Missouri, Chase through his anti-slavery correspondents in Missouri and Kentucky was better able than he to gauge the feeling of those two States, and to influence their destiny. He felt that he had a right to send to Lincoln a vigorous and sensible letter, begging him to use force to prevent the secession of Maryland; and in Virginia and West Virginia he exercised a semi-military responsibility. There are abundant evidences that he had special authority in the first months of the war to organize the Western troops and even to suggest their destination.

To a West Virginian he writes, as by authority, promising to accept and maintain such troops as his correspondent may raise. He writes to General Sherman as though the general were subject to his orders, promising commissions for his subordinates, and a supply of arms. To General Nelson he writes: "I will go to the War Department at once on the subject of your wants, and do all I can to urge the department to action;" and a little later: "As to popularity growing or diminishing I care little. I want to support everybody who has tried to do something." Toward McClellan he was at the beginning much attracted, and he assured the young commander that his commission of major-general was in large degree due to his representations; he even suggested a plan of campaign for him, and later wrote to him that "The army and the treasury must stand or fall together." In fact, until Stanton became Secretary of War, Chase continued to consider himself, and appears to have been considered by the President, the special administrator of operations in the West. Perhaps he hoped to be Cameron's successor; at any rate, in September he wrote to a friend: "Who is sufficient for the great work of the War Department? I see and deplore its defective organization, but when I look around and ask myself who will bring to this great work the needed ability, or indeed more ability and fidelity than its present head, I confess myself perplexed."

Throughout the war Chase kept up his great interest in the conduct of the army, and he maintained close correspondence with many of the commanders, — at first with McClellan, later with Hooker, Lander, H. B. Carrington, Mitchell, Garfield, McCook, W. B. Smith, Benham, and many others. Western officers and politicians were especially fond of seeking his military influence. Doubtless all the members of the cabinet were beset by requests for commissions and military favors, especially for paymasterships; certainly they poured in upon Chase by hundreds. One man complains to him that others are promoted over his head; another informs him that the governor of a Western State is "drunk and incapable all the time;" another urges the immediate raising of 300,000 men; another wants Chase to control the contracts for gunboats on Western rivers; another pleads that General Lyon be kept in Missouri; and another advocates a new government in West Virginia.

In other fields of politics and administration Chase was much less interested than in the military department. Notwithstanding the threatening aspect of foreign relations, he took but little part in external affairs, except to represent strongly to Seward that he expected a share of the foreign patronage; he figured out that his State was entitled to 33 of the 269 diplomatic places. He secured desirable berths for his own intimate friends, Richard C. Parsons and James Monroe, as consuls to Rio, and he influenced some diplomatic appointments. He even transmitted to the President in October, 1861, a curious suggestion that "Honorable Andy Johnson" be sent over "to conciliate public opinion in England." Throughout the war, Chase had some special channels of foreign information through the letters of a shrewd correspondent, Mr. Wood, then our minister to Denmark, and through the impressions in foreign financial circles which came to him from time to time through New York bankers engaged in placing American loans abroad. The one subject in foreign diplomacy in which Chase took a marked interest was the settlement of the Trent affair. In a cabinet meeting of December 26, 1861, he strongly urged the return of Mason and Slidell, on the ground "that the technical right was clearly on the side of the British government;" and he had an honorable part in settling that controversy.

The significance of the national finances was not felt by the secretary till December, 1861; but during the anxious earlier months of that year Chase found time to rehabilitate the disorganized and almost bankrupt Treasury, to make the necessary appointments, to come into relations with the capitalists of the country, to suggest new taxes, and to borrow the money necessary to carry the country through the first period of the war. In a letter of April 6 he writes: "Certainly I never worked nearly so hard before; twice this week I have been at the department till after midnight from nine in the morning, with an interval for luncheon only. Every night except one I have been there till after ten."

Hard work was necessary, first of all, in order to reorganize the personnel of the department, and to reform the complicated and inadequate system of accounts. Since the end of Robert J. Walker's term in 1849, there had been no efficient Secretary of the Treasury, and the whole civil service at Washington was demoralized by the breaking out of war, and the consequent resignation of many Southern clerks and officials; while some who remained in office used their opportunities to send information to the enemy. It was necessary to purify the Treasury service; and had it been less necessary, no man could have altogether resisted the tremendous pressure for office which came upon Secretary Chase. The New York "Tribune" of March 9 said: "Chase intends to insist that the law requiring subordinates in his department [to] be examined before their appointment shall be strictly enforced; and no applicant will be admitted to office without entire qualification. This rule will purge the public service of drones and incompetents."

In making appointments, Chase in good faith sought to apply the system of pass-examinations, which had been set up under the act of 1853, and there were instances of appointees who were not allowed to qualify because of failure to pass. Nevertheless, large numbers of appointments were made on the personal judgment of the secretary himself; and many others on political recommendations. Several heads of bureaus and some clerks were allowed to remain in service, and new bureaus were speedily organized, as the business of the department increased. Perhaps the most important of the "hold-overs" was Mr. John J. Cisco, who at the express request of both Chase and Lincoln continued as assistant treasurer in New York City throughout and beyond Chase's administration. Out of one hundred and fifteen heads of custom-houses ninety were lopped; and twelve of the fifteen naval officers, and every appraiser disappeared. Nearly all the subordinates of such officials went with them; and where there were no removals, as fast as commissions expired new men were almost invariably appointed.

The greatest prize within Chase's department was the collectorship of the port of New York, a place highly paid, honorable, and, through its large number of employees, a means of affecting the politics of New York City and State. To this office Mr. Hiram Barney was speedily appointed. He had been one of the small circle of Chase men in New York in 1860; when the New York delegation came to the President with a slate of appointments, Lincoln informed them that he had himself chosen to nominate Barney. This appointment was out of the regular course, for Barney was not in the favor of the Seward-Weed combination, and, on the other hand, he was not sufficiently active as a politician to please Mr. Chase's eager friends; hence in the end it proved satisfactory to neither faction, and gave occasion for many bitter attacks upon the secretary.

Long before the beginning of his administration, Chase's intimates, his acquaintances, and sometimes his enemies, began to make suggestions to him as to appointments. Among them his far-sighted and public-spirited friend, Joshua Hanna, the Pittsburg banker, desired him to urge Lincoln to "inaugurate a new era in this government by selecting from among the business men of the country those best qualified, who would honestly and intelligently fill their several positions." The editors of the local party papers had a different set of principles, and clamored for office of every kind for themselves and their friends; and almost every place in New York was hotly contested between Weed and anti-Weed factions.

As soon as Chase was settled, members of Congress began to insist that he should make no appointments in their districts without their consent. Many of his political and personal friends furnished him with a variety of amusing reasons why they should have offices: one writes to ask for "a place in Abraham's bosom," and suggests the embassy to Chili; another must be appointed because he cannot make a living in any other way; another, because of his great public services; another, because Mr. Chase has in a moment of undue warmth offered him any office in his gift; another because he is from Ohio; another, because he will work up a presidential influence for the secretary; another, a lady, asks a place for her son, because his father would have been competent had he lived. Chase got appointments in other departments for his old law partner, Ball, for his brother, and for other kinsmen, and he himself appointed many other old friends; but the evidence shows that he made it a principle to recognize merit and efficiency, and was glad to find it among his own friends and adherents, all of whom were of course Republicans or strong war Democrats.

The patronage of the Treasury, already large and to be increased by the creation of new and lucrative offices, was to an unusual degree left by Mr. Lincoln in the hands of his secretary. Occasionally a candidate appeared at the department with such a note from Mr. Lincoln as the following: "Ought Mr. Young to be removed? And if Yea, ought Mr. Adams to be appointed? Mr. Adams is magnificently recommended, but the great point in his favor is that Thurlow Weed and Horace Greeley join in recommending him; I suppose the like never happened before, will never happen again, so it is now or never. What think you?" But the President very rarely pushed an appointment hard, or disregarded a recommendation made by Chase.

While the new men were fitting into their offices

Chase began to reorganize the routine of his department. He was always fond of arranging and analyzing, and showed an aptitude for distributing the work of his great office among the various bureaus. Himself untiring, he expected hard work from those about him. One of the great changes which he introduced into government business was the employment of women in the public service, first as counters of currency, later as assistants in many clerical occupations. But though he thus won the distinction of opening up an important line of employment to women, he very much disliked to do business with them, and hated to be made the object of their personal demands for appointment or other use of his influence.

Although the Treasury operations were larger during 1861 than ever before, the available methods were those which had always been employed whenever the expenditures outran the resources: loans, treasury notes, and delayed settlement of accounts. The panic of 1857 so cut down the income of the United States that it had to borrow to make up running expenses; and by November, 1860, the debt had risen to about $62,000,000. Impending secession reduced the credit of the government, so that when, toward the end of 1860, Secretary Cobb advertised a loan of $10,000,000, only about $7,000,000 was taken, and on January 1, 1861, in order to meet interest payments, money was borrowed on treasury notes at twelve per cent. The net result of these operations during the last four months of Buchanan's administration was an addition of $14,000,000 more of debt, with nothing to show for it.

Chase was obliged to begin his administration by contracting new loans. April 2, 1861, he accepted tenders for $8,000,000 of six per cent bonds, ranging from par to 94; but on May 21, after the war had actually begun, he was obliged to borrow a further sum of $7,000,000 in six per cents, at rates from 93 to 85, besides issuing new treasury notes for present needs.

The meeting of Congress in July, 1861, gave the secretary his first opportunity to suggest a financial plan for the government, and to discover how much criticism and change he must endure from Congress before any efficient legislation could be had. At this time he desired authority to contract for only such loans as the country might speedily expect to extinguish. "The idea of perpetual debt," said he, "is not of American nativity and should not be naturalized." He therefore recommended such increased taxation as would raise the ordinary annual revenue of the government from $50,000,000 to about $80,000,000, including a direct tax of $20,000,000, to be apportioned among the States, and an income tax of three per cent. He favored also an extensive measure of confiscation. All these measures were enacted by Congress; but down to December, 1861, not more than $2,000,000 was actually paid into the Treasury from direct taxation, and nothing from the income tax.

The most important financial measures during the first year were arrangements for new loans, and the actual borrowing of money — both matters in which the brief legislation of Congress was very significant, for there was laid the foundation for large issues of bonds, of interest-bearing notes, and of circulating notes. During the short summer session, Chase was authorized to borrow an additional $250,000,000 in any or all the three forms, the non-interest-bearing notes not to exceed $50,000,000; and it was upon the basis of this authority that the funds necessary for the prosecution of the war during the second half of 1861 were obtained.

One of the first steps taken by the new secretary was to seek the acquaintance of the financiers in Philadelphia, Boston, and especially New York. His retention of Mr. Cisco as local treasurer helped him to win the confidence of bankers; and several of the metropolitan capitalists and bank presidents were Chase's personal friends, especially George Opdyke, later mayor of the city. Armed with his new authority from Congress, in July Chase had a conference with the heads of the banks in the three great financial centres, and arranged for the placing of $150,000,000 of three-year treasury notes, bearing interest of seven and three-tenths per cent. Chase has left an account of the language in which he stated to the bankers the only alternative for this loan: "I was obliged to be very firm, and to say, Gentlemen, I am sure you wish to do all you can. I hope you will find that you can take the loans required on terms which can be admitted. If not, I must go back to Washington and issue notes for circulation; for, gentlemen, the war must go on until this rebellion is put down, if we have to put out paper until it takes $1000 to buy a breakfast.'" This suggestion of government notes in denominations and on terms which would cause them to circulate, was a threat of much import to the state banks; but without it they stood ready cheerfully to take the first installment of $50,000,000 in seven and three-tenths per cent treasury notes.

The money was spent almost faster than it was received, and a few weeks later Chase arranged for a second call of $50,000,000 on the same terms. But investors showed less confidence than the banks, and when a third call was made for $50,000,000, the bankers could no longer advance upon the "seven-thirty" notes at par, and Mr. Chase reluctantly issued $50,000,000 in six per cent bonds at about 92. A part of his loan system had been the appointment of one hundred and forty-eight agents for the placing of the loan; of these, only one, Jay Cooke of Philadelphia, distinguished himself by his success in distributing the treasury notes. Though the system of agents was for the time abandoned, his efficiency was not forgotten, and he later became Chase's special loan distributor.

Thus far, during the nine months of his stay in the Treasury, Chase had had little opportunity to show his qualities either as a great leader in the

Civil War or as an originator of schemes for finance. His military activity in the East was much diminished when McClellan was appointed to the command of the Army of the Potomac and began his system of military organization. After some attempts to form a friendship with the general, Chase found that he was little consulted on the affairs of the Eastern army. The question of slavery, in which Chase was by his history and his convictions a leader, was as yet kept in the background, and national finance thus far had consisted in organizing the machinery of the Treasury, in taking up the small amount of available capital at high rates of interest or at a humiliating discount, and in issuing a few millions of so-called "demand notes," which circulated as currency, and were receivable for debts to the government. Had the war ended early in 1862, as was hoped, Chase would never have had an opportunity to show his powers as a financier, or to urge his banking scheme. So long as specie payments continued he had no harder task than that of several secretaries of the Treasury before him.

During 1861 began one of the peculiar functions of the Treasury which, though it went on throughout the war, may be conveniently discussed here. It has already been noted that Mr. Chase looked forward to a large income from the confiscation of the property of rebels: this measure seemed an easy mode of combining revenue with punishment. By the first confiscation act, August 6, 1861, the President was authorized to seize any property used in promoting insurrection; but it proved difficult to get legal proof against such property, and hence the act, in its practical application, had to do principally with slaves. A second act of July 17, 1862, authorized the taking of property belonging to civil and military officers of the Confederacy, or to any persons who had given aid and comfort to the rebellion. In both cases some kind of legal proceeding was necessary for condemnation; but as Federal lines were extended, plantations, buildings, live stock, and especially cotton, were often found without a visible owner; and since this property was expected to come into the Treasury, it fell within the jurisdiction of Secretary Chase. By a series of orders, approved by the President, he made provision for the collection, sale, and record of such property; and in order to manage this immense business he was authorized to appoint a special body of Treasury agents, who followed close behind the armies, and sometimes went ahead of them.

It was also the function of the Secretary of the Treasury to make and enforce regulations for external commerce, so as to prevent goods sent out of the United States from finding their way eventually to the enemy; and this important power was extended to the control of trade on the land border. Movements of trade which had been established half a century were interrupted by the war, and the traffic from Southern to Northern

Atlantic ports by sea was resolutely and completely suppressed; but along the whole military land frontier from the James River to the mouth of the Mississippi, there was an unceasing effort to carry on traffic as if there were no war. On one side, the Northwestern States were cut off from their valuable provision trade to the South; on the other side, cotton accumulated behind the Confederate lines without any home market. Even within the Union lines the condition of the border States was desperate, for sympathizers with the South were so intermixed with loyal men, and the facilities for forbidden trade across the broken country which constituted the military frontier were so abundant, that it became necessary to regulate, and in some cases almost to cut off, the commerce of whole communities. Hence a great pressure was put upon the secretary to grant permits to furnish supplies for particular places and regions; and rigorously limited permissions were given to furnish $5000 a month in drugs to such a city, and $10,000 in dry goods and groceries to such another.

By a series of Treasury regulations in May and June, 1861, Chase directed the officials of his department to refuse clearances to places within the hostile lines; but under the act of July 13, 1861, the President was authorized to license commercial intercourse with parts of the seceded States, and the regulation of this trade was turned over to the Secretary of the Treasury. When he came to apply the principle in Kentucky and Missouri,

Chase laid the foundation of a most bitter hostility to himself; for the Ohio River trade to all places on the south side of the stream was for some time prohibited, and the commerce of Louisville was checked; while by cutting off the traffic down the Mississippi from St. Louis, the opposition of the business men of that city was roused. In New Orleans, under General Butler's rule, a brisk traffic began across the Gulf to the Confederacy, salt going in and cotton coming out; and agents were despatched to bring down cotton from the tributaries of the Mississippi.

Such a system of agents, acting so far from Washington and in the midst of war, was certain to lead to abuses; for to the special agents of the Treasury had been given an authority independent of the military commanders, and capable of gross misuse. The confidential reports of several of Chase's agents are still in existence, and they show his own earnest desire that the business should be done honestly, and at the same time the impossibility of carrying it on at such a distance without fraud and corruption.

The most profitable trade was in cotton and sugar. Cotton inside the Confederate lines was worth not more than ten cents in specie, but once on its way North or abroad it was worth seventy cents and upward. The temptation was too strong to be resisted. George S. Denison, collector of the revenue, Chase's confidential and upright representative in New Orleans, wrote him letter after letter about the trade across the border, which was going on under his own eyes, but which he could not check because it was authorized by the general in command. General Butler professed indignation, and promised amendment; but Mr. Denison reported — what everybody in New Orleans suspected — that the brother of the general was profiting by this unwarrantable trade, and that the general winked at it. A statute of March, 1863, attempted to correct these abuses by affixing a penalty to the reception of anything which was brought out of the Confederacy except, by the authorized agents of the Treasury; and Chase followed up the statute by renewed regulations, approved from time to time by the President. In 1863 a comprehensive plan was drawn up by which the country was divided into special agencies with a hierarchy of agents. By the removal of persons proved to be unsound, Chase tried to check the corruption of the agents, and in September, 1863, after the capture of Vicksburg, he successfully resisted a committee from St. Louis backed by Attorney-General Bates, which demanded that the Mississippi be opened to trade throughout its length.

The administration of the Treasury during the war has no more unsavory side than the scramble for permits and the collusion of military officers in getting out property from the enemy's lines; yet for no object did the secretary more honestly bestir himself than to regulate the trade. The circumstances were too much for him, as they were for the most upright commanders in the field. A few days before Chase's resignation in 1864, General Sickles wrote: "The real truth is that it has come almost to a direct trade with the enemy. In Kentucky, Tennessee, and Mississippi and Arkansas immense quantities of merchandise go through our lines, often in unbroken packages." Though the Treasury was defeated in its effort to keep the trade in proper channels, it would be unjust to hold the secretary culpable. Chase could and did remove delinquent agents; but he could not guarantee that their successors would be proof against the temptations of their unrivaled opportunities.

In later chapters the attempt will be made to describe Chase's financial policy. The fiscal and financial history of the Civil War is yet to be written; but it is possible to show the plans, hopes, and fears of the secretary, to bring out the personal side of his administration, to discuss his problems. Throughout the financial chapters the reader will find useful the brief financial tables, printed as an appendix to this book.

CHAPTER IX

TAXATION, LOANS, AND LEGAL TENDERS, 1862-1863

WITH the meeting of Congress in December, 1861, there came upon Chase a new set of anxieties, both financial and political. Upon him lay the responsibility of suggesting a financial system which should keep up the government's credit on $267,000,000 of outstanding loans and notes; which should provide at once for a deficit, already incurred, of $143,000,000; and which should make possible the prosecution of the war upon the scale which it now assumed. It was his duty also to convince the capitalists of the country that his schemes would work; and — perhaps more difficult still — he must persuade Congress of his superior wisdom.

His first annual report appeared December 9; but before it could produce any effect, his hand had been forced by a crisis in the currency. The three successive interest-bearing loans of $50,000,000 each had drawn heavily on the specie reserves of the country; and at the same time, $27,000,000 of treasury notes were in circulation as a currency, in competition with state bank notes. Feeling the drain upon their gold, the banks urged the government to receive their bank notes for bonds, a proposition which meant that the state bank issues were to be bolstered up by government credit. To this suggestion Chase replied with firmness: "If you can lend me all the coin required or show me where I can borrow it elsewhere at fair rates, I will withdraw every note already issued, and pledge myself never to issue another; but if you cannot, you must let me stick to United States notes, and increase the issue of them just as far as the deficiency of coin may require." The real difficulty was not scarcity of specie, but a want of public confidence in the success of the war, which affected both the government notes and the new securities still held in large quantities by the banks.

In 1812, in 1837, in 1839, and in 1857, the banks had all refused to redeem their own notes in specie, and it was plain that they were likely to suspend specie payment again. It was a painful suggestion to Chase, for he had insisted that no suspension would be necessary; but he had no power to control public confidence, and had made no preparations for such a crisis. On December 30 all the banks by general agreement suspended payment of their demand notes, and the government followed, with the result that after a few days a small premium was exacted for specie, gold became a commodity, and the government issues of notes and bonds began to decline in value.

Looking backward over the experience of nearly forty years, it is easy to criticise the banks, the country, and the secretary for this suspension.

Ought not resolution, bold taxation, or loans at high interest to have held the country up to the specie standard? So far as the previous experience of the United States shows, a suspension was inevitable, and would have come about had there been no government circulating notes. But considering the special difficulties of the time, none but an extraordinary financier, a Hamilton, could have prevented this misfortune. The banks of issue had state charters, and were subject to no control and no penalties from the general government if they failed to redeem their notes. When the banks gave up specie for Chase's seven-thirty notes, they expressed their own confidence that the government would punctually pay interest and principal; but so far as they held those notes, and had not sold them to investors, they were basing their own solvency on the national confidence that the government would speedily break down the Southern Confederacy; and neither banks nor investors were keyed up to the enormous expenditures which had begun to appear essential.

The government notes affected the question of suspension indirectly, because they showed that borrowing had already begun to lag, and because the United States could not keep them afloat as a special gold-value currency; but the real reason for the suspension of specie payments was that nobody could see where the specie was coming from to keep up the reserves, in view of the probable demands by the federal government. Vigorous and immediate taxation would have checked the fall of paper money, but it could not have provided for the expenses of 1862; and both private and public finance were disorganized for a time by the conditions of a civil war. Business was disconcerted by loss of foreign trade, by the closing of the Southern market, and by the cancellation of most of the debts due from Southern merchants.

As for the Treasury, in 1861 the administration had to feel its way; it had not foreseen the necessary changes in its financial system, because it had not foreseen a long war. As yet there was no powerful syndicate of American money lenders to absorb loans or sell abroad; no machinery for placing popular loans; no experience of the capacity of the people for bearing taxation; no knowledge of the terrible war expenses which ate up the revenue long before it was available; no sufficient understanding between secretary and Congress. The only thing of which Chase could feel reasonable certainty in December, 1861, was that the country would carry on the war through the next campaign; the task of straightening out the national forces and causing them to run parallel was the work of many months to follow.

Chase's position would have been stronger had the beginnings of a consistent financial system been presented to the July session of Congress; but the finance of 1861 was practically a series of makeshifts. First, there were the scanty proceeds of peace taxes; then loans, till they broke the market; then treasury notes, to tide over a few months. The crude devices of direct tax, of confiscation acts, and of income tax had as yet produced little; and when in December, 1861, the secretary was ready with a comprehensive scheme — taxes, loans, notes, and banks — his plans were pushed aside by Congress, till the mischief of the suspension of specie payments had been done, and the Treasury was empty; and then began a hurried course of legislation in which the plans of the secretary were treated with little respect.

It was not in Chase's nature to be persuasive; in all his public life his successes were those of the downright man, convincing without pleasing. Himself a most capable legislator when in the Senate, he had little patience with slow intellects, and less of that urbane yielding of non-essentials which secures the adoption of the larger matters of principle. The Congress of 1861–63 was at best a body hard to conciliate; the majority was made up of elements suspicious of each other, and the eventual crystallization was around very aggressive men, like Wade and Thaddeus Stevens; moreover, the temper of Congress shortly became so radical that, even on such a question as slavery, men like Chase were found among the conservatives. The lack of harmony between appropriations and "ways and means," which had been of small consequence before 1861, became dangerous during the war; for to vote supplies seemed a patriotic duty, to be performed instantly and without too much discussion, while the raising of money required long debates, and affected a member's popularity in his own district.

To deal with Congress Chase needed lieutenants, and he never had them. Senator Fessenden of Maine was sincerely interested in financial questions, and was as helpful as any member of Congress; but Chase had few personal friends in either house and fewer spokesmen. He had to keep in relations with the Committee of Ways and Means of the House, and the Finance Committee of the Senate; and he argued before them, button-holed members, wrote letters, placated them with minor appointments, and brought pressure to bear from constituents and newspapers; but he understood not the arts of lobbying, and he never could bring Congress to accept his financial scheme in an entirety, or any part of it without great modification of details.

So far as expenditures went, Chase never had any control over them, and yet he was held responsible for at least the suggestions of means to meet them. An example or two will show how far out of the way his estimates sometimes were. In July, 1861, it seemed to him safe to predict that the expenditures for the fiscal year 1861–62 would be $318,000,000; but the revised estimates in December were $543,000,000, and the actual sum eventually shown to have been expended was $475,000,000. For the year 1862–63 the secretary estimated $475,000,000, and in the end paid out $715,000,000. Both the committee system and the exigencies of the war made it impossible for Chase to impress upon Congress a conviction that he had a firm grasp of the problems of national finance.

All the elements of Chase's whole system of finance are to be found in his careful report of December, 1861. In expenditure he urged an economy which he was never able to secure. For receipts he recognized five possible sources: taxation, time loans, confiscation of property of the insurgents, treasury notes to be issued for brief periods on interest, and demand notes circulating as currency; out of these sources he meant soon to eliminate the government notes of both kinds, except for temporary uses; and he intended to rely on taxation, long loans, and confiscation. The questions which most exercised his mind were: in what proportion to use loans and taxes, and how to find a market for his loans? The force of circumstances, however, speedily forced upon him as his main resources short term loans bearing high interest; and treasury notes, circulating as currency, irredeemable, and a legal tender.

At the moment, the most serious problem seemed to be whether the Treasury should rely on heavy taxation to furnish a considerable part of its revenues, to create confidence in the payment of interest, and to form the basis of a sinking fund for the bonds. Chase did not in either 1861 or 1862 urge high taxation, and in December, 1863, he very distinctly stated his reasons. "I can see clearly that we can go no further without heavy taxation; and he has read history to little purpose who does not know that heavy taxes will excite discontent."

The experience of 1864 and 1865 proved that the country could pay enormous taxes; hence it is a serious question whether Chase ought not to have made taxation the basis of his whole scheme. It must not be forgotten how unused people were to any national taxes except indirect customs, and how light even state and local taxation had been for many years. From 1837 to 1861 the national revenue was practically derived from import duties, except a few millions from public lands. The excise had twice been laid, but the second excise expired in 1817, and it had always been a very unpopular impost. No direct tax had been levied since the War of 1812, and it was a device which bore hardest on the poorest communities. Chase's political instincts were against high protective duties, and Congress never knew how to force up the tariff to a basis which would be productive and yet not impair its revenue capacity. The strongest reason for holding off from war taxation in 1861 was the expectation that the war would be over in twelve months; Chase hesitated, and Lincoln hesitated with him, to lay a permanent war tax, and both deliberately faced the prospect of going through the calendar year 1862 chiefly on loans and on the expected proceeds of confiscations.

In his report Chase expressly disclaimed a purpose of depending on government circulating notes. He expected to borrow, but on obligations running many years, and he brought forward in its first form his great project for a system of national bank corporations, which should give the country a stable currency and at the same time become large lenders to the government. To his mind the new banks were to be the keystone of his financial arch; they were to interest the financiers in the success of the government, to take away the competition between state bank notes and government issues, to absorb and sell the government securities, and to replace the temporary treasury notes.

As soon as the recommendations of the secretary were sent to Congress it became evident that that body was little disposed to follow his lead. The customs duties had produced $64,000,000 in 1856–57, but only $40,000,000 in 1860–61. The Morrill tariff took effect April 1, 1861; but as it could be applied only to the loyal States, on Chase's recommendation a special act of August 5 had imposed revenue duties on tea, coffee, sugar, and molasses; and on December 24, also on Chase's suggestion, Congress further raised those rates so as to add at once to the revenue. As new sources of revenue, Chase proposed direct, income, and internal taxes to the amount of $50,000,000 a year, which, with the increased customs, would make an income of $90,000,000.

Although he apologized for asking such large

sums, Congress parted from him at this critical moment, and under the leadership of Thaddeus Stevens the House directed the Committee on Ways and Means to lay new taxes which should produce $150,000,000. But if Chase asked less than the country was willing to give, at least he wanted speedy action; and Congress let six months slip away before the comprehensive internal revenue act of July 1, 1862, was passed. In this statute a large number of articles, processes, and evidences of wealth were included; and a necessary part of the scheme was a new tariff, by which additional duties were placed on imported goods, to correspond with the new burdens placed on American manufactures. This act required a wholly new and very elaborate machinery, which could not be improvised. Hence the net result of the disregard of the secretary's suggestion was that during the fiscal year 1861–62 he had no income from new taxation except driblets from the direct tax to the amount of about $2,000,000; and in 1862–63 he got less than $40,000,000 from new taxes, while the tariff receipts for that year were hardly greater than for 1856. Chase's own modest plan would have yielded from $60,000,000 to $70,000,000 a year during the same period, with an immediate good effect on the public credit.

The full influence of the legislation of 1862 was not felt till the fiscal year 1863–64, when customs and internal revenue raised the income at last to more than the $200,000,000 which Chase had expected in 1862, and with the aid of $30,000,000 of confiscations the revenue ran up to $260,000,000. In 1864–65, after Chase's retirement, the taxes rose to $300,000,000, and in 1865–66 to $490,000,000; and the country from which Chase hesitated to ask $90,000,000 in December, 1861, five years later furnished $570,000,000 to the federal treasury, besides tremendous sacrifices of men and money.

It would not be fair either to the secretary or to Congress to think the conditions of 1866 like those of 1861. Flush times, sudden revival of business, resumption of immigration, national self-confidence, the restoration of the South, had by that time taken the place of distress and forebodings. Chase might have struck a higher note in his policy of taxation, and every dollar raised in 1862 would have saved three dollars in 1864; but he had an intelligent plan of successive increases of taxation, which would have accustomed the country to the machinery of collection, while the congressional system of taxes was slow at a critical time, and in the end bore harder than was intended.

In all the previous crises in the finances of the United States, — 1776, 1794, 1812, 1837, 1842, 1857, — taxation had been both inadequate and slow; and three other means of raising money had been employed, — temporary loans, funded loans, and a form of paper currency. The easiest method was to issue the so-called "treasury notes," usually in large denominations and bearing interest. They were used to satisfy for the time being the claims of contractors, and also to attract idle capital, since they had commonly but a few months to run, and were as sound as any security in the country. They were almost always treated as an investment, and did not circulate except among banks and capitalists.

Chase found outstanding when he came into office more than $10,000,000 in one-year notes; and he also found authority, by an act of March 2, 1861, to issue more treasury notes; and before December 1, 1861, he had put out $22,000,000 of two-year notes, besides a large amount of very short-term notes, which were redeemed as they fell due. Under the discretion given him by the statutes, he revived a form of note devised in the War of 1812, — a $7\frac{3}{10}$ per cent three-year "bond," as he called it, issued in denominations of $50 and upwards. The rate of interest was high; it was easy to calculate, and it was hoped that the people would hoard the notes: as a matter of fact they were taken chiefly by banks and large investors. In July, 1865, $810,000,000 of these notes were outstanding, and they were not all extinguished till 1870.

Several other forms of temporary obligations were worked out by the ingenious secretary: such were the ordinary one-year and two-year notes at five per cent and six per cent interest; "certificates of indebtedness," bearing six per cent and running a year; and "temporary loans," payable on ten days' notice, with four per cent, five per cent, or six per cent interest, — a very popular method of obtaining interest on temporary deposits. A favorite form with Chase was the "demand notes," as issued under acts of July 17 and August 5, 1861, the authority to terminate December 31, 1862. These were in denominations as low as five dollars, bore no interest, and were not legal tender; eventually they reached $60,000,000, but they were superseded by the legal tenders and retired in 1862 and 1863. The demand notes were the forerunners of the United States paper currency, or "greenbacks," and were from the first intended to circulate side by side with state bank notes. Even after the suspension of specie payments they stood at par in gold, because they were receivable for customs.

The whole system of short loans was an unfortunate makeshift. Since it was impossible to foresee expenses a year ahead, Chase's budgets were all estimates. What he did was to raise all the money he could, in every possible way; to refund his temporary loans into bonds, so far as he could, and then to resort to new short loans for pressing needs. When everything else failed he issued more legal tenders.

In December, 1861, the funded debt of the United States (not including notes) was $280,000,000, of which about $200,000,000 had been contracted since March, 1861. While the question of taxes was pending, and indeed during the many months before they could become productive,

Chase was by the necessities of the case obliged to put forth new issues of bonds. The second great loan act, February 25, 1862, authorized the issue of $500,000,000 in the so-called "five-twenty" bonds. Chase himself proposed the two limitations in the issue — the fixing of the interest at six per cent, and the payment of interest in gold. A twenty-year bond at such rates of interest as were usual in the country during the Civil War should have been a good investment; but neither of the two provisions worked as had been expected. To furnish the specie for the interest the import duties were levied in gold, a provision reasonable in itself and helpful to the Treasury; but the bonds would not sell at par on a specie basis, because the investing public in the United States and abroad thought six per cent too little for the risk; and by making the legal tenders convertible into the bonds, Chase did not raise the credit of the notes, and did inevitably depress the price of his bonds to par in greenbacks. The continued effect of these causes was that large blocks of Civil War bonds were sold at gold values of 50 or even 40, on which was paid an interest which, measured in greenbacks, was 12 per cent to 15 per cent, with the obligation of eventually redeeming in full in gold. The purchaser of a "ten-forty" five per cent bond in 1864 had therefore virtually a 20 per cent investment for at least ten years.

In placing the bonds, Chase wisely determined not to depend longer upon banks, but to put the whole matter in charge of a general agent. The person selected for this important national service was Jay Cooke, a man of great energy, which he infused into local agencies established with banks and bankers throughout the United States. But in order to place the bonds at all, it was necessary to allow a commission of three-eighths of one per cent; which, however moderate in itself, was a monopoly privilege, and caused plenty of hard feeling and some reflections on the secretary. With every exertion, the actual subscriptions to permanent loans during 1862-63 amounted to only $175,000,000, while the taxes produced only $111,000,000; the expenditures were $704,000,000, leaving $418,000,000 to be raised by temporary loans and paper money. For two years, from July, 1861, to July, 1863, the total expenditures were $1,189,000,000, the receipts from taxation $163,000,000, and from funded loans only $235,000,000. This leaves $791,000,000, or more than two thirds of the whole, which had to be made up by temporary loans of various kinds and by legal tender notes which were a forced loan. In the next year, 1863-64, much of the floating obligation was at last funded, and the rising taxes came to the relief of the government, so that when Chase went out of office, in July, 1864, he left a funded debt of $769,000,000, short-term debts of $516,000,000, and paper currency to the amount of $455,000,000. This was simply hand to mouth finance, issues of notes from time to time making up for fluctuations in the various forms of temporary debt; and the proceeds of loans anticipated long before they were paid in.

Except certain one, two, and three year interest-bearing legal tender notes first authorized March 3, 1863, the obligations just described might be refused by any creditor of the government who did not choose to accept them; and the early demand notes were the only ones that freely circulated during 1861. But in November, 1861, Chase was cogitating a larger issue of some kind, and he said to the banks: "You ask me to borrow the credit of local banks in the form of circulation. I prefer to put the credit of the people into notes and use them as money."

The necessity for some kind of regular currency had been felt throughout 1861, when the Western bank circulation was giving way; and it was accented in January, 1862, when the specie began to disappear from circulation. The state bank notes then amounted only to $184,000,000, which was not sufficient for the needs of the country; and many of them were of doubtful value. The patient secretary was at once beset by all sorts of wild schemes for replacing or supplementing them by a government currency. One friend suggested circulating notes with accumulating interest at $3\frac{65}{100}$ per cent; another proposed a system of government notes redeemable in land; another thought that the United States should take up the outstanding bank paper; and others that the secretary should ask for authority to issue legal tender government notes. For some months the premium on gold was very slight, but after the military disasters of July, 1862, the United States notes sank to 84 per cent, measured in specie.

Two rival plans now presented themselves to Congress. Mr. Chase was willing to issue large amounts of demand notes, taking the chances of their deterioration; on the other hand, Judge Spaulding, the chairman of the sub-committee of the Committee of Ways and Means, was convinced that the only way to sustain such issues was to make them legal tender. After a long fight in Congress, an act was passed on February 25, 1862, authorizing the issue of $150,000,000 in notes, to be reissued as they were presented for redemption, "and to be lawful money and a legal tender in payment of all debts, public and private, within the United States, except duties on imports and interest on the public debt." The country was thus committed to a policy of government legal tender notes, and throughout the war, whenever taxes and loans proved insufficient, recourse was always had to this expedient; when the war ended, $431,000,000 of these legal tender notes were in circulation. As silver suddenly disappeared from circulation, acts of July 17, 1862, and March 3, 1863, authorized also the issue of fractional currency in paper, and the amount eventually reached $45,000,000.

No act in Chase's life has caused so much discussion as his attitude on the legal tenders; he has been held up to odium as yielding to a pressure from an uninformed Congress, which he might have safely resisted. In his report of December, 1861, he had dwelt upon the dangers of a national paper currency, even without the legal tender quality, saying that "in his judgment possible disasters so far outweigh the probable benefits from the plan, that he feels himself constrained to forbear recommending its adoption." Judge Spaulding prepared the draft of a statute to authorize in terms the issue of legal tender notes, and thereby raised the question of constitutionality; whereupon Attorney-General Bates gave the informal opinion that Congress had the power to issue legal tenders. Chase saw that Congress was outrunning his recommendations, and he called a conference of bankers and members of the committees of Congress to find some counter plan upon which all might combine. On January 15 the representatives of the banks agreed to a plan which was to relieve the country from the necessity of a legal tender act; but on January 22, when the currency bill was sent to Chase for his comments, he had no argument to make against the legal tender clause further than to express the regret that it was considered necessary; thenceforth the opponents of the measure were deprived of his powerful influence. On a test vote in the House, the legal tender clause stood 93 to 53; and on February 4 Chase gave up the struggle, "on condition that a tax adequate for interest and sinking fund and the ordinary expenditures be provided, and that a uniform banking system be authorized."

The responsibility for the issue of legal tender notes, and especially for the continued and excessive issue, is difficult to place. It has often been urged that by insisting on high taxation and by issuing demand notes without the legal tender quality, the war might have been fought through without recourse to this expedient. The responsibility for the delay in new taxes certainly lies with Congress, or perhaps with the administration as a whole, rather than with the secretary; though it must not be forgotten that the new taxes of 1862 were supposed to be severer than they proved, for all authorities much overestimated their probable proceeds. When their inadequacy was seen in 1863, Chase urged "the enactment of such laws as will secure the increase of the internal revenue to the amount originally estimated, of $150,000,000 a year." From the tariff alone adequate revenue was not to be expected; for Congress was much more disposed to add to the protective than to the revenue schedules. The real difficulty, so far as taxation was concerned, was the continued underestimate of the probable duration of the war, and the lack of experience of the ability of a prosperous and energetic people to bear the burdens of a long conflict. Without high taxes to give a basis for the credit of the government, borrowing was difficult and the time loans expected in 1862 could not be obtained in sufficient sums. There was plenty of capital, as was shown by the large temporary deposits with the government, but the capitalists had many profitable investments before them, and felt doubtful of the outcome of the war. So far as taxation is concerned, Chase showed little initiative, and as a consequence, lost his leadership at the outset.

Nobody then or since has been able to point out a way whereby the issue of government notes of some kind might have been averted. There was, however, a very strong objection to giving them the legal tender quality, although the idea was by no means new, and was proposed in Congress about the end of the War of 1812. Chase had evidently been turning the objections to the plan over in his mind, for on June 3, 1861, a friend sent him a scheme for legal tender notes redeemable in gold, silver, or interest-bearing treasury notes; but the secretary's instincts were against any system which stretched the national powers and impaired preëxisting contracts. For two months before the act passed he stood out against a legal tender clause, first by direct argument, then by trying to organize a counter scheme, and finally by refusing to give his influence in favor of the plan; but as has been seen, his arguments did not convince Congress, his counter scheme did not satisfy the bankers, and in the end the clause was put into the bill whether he would or no.

Undoubtedly it was the duty of a finance minister to lead, and of Congress to defer, in such a discussion as that on legal tenders; but if Chase ever thought of appealing to the country over the head of Congress, he quickly gave up the idea; for when the question came to the test, he found against him, not only the Committee on Ways and Means, but the great banking interests of the country; and the imperious need of speedy provision for the Treasury did not allow delay. Chase was simply overborne by the weight of his counselors, and further opposition would only have emphasized his defeat.

Besides the testimony of shrewd observers at the time, there are still in existence letters from many bankers and business men in all parts of the country, and especially in New York, Philadelphia, and Boston, insisting on the legal tender clause. Among these men were Assistant Treasurer John J. Cisco; and George Opdyke, who in an elaborate memorial of January 28, 1862, set forth the argument that the legal tender clause would strengthen the interest-bearing securities of the government, and urged that without it the government would soon be unable to purchase supplies for the army or to keep its bonds from a rapid fall. Another phase of the question is set forth in a letter from T. C. Henry of Philadelphia, who insisted upon a legal tender quality in order to prevent the government notes from sinking below bank paper; for some of the banks at this time adopted the ill-timed practice of refusing to take the demand notes in ordinary deposits, with a view to show that the credit of their own notes was better than that of the Treasury; while other concerns, especially the savings banks, were furious at this attempt to throw them back upon wholly irredeemable bank notes. A few men, like William Welsh of Philadelphia, urged the secretary not to yield the point; but had he continued to hold out against Congress, he would have parted company with the men through whom alone he could expect to place loans. He yielded, not to an uninformed Congress, but to the wisest men with whom he could consult; and he yielded because he expected to hold the legal tender notes near par.

The constitutional question played a great part in the debates in Congress, giving rise to indignant remonstrances and denunciations; but this side of the problem seems at the time to have had less weight in Chase's mind than the disorganization of contracts and the danger of a depreciated currency. In his thought this latter danger was to be removed by his national bank project, through which a new and sound currency was speedily to take the place of the government issues. He and his friends expected a moderate issue of the new notes to tide the government over until the rising flood of taxes, the large subscriptions to loans, and the credit of national banks should make it possible to refund the notes and at the same time to meet the expenses of the government.

It is remarkable that Chase did not foresee the

two interactive features of the legal tender act which gave him much trouble in the long run, namely, the coin duties, and the conversion of legal tenders at par into six per cent bonds. Since gold was necessary for the payment of duties, it must be had by the importers at any price, and the arrangement therefore lent itself to a speculation in gold, which was really a speculation in depreciation of the legal tender notes. But, on the other hand, the scheme was really a somewhat clumsy system of redemption, since the holder of legal tenders could always turn them into a coin-bearing security.

CHAPTER X

SLAVERY IN THE CIVIL WAR

TOWARD the end of 1861 slavery became the central point, both of divergence between parties and of differences within the parties; and thereafter the question became more and more momentous, till it culminated in the second Emancipation Proclamation of January 1, 1863. From that time on, the anti-slavery forces were in the ascendant, and did not rest till in March, 1865, the Thirteenth Amendment to the Constitution was laid before the state legislatures.

At the beginning of the war the Republican party was not an anti-slavery party, its most advanced principle being that no new slave Territories or slave States should be permitted; and in the tumultuous tides of public feeling after the firing on Fort Sumter, the greatest efforts were made to prevent the slave question from coming to the front. At least four different elements may be distinguished in the supporters of Mr. Lincoln's administration: first, the anti-slavery Republicans, of whom Chase was the only distinct representative in the cabinet; second, the moderate Republicans, of whom a type, if not a leader, was

Seward; third, the war Democrats, at first headed by Stephen A. Douglas, who offered his personal support and aid to the President, and who, with his followers, believed and expected that the war would be finished without affecting slavery in the States; fourth, the loyal border-state men, many of them slaveholders, represented in the South by Crittenden, and in the cabinet by Bates and Montgomery Blair. Such men adhered to the Union under the assurance that their property rights would be safeguarded.

To reassure both war Democrats and border-state men, the House of Representatives, on the day after the battle of Bull Run, by a vote of 107 to 2, passed the following resolution: "*Resolved by the House of Representatives of the Congress of the United States*, That the present deplorable civil war has been forced upon the country by the disunionists of the Southern States, now in arms against the constitutional government, and in arms around the capital; that in this national emergency Congress, banishing all feelings of mere passion or resentment, will recollect only its duty to the whole country; that this war is not waged on their part in any spirit of oppression, or for any purpose of conquest or subjugation, or purpose of overthrowing or interfering with the rights of established institutions of those States, but to defend and maintain the supremacy of the Constitution and to preserve the Union with all the dignity, equality, and rights of the several States unimpaired, and that as soon as these objects are accomplished the war ought to cease."

In most of the States an attempt was made to find a common political ground for Republicans, and for those war Democrats who could not accept the party designation of their former opponents. Throughout 1861 and 1862 this fusion was kept up, and in 1863 for a time took the name of Union Party. Not until 1864 did the Republican party again come forward as an entirely independent organization, and rid itself of such of the remaining war Democrats as preferred to return to their own Democratic organization.

That the war might be fatal to slavery was, however, evident to some minds from the first; and in April, 1861, a correspondent pointed out to Chase the precise method which was to be the solution of the question. "Why should not this administration place itself upon the construction given to the Constitution by John Quincy Adams, that the state of war would confer a constitutional power upon the government to proclaim emancipation; then declare the seceded States in a condition of rebellion, and by a proclamation of emancipation obtain a power over the subject race to assist in the restoration of order in the rebellious States?"

At that time Lincoln was not ready to take up either the idea of emancipation by proclamation or the enlistment of negro troops; he still believed that the solution was to be emancipation by the voluntary action of the States, through the assistance of the general government. Throughout 1861 his mind dwelt on schemes for compensated emancipation and the deportation of the freedmen to some other part of the world, schemes which had been favorite ideas with him for ten years; and nothing but the relentless logic of events convinced him that more violent methods were both possible and desirable.

The hostilities of 1861 brought out several points of altercation concerning slaves, especially the confiscation of slaves belonging to rebel masters and the status of fugitives who had come within the Federal lines. It was a grief to Chase that he could not support General Frémont's proclamation of August 30, 1861, which declared free the slaves of all persons in the State of Missouri who were taking an active part with the enemy in the field. Chase defended the action of the President in annulling this pronunciamento, partly on the technical grounds that the recent confiscation act of Congress had limited the confiscation of slaves to such negroes as had actually been used in the rebellion, and partly because, as he wrote, "I am sure that neither the President nor any member of his administration has any desire to convert this war for the Union and for national existence . . . into a war upon any state institution."

Butler's shrewd solution of the fugitive question in May, 1861, held the negroes who had come within his lines to be "contraband of war;" this declaration had Chase's sympathy and support, and on October 8 he took the unusual step of sending to the "National Intelligencer" a leading article, in which he approved using the service of the fugitive negroes in the same way in which it had been employed on the other side; but suggested that in the end such persons ought to be transported to some tropical region, in order that "all injurious influence from their emancipation would be averted, while loyal masters, provided that they remain loyal, can be, and doubtless will be, fully indemnified."

The same Congress which in 1861 and in 1862 showed a disposition to make a financial policy of its own, also outran the President and his cabinet on the question of slavery. On December 16, 1861, a bill was offered for the total abolition of slavery in the District of Columbia, and on April 16, 1862, the act was passed, including a compensation to the owners. As a consequence the three thousand slaves in the District were shortly emancipated at a cost to the government of about $1,000,000. The District of Columbia act was an assertion of a constitutional right which had always been claimed by the North; but before that bill became law another proposition was introduced, nominally "to render freedom national and slavery sectional," but really to put into practice, in defiance of the Dred Scott decision, the doctrine that Congress could and should prohibit slavery in the Territories. Eventually this bill became a statute, prohibiting slavery and involuntary servitude in all the Territories of the United States then existing or which thereafter might be formed. On July 17 a second confiscation act provided that the disloyalty of a master should be a bar to any legal proceedings which he might bring to claim the service of his slave. By another statute, officers of the army were forbidden to render any assistance in the return of fugitives even to loyal masters.

Though slavery was undermined by this series of acts, all passed within a year from the beginning of active hostilities, it still remained legal in the loyal border States, and the machinery of the Fugitive Slave Act of 1850 was in operation; while slaveholders in the seceded States remained in legal possession of their slaves, provided the masters had taken no actual part in the war. Nevertheless, on both sides of the military lines the institution was disorganized and in danger; thousands of negroes flocked to the camps from the border States, and in the disturbed conditions of the time could not be recovered by their masters; other thousands found their way out of the Confederacy across the front, and gathered about the headquarters of the Northern armies.

By this time Chase had come forward as the leading anti-slavery spirit in the cabinet, and sought an opportunity to make his principles felt. Through his functions as the head of the department which dealt with confiscated and abandoned property, he had a special relation with the refugees from the South; and after the taking of Port Royal, on the coast of North Carolina, in November, 1861, he was allowed to direct the first experiment in organizing and civilizing the former slaves. In January, 1862, he sent down his friend, Edward L. Pierce of Boston, an old-time abolitionist, who had already been at Port Royal and hence knew something of the conditions there. When Pierce, at Chase's request, waited upon Lincoln to discuss with him what might be done for the freedmen, the President broke in upon him impatiently with the inquiry, "What's all this itching to get niggers into our lines?" and he reluctantly authorized the Secretary of the Treasury to give to Pierce such instructions as might be necessary. In these instructions Chase expressed his judgment that "the persons who have thus been abandoned by their masters, and who are received into the service of the country, can never, without great inhumanity on the part of the government, be reduced again to slavery." In his mind, therefore, military emancipation had begun, and the problem of caring for the former slaves must be assumed by the government. He took a great interest in the gathering and training of the refugees, and several times visited the station in person.

In the spring of 1862 the direction of the work was transferred to the War Department, but Chase, through his special control of the collection of cotton, kept in close touch with the missionary enterprise. General Hunter was put in command of the troops, but General Saxton was by Chase's personal request appointed military governor of South Carolina, and supervised the fugitives who occupied most of the little district within the Federal lines. The sea islands were again brought under cultivation; plantations were started, and lands in small plots were assigned to individual negroes. Schools were established by benevolent societies in the North, and, in spite of many discouragements, the experiment of making former slaves self-supporting was on the whole successful. In this work Chase felt that he had had neither support nor sympathy from the President; but when negro troops began to be organized, the settlement at Port Royal became important as a recruiting station, and at the end of the war a prosperous community appeared to have been founded. Then questions were raised as to the title to the lands distributed to the freedmen; and in time most of them were dispossessed of the little holdings for which they had worked so hard, and the experiment came to an unhappy end. The Port Royal principle of special supervision and protection by the government was, however, continued to the end of reconstruction times.

Neither fugitives nor refugees could much affect the other great problem of slavery, — the status of the slaves in the seceded States. President Lincoln, himself a native of Kentucky, had always had a strong sense of the practical difficulties and dangers of emancipation in regions where the negroes were numerous; hence from 1861 to 1864 he continued to press his influence to the farthest point possible in favor of compensated emancipation, at least in the border States. Although Chase had looked with some favor on this plan in 1861, he finally set himself distinctly against Mr. Lincoln's corollary scheme for colonization of the freed negroes in the West Indies or in Central America. Chase felt that the Port Royal experiment had been neglected because "the colonization delusion and negrophobia dread are too potent yet." Upon this point his view was clearer than that of the President; for colonization involved depriving the South of its laborers and the North of needed soldiers, and Chase was quicker than Lincoln to reach the point where he was willing to risk defection of the border States and political disturbance in the North, by setting free all the slaves in the Confederacy.

Before the war had been going on many months the usefulness of the negroes as laborers on the fortifications began to be seen, and a few early voices were heard urging their enrollment as troops. Probably one of the earliest of these suggestions was made in May, 1861, by Elizur Wright. "At its foundation the war is all about the black man. Between magnanimity and contempt, we Northerners may be willing to fight it out for him, and entirely without his aid. But events are not ruled by men, and before the war is through the black man is pretty likely to be fighting for himself on one side or the other." Notwithstanding the fundamental objection to using slaves as soldiers, they were gathered in large quantities by the Southern authorities for work on fortifications, and free negroes were in a few cases actually enlisted and disciplined in the rebel army. At the capture of New Orleans a regiment of such negro troops was found there.

Serious political objections stood in the way of negro enlistments either in Northern States or in conquered territory: white troops objected to service alongside negro soldiers; and it was feared by many and hoped by a few that the effect of enlistment would be to stir up slave insurrections in the South. On May 9, 1862, General Hunter at Hilton Head raised the issue by proclaiming that "slavery and martial law in a free country are altogether incompatible. The persons in these three States,—Georgia, Florida, and South Carolina,—wherever held as slaves, are therefore declared forever free;" at the same time he began upon his own responsibility to organize colored troops. With this action, which was as insubordinate as the similar proclamation of Frémont the year before, Chase sympathized, and he exerted his influence, though without avail, against its revocation by the President. "I have never been so sorely tried," he wrote to Horace Greeley, "in all that I have seen in the shape of irregularities, assumptions beyond the law, extravagances, deference to generals and reactionists which I cannot approve, . . . as by the nullifying of Hunter's proclamation." From this time on Chase remained a strong advocate of arming the negroes, and of making them eventually full citizens. Congress soon came to the point of authorizing the enlistment of negroes, by the act of July 17, 1862, which empowered the President "to employ as many persons of African descent as he may deem necessary and proper for the suppression of the rebellion, and for these purposes he may organize and use them in such manner as he may judge best for the public welfare." A few weeks later Secretary Stanton authorized the enlistment of troops at Port Royal, and in the Emancipation Proclamation of January 1, 1863, the President formally promised to receive negroes into the military service of the United States.

Though Chase had no strong influence in any of the legislative or executive measures relative to slavery, he was always the mainspring of antislavery influence within the councils of the President; to him the abolitionists throughout the country appealed for such action by the President as should forever stamp the institution of slavery with the crushing disapproval of the people in arms. Every week brought suggestions not only that the government had a duty in protecting fugitives and in punishing disloyal masters by freeing their slaves, but also that the great opportunity had come for a declaration that the war was a war upon slavery; that, as Chase told Motley in June,

1861, if the North was otherwise unable to put down the rebellion, "we shall then draw that sword which we prefer at present to leave in the sheath, and we shall proclaim the total abolition of slavery on the American continent. We do not wish this, we deplore it because of the ruin, confiscation of property, and of the servile insurrections, too horrible to contemplate, which would follow."

That the negroes would rise if there was a good opportunity seems to have been accepted as an axiom on both sides; but the South understood the character of the negro better than did the North, and confidently denied its own axiom, withdrawing its able-bodied white men from the plantations, for military service. In the whole history of the Civil War, there is no case of a rising of slaves, though, till the first proclamation of emancipation was actually issued, Lincoln shrank from what seemed a desperate and dangerous appeal to their passions. Chase never faltered, but used all the influence that he possessed upon the President and his fellow members of the cabinet to secure the desired proclamation; and he so far realized the importance of the issue that he made in his diary from day to day those careful entries of the discussions in the cabinet which are the most definite source of our information about the motives of Lincoln and his advisers at this crisis.

In July, 1862, the political situation was threatening for the Republican party. The country was alarmed by disasters in the field, by new taxation, and by heavy loans, and it saw no likelihood of concentrated military energy. Chase himself was out of patience, and thought seriously of seeking a senatorship. In this gloomy period Chase earnestly supported and even outran Lincoln's purpose to take a definite step which would be unmistakable to the country and to foreign nations. His record of the discussion in the cabinet runs as follows: —

July 21, "I went at the appointed hour, and found that the President had been profoundly concerned at the present aspect of affairs, and had determined to take some definite steps in respect to military action and slavery." To such a step most of the members of the cabinet were favorably inclined. August 3, "I expressed my conviction . . . that the time for the suppression of the rebellion without interference with slavery had long passed. . . . Mr. Seward expressed himself as in favor of any measures likely to accomplish the results I contemplated, which could be carried into effect without Proclamations; and the President said he was pretty well cured of objections to any measure except want of adaptedness to put down the rebellion; but did not seem satisfied that the time had come for the adoption of such a plan as I proposed."

In September Chase was discouraged, and says: "I have urged my ideas on the President and my associates, till I begin to feel that they are irksome to the first, and to one or two, at least, of the second." September 21, hearing that the President was busy, he conjectures, "Possibly engaged on Proclamation." September 22 another cabinet meeting was held, the result of which was the proclamation of 1862. Of this important meeting we have a full and animated account in Chase's diary and memoranda: —

"To Department about nine. State Department messenger came, with notice to Heads of Departments to meet at 12. Received sundry callers. Went to White House.

"All the members of the Cabinet were in attendance. There was some general talk; and the President mentioned that Artemas Ward had sent him his book. Proposed to read a chapter which he thought very funny. Read it, and seemed to enjoy it very much — the Heads also (except Stanton) of course. The chapter was 'High handed Outrage at Utica.'

"The President then took a graver tone and said: —

"'Gentlemen: I have, as you are aware, thought a great deal about the relation of this war to Slavery; and you all remember that, several weeks ago, I read to you an Order I had prepared on this subject, which, on account of objections made by some of you, was not issued. Ever since then, my mind has been much occupied with this subject, and I have thought all along that the time for acting on it might very probably come. I think the time has come now. I wish it was a better time.

I wish that we were in a better condition. The action of the army against the rebels has not been quite what I should have best liked. But they have been driven out of Maryland, and Pennsylvania is no longer in danger of invasion. When the rebel army was at Frederick, I determined, as soon as it should be driven out of Maryland, to issue a Proclamation of Emancipation such as I thought most likely to be useful. I said nothing to any one; but I made the promise to myself, and (hesitating a little) to my Maker. The rebel army is now driven out, and I am going to fulfill that promise. I have got you together to hear what I have written down. I do not wish your advice about the main matter—for that I have determined for myself. This I say without intending anything but respect for any one of you. But I already know the views of each on this question. They have been heretofore expressed, and I have considered them as thoroughly and carefully as I can. What I have written is that which my reflections have determined me to say. If there is anything in the expressions I use, or in any other minor matter, which any one of you thinks had best be changed, I shall be glad to receive the suggestions. One other observation I will make. I know very well that many others might, in this matter, as in others, do better than I can; and if I were satisfied that the public confidence was more fully possessed by any one of them than by me, and knew of any Constitutional way in which he could be put in my place, he should have it. I would gladly yield it to him. But though I believe that I have not so much of the confidence of the people as I had some time since, I do not know that, all things considered, any other person has more; and, however this may be, there is no way in which I can have any other man put where I am. I am here. I must do the best I can, and bear the responsibility of taking the course which I feel I ought to take.'

"The President then proceeded to read his Emancipation Proclamation, making remarks on the several parts as he went on, and showing that he had fully considered the whole subject, in all the lights under which it had been presented to him.

"After he had closed, Gov. Seward said: 'The general question having been decided, nothing can be said further about that. Would it not, however, make the Proclamation more clear and decided, to leave out all reference to the act being sustained during the incumbency of the present President; and not merely say that the government "recognizes," but that it will maintain, the freedom it proclaims?'

"I followed, saying: 'What you have said, Mr. President, fully satisfies me that you have given to every proposition which has been made, a kind and candid consideration. And you have now expressed the conclusion to which you have arrived, clearly and distinctly. This it was your right, and under your oath of office your duty, to do. The Proclamation does not, indeed, mark out exactly the course I should myself prefer. But I am ready to take it just as it is written, and to stand by it with all my heart. I think, however, the suggestions of Gov. Seward very judicious, and shall be glad to have them adopted.'

"The President then asked us severally our opinions as to the modifications proposed, saying that he did not care much about the phrases he had used. Every one favored the modification and it was adopted. Gov. Seward then proposed that in the passage relating to colonization, some language should be introduced to show that the colonization proposed was to be only with the consent of the colonists, and the consent of the States in which colonies might be attempted. This, too, was agreed to; and no other modification was proposed. Mr. Blair then said that the question having been decided, he would make no objection to issuing the Proclamation; but he would ask to have his paper, presented some days since, against the policy, filed with the Proclamation. The President consented to this readily. And then Mr. Blair went on to say that he was afraid of the influence of the Proclamation on the Border States and on the Army, and stated at some length the grounds of his apprehensions. He disclaimed most expressly, however, all objection to Emancipation *per se*, saying he had always been personally in favor of it — always ready for immediate Emancipation in the midst of Slave States, rather than submit to the perpetuation of the system."

The proclamation was preliminary, but its effect was immediate: it caused parties and individuals to declare themselves. Nevertheless in the October and November elections for the next House no Republican majority could be secured out of the free States: but a silent and drastic process was applied by the military in the loyal border States, which caused them to furnish enough Republican members to make up the majority without which the war must fail. Upon the South and the slaves, the proclamation had no immediate effect; contrary to Chase's judgment, it excepted the only territory where it could at once be applied,— those portions of the seceded States then occupied by Northern forces.

At the cabinet meeting of December 31, 1862, the President called for suggestions on a final proclamation, and Chase proposed two alternatives: to make the proclamation apply to all parts of the seceded States except to West Virginia, and to omit any phrases which might be construed to incite servile insurrections. Neither of these suggestions found favor with the President, but he did adopt almost verbatim the dignified final paragraph written by the Secretary of the Treasury: "And upon this act, sincerely believed to be an act of justice, warrantable by the Constitution, upon military necessity, I invoke the considerate judgment of mankind, and the gracious favor of Almighty God." With that invocation it went to the world on the first day of 1863.

Whether the proclamation of emancipation had legal effect as a constitutional exercise of the war power, or whether it was only a declaration of political policy, to be finally carried out by the action of the Southern States and the Thirteenth Amendment, was a question which gave little concern to anti-slavery men during 1863 and 1864. The purpose of the administration was thenceforward undoubted, and the whole controversy entered upon a new stage, in which the principal issues were the emancipation acts of Maryland and Missouri, the political status of the emancipated negroes, and the use of negro troops.

In the movements for constitutional amendments against slavery in the border States, Chase had great interest and little influence. Though opposed by the powerful influence of the Blairs, he continued a most efficient friend of the Southern negroes, and he used his opportunities as Secretary of the Treasury in special charge of border traffic, to support schemes for reconstruction intended to protect the freedmen. His interposition was asked in cases in which negroes floating about the border States were taken up and sold for their jail fees; in February, 1863, he assumed the right to supervise contracts between whites and negro laborers within the Union lines; and he sought the creation of a proposed Bureau of Emancipation, which eventually developed into the Freedmen's Bureau.

Serious questions arose out of the enlistment of black troops, which proceeded rapidly during 1863.

Through Denison and other federal officeholders and correspondents Chase did his utmost to stimulate the enlistment of negroes. General Butler to some degree sympathized with this purpose, and enrolled several thousand negroes; but his successor, Banks, held back, notwithstanding Chase's efforts to encourage him. In March, 1863, Jacksonville was taken and held by Northern troops, and Chase urged that it be made a centre of recruiting. His purpose in both States was not only to recruit needed troops but to draw negroes out of the Southern lines, and in the persons of the negro soldiers to furnish object lessons of the necessity of supplementing emancipation by sweeping away all the legal distinctions which hedged the negro about.

Plainly, Chase's system must in the end come to an insistence on negro suffrage. It took a long time for him clearly to see that this was the logical result, but in December, 1863, he urged his friends in New Orleans to recognize the principle of "reorganization on the free labor and free suffrage basis." "How would it do," he asked of Horace Greeley, "to advocate something like this: that the new constitution [of Louisiana] contain a suffrage article; . . . that all citizens not imprisoned for crime in the country, who desire to exercise the right of suffrage, being twenty-one years of age, present themselves for examination to these commissioners, and on being found able to read and write, and possessed of a competent knowledge of the Constitution of the State and the United States, receive certificates, describing each sufficiently so as to identify him, in virtue of which the citizen receiving it shall be entitled to receive the right of suffrage? Would it not be very honorable for Louisiana and Florida to lead the way in this country to an electoral community with no test except virtue and intelligence?"

So long as Lincoln lived, little progress was made in this direction, and a year later Chase wrote: "I fear our good President is so anxious for the restoration of the Union that he will not care sufficiently about the basis of representation. In my judgment there is none sound except absolute justice for all, and ample security of justice in law and suffrage." The progress of public sentiment on this subject is a part of the story of reconstruction.

CHAPTER XI

NATIONAL BANKS AND THE GOLD QUESTION

In his first formal report to Congress, Chase foreshadowed that part of his financial system which was most original, most permanent, and perhaps most serviceable to the country, — the national bank scheme. From the beginning of the government, the States had chartered banks of issue upon such terms and with such security as seemed good to the legislatures. The United States Bank of 1791 had been a competitor with these state institutions; and the second United States Bank (1816 to 1836) was chartered with the express purpose of furnishing a safe note circulation, which, by competition, should compel state banks to keep their currency on a specie basis. In 1861 the number of such banks was 1600, with a capital of $430,000,000 and a circulation of over $200,000,000, of which nearly $150,000,000 was in Northern States.

Some of the more conservative New England and Middle States required a deposit of securities, in order to redeem the circulating notes in case of the failure of the banks, and Louisiana and Kentucky had two of the securest systems in the Union. The best Western banks had redemption agencies in Eastern cities; and several of the Western States had each chartered a bank as a state institution, for which the ultimate security was the credit of the commonwealth. Multitudes of other banks had no separate or adequate security for their circulating notes; while hundreds of kinds of bills were in circulation, and new counterfeits appeared every day. The result was that in 1861 more than five thousand sorts of altered, raised, or spurious notes were afloat, and such was the suspicion of an unfamiliar bill that cases have been known where the owner of a perfectly good fifty-dollar note, exchangeable for specie on demand, has traveled for days before he could find any one who would so much as change it.

The experience of the eight months of 1861, when great difficulty was found in placing loans through even the best of these banks, convinced Chase that they were not to be depended upon to stand as the permanent intermediary between the government and the people; and we have already seen that the legal-tender controversy was, in his judgment, precipitated by the existence of the bank currency. From session of Congress to session, and from year to year, Chase insisted upon a new bank system, till in 1865 he saw his project carried out in all the details which he thought essential, and the system still remains a monument to its founder.

Just when or why Chase first resolved to break up the state bank currency is uncertain. In his report of July 4, 1861, appears an innocent recommendation of taxes "on distilled liquors, on bank notes, on carriages, and similar descriptions of property;" but in a letter a few months later he explains the recommendation as intended to break down the competition of the poorer currency with government notes, then redeemable in gold. He also fearlessly asserted "the duty of the general government to furnish a national currency. . . . Its neglect of this duty has cost the people as much as this war will cost them." In his report of December, 1861, Chase laid down his favorite principle, that a paper circulation was a loan without interest made by the people, and that the government was fairly entitled to the profitable privilege. He followed this up by a clear statement, from which he never wavered, "that Congress under its constitutional powers to lay taxes, to regulate commerce, and to regulate the issue of coin possesses ample authority to control the credit circulation." The characteristic features of the system which Chase outlined, and for which he presented the draft of a bill, were three: the issue of demand bank notes redeemable in coin; the requirement that United States bonds should be the only non-metallic basis for circulation; and the preparation and issue of all notes under the direction of the government. He thus intended to secure simultaneously the three advantages of a safe currency, of loans to the government, and of a simple and uniform system of notes, under the guaranty of the nation.

It was one thing to propose so sweeping a reform, and to point out the ease with which the change might be brought about through a simple transformation of the state bank currency into a currency founded on national authority; it was quite another to meet the conservatism of Congress; and it was still more difficult to overcome the opposition of the banks themselves to the transformation thus suggested. Though Hooper of Massachusetts, one of the few approvers of the proposition, was a member of the Committee of Ways and Means, Thaddeus Stevens, as chairman, reported against the project early in 1862; and Chase thus lost the opportunity to enter on what in private conversation he declared to be "the only way by which we can raise the means to carry on the war and save the country."

During 1862 the legal-tender notes were freely poured out, till by October 1 they reached $200,000,000. The expectation that they would be converted in large quantities into interest-bearing loans was not realized. On the other hand, the state bank circulation also increased, and the state banks grew more determined in their opposition to the renewal, at the next session of Congress, of the effort to charter national banks. Again, in his second annual report, December, 1862, the secretary feelingly pointed out that government legal tender notes were being used instead of specie to form bank reserves, and were thus withdrawn from circulation and replaced by state bank notes; and he proposed in round terms that "the circulation furnished by the government be issued by banking associations, organized under a general act of Congress."

Several factors combined to give the whole project greater strength than in the previous year. The delay of Congress had the excellent effect of showing that the weaker banks would not voluntarily give up the privileges of their state charters and accept a currency under national auspices; but that the cohort was broken by the decision of some of the strongest banks to take federal charters as well as federal circulation. Men like President Walley of the Revere Bank of Boston saw no objection to creating national banks in the great financial centres; and some of the savings banks discovered the preference of their depositors for government notes, and were plagued by the miscellaneous state bank notes which they had to receive from the regular banks of issue. Meanwhile Chase's renewed effort to get a tax on state bank notes gave some alarm to the regular banks; and his personal friends went to various state legislatures urging them to indorse his plan. At length, on January 17, 1863, Chase secured from Lincoln a special message asking Congress to pass a national bank act; and by the middle of February, amateur lobbyists were asking Chase's favor on the ground that they were influencing votes for his scheme. Finally, on February 25, 1863, the National Bank Act was passed by the narrow votes of 23 to 21 in the Senate, and 78 to 64 in the House.

The statute, however, did not go to the point which Chase felt to be absolutely essential. It authorized the chartering of associations which should deposit with the Treasury of the United States bonds of the United States to the amount of not less than one half of their capital; it permitted such banks to receive notes to the amount of ninety per cent of the par value of the bonds thus deposited, the total amount of notes to be limited to $300,000,000; and it exempted the new banks from taxation, a privilege which tended to make them unpopular in the States. But the act also authorized the issuance of similar notes to the amount of eighty per cent of the face value of United States bonds deposited by state corporations. The bill was therefore little more than a permission to new institutions to enter into competition with state banks, or to existing state banks to reorganize under a national charter.

A few months' experience showed how little the privileges were valued; and the old state bank notes continued to increase. In vain did Chase's friends, political and financial, make a personal effort to found new banks; in vain did Jay Cooke give a dinner to all the editors in New York, in the hope to swing them into line. The bankers thought the old system more profitable; and men like Chase's friend George Opdyke, who tried to organize national banks, found themselves hampered and chilled by political opposition.

After more than two years of effort Chase's national bank scheme had actually done little for the government and less for the public. By December, 1863, thirty-four of the new banks had been formed; but their whole capital was only $16,000,000 and their notes actually issued were not much above $3,000,000, while $450,000,000 of legal tender had been authorized and $447,000,000 had been issued. In his third annual report, in 1863, Chase indefinitely suggested "proper measures" to induce the conversion of the state banks into national banks, though he still expected that large numbers of the banks would voluntarily accept the change. A few months more of experience convinced him of the contrary, and early in 1864 he proposed a prohibitory taxation of state banks, on the ground that the effect of the legal tender act had been to relieve them from their charter obligation to redeem their notes in specie, and that therefore they had provided themselves with reserves of legal tenders, with the result that the irredeemable notes of the United States were made the basis of a second issue of paper money of greater amount than the paper reserve of the banks.

In March, 1864, Chase brought forward an amendatory national bank bill, ill-naturedly characterized by an opponent as made up of a special clause for the benefit of the Bank of Commerce in New York city, an admission that the original bill had failed, and an appeal to adopt the principles of the first bill. Even now the secretary had not thought it prudent to introduce a prohibitory clause against the state institutions, contenting himself with a bill which would make easier the transition from state to national charters; but this moderate measure, though it much improved the original bank act, failed mainly on the question of the exemption of the national banks from all state taxes; and on April 6, with the assent of its friends, it was laid on the table. Chase exerted himself desperately in behalf of his favorite measure. He urged Horace Greeley to "say in the 'Tribune' that it is as wrong in principle to issue and circulate . . . paper money without the imprint and sanction of the nation as it is to issue and circulate a piece of metallic money." A few days later he addressed a remonstrance to Thaddeus Stevens, urging that the "emission of notes of circulation by private, municipal, or state authority is as indefensible as the emission of coin by the same authority." To Greeley he had also thrown out suggestions that the state banks must be taxed "as much as they can bear," and he appealed also to the President to stand by the prohibition of bank issues.

Under these influences, Chase's bill was revived and passed, June 3, 1864, including a special clause permitting the transfer of the anomalous Bank of Commerce of New York, with its $10,000,000 of capital, into a national bank; and the taxation question was stilled by allowing taxes on the shares of a national bank only in the State where it was located, at the same rates as for other similar institutions; while a tax of about one per cent was also laid on the national banks by the national treasury. The new system stimulated conversions, and in December, 1864, there were nearly six hundred national banks, with a circulation of $65,000,000.

The final step was taken long after Chase's resignation, by the passing of the act of March 3, 1865, which embodied the provision which had been in Chase's mind more than four years earlier,—a tax of ten per cent on all state bank notes. Although many of the state institutions never accepted government charters, they were obliged to give up their issues; and when the tax took effect, the whole issue of bank paper notes was transferred to 1650 national banks, having a circulation of over $400,000,000.

The plan of a national bank system is indubitably Chase's. His was the first definite conception of a circulation under national authority, backed up by a prohibitory, or at least a discriminating, tax on other issues; and in 1862 he added the necessary feature that all the banks of issue should owe their charter to the United States and be subject to national supervision. In Chase's mind a great advantage of the scheme was the demand thus created for government bonds, and the consequent relief of the legal tender notes; and it was not his fault that during his administration little progress was made in the actual accepting of United States securities as a basis for notes. A second consideration which Chase had always in mind was the national need of a currency at once uniform and safe. He approved of all three of the measures which were finally passed into law; and much of the present organization of the national banks is due to his invention. He had many disappointments in dealing with Congress; but his is the triumph of conceiving a working national bank system, of showing its possibilities, and of putting it into force.

Though a central idea of the national bank system was that the notes should always be redeemable in specie, Chase had the mortification to see the circulating notes of the government gradually sink. In April, 1862, the depreciation was less than two per cent; but after the failure of the Peninsular campaign greenbacks fell to about eighty-seven cents on the dollar, and by December, 1862, to about seventy-five cents.

This depreciation was a sore point with Chase, and in his reports he attempted, with but poor success, to show, first that it was less than it appeared to be, and second, that it was not due to excess of government paper. "Gold," he said, "had become an article of merchandise, subject to the ordinary fluctuations of supply and demand and to the extraordinary fluctuations of mere speculation." In December, 1862, the aggregate circulation of paper, national and state, was about $400,-000,000, which he considered hardly more than was necessary, considering the active condition of business; any excess of currency he attributed to the state banks. During 1863, however, while the bank issues were about stationary, the government increased its legal tenders and fractional notes by nearly $300,000,000. Once more the secretary could not believe that "the increase in price is attributable wholly or in very large measure to this circulation," and he still asserted that not his notes but those of the banks were at fault.

Though Chase could argue that paper money did not fall, he could not deny that "gold was rising," and various expedients were suggested for stopping the process. In November, 1862, a plan was sent him for issuing gold and silver notes, to be always redeemable in specie, and available for the payment of customs and other specie obligations. But some bankers and public men kept calling for issues of government paper, even to the extent of replacing all the interest-bearing bonds; and in February, 1863, owing to some temporary flurry, a small premium was offered for state bank notes over United States notes, and some creditors of the government even declined to receive those treasury notes which were not specifically legal tender. The only part of the country where gold continued to circulate was the Pacific coast, and through his special agent in San Francisco Chase made several unsuccessful efforts to introduce the legal tenders there and thus to drive out the gold. Gold stood January 31, 1863, at 160, and during the year various devices were proposed for checking the depreciation of paper. One was Colfax's scheme,—tried and found wanting in the Revolution,—that of fixing the legal tender notes at a depreciation of one third their face, with the hope thus to prevent their sinking lower. Wilder schemes were suggested, such as the sending out of treasury agents to corner all floating gold and force down its price by drawing on the reserve of the Treasury; or to tax the business of gold speculation.

In March, 1862, the first legislation on this subject was obtained in the form of a statute authorizing the government to purchase gold with bonds or notes; and in March, 1863, the secretary received authority to pay gold interest in advance; and a tax was laid on all contracts for the purchase of coin or bullion. In the spring of 1864 the public uneasiness had reached such a point that the secretary attempted first one and then another measure of repression. His first idea was the selling of treasury gold, in order to "bear" the gold market; and in the middle of April, he himself went to New York, where, by the sale of $11,000,000, he did succeed for a few days in running the premium down from 189 to 165, though he soon saw that he could not achieve a permanent effect. Only one means seemed left: through the President and through Congress, he pushed again his favorite scheme for prohibiting state bank notes, a plan which might have had some effect, but found no favor; at the same time he urged a statute for punishing criminally the business of dealing in gold futures.

The "Gold Bill," long delayed in the House, did not become law until June 17. It provided penalties for effecting contracts in gold coin or bullion or foreign exchange for future delivery, and also declared all such contracts absolutely void. The result was that in ten days, from June 20 to June 30, gold rose from about 200 to 250. It was useless for Chase to write to his financial supporters in New York that "there is not the slightest reason for any rise in the price of gold, either in the financial or military situation;" and it was equally futile to draft a new bill for the sale of gold and silver mining lands, as a means of restoring confidence in the ultimate payment of the notes. The great bankers of New York came to Congress to demand the repeal of the act, on the ground that it only made it easier for gold speculators to monopolize their commodity; and they secured a hasty repeal of the Gold Bill on July 2, 1864. The almost simultaneous resignation of Chase further excited the gold speculators, causing gold a few days later to reach its highest figure of about 285; in August and September it began to decline, with irregularity. In February, 1865, it fell to 200; and in March to 150.

It has often been asserted that the real cause of

Chase's withdrawal from the Treasury was the failure of this measure and the revealed inability of the secretary to keep up the public credit; but there is nothing in the private papers of either Chase or Lincoln to show that the President felt his secretary responsible for the fall of the legal tenders or that Chase had lost the confidence of the financiers of the country. The premium on gold was an index of the distress and uneasiness of the people at the long progress of the war; and the reason for the gradual recovery of the public credit, after Chase's withdrawal, was simply the conviction that the military commanders then at the head of the army would carry the war to a successful end.

No doubt one reason why Chase offered his resignation was his conviction that he was rendering so great a service to the country that he could not be spared and must be conciliated. How far did the events of his secretaryship justify this confidence in Chase's financial abilities, held not only by himself but by multitudes of his admirers throughout the country? The question is not simply what he did, but what he did under the circumstances and conditions of the times. Chase took the Treasury when the country had for more than forty years known no sort of a national taxation except customs duties, when state taxes were also very low, and when the private finance of the country was as yet little organized in powerful associations or syndicates. He suffered from the lack of adequate personal backing in Congress, through which he might have more urgently presented his financial schemes. He suffered also from the lack of previous acquaintance with the bankers and lenders of the country; and he was most of all hampered by the inability of all the leading public men, including himself, to foresee how long and how desperate the Civil War must be. He was not fairly aroused until 1863, and by that time the Treasury was too deep in its legal tender notes to free itself, either through taxation, or through the better market for loans which resulted from the victories of Vicksburg, Gettysburg, and Chattanooga, and from the success of the blockade of the Southern ports. His loans were wisely and shrewdly managed, and would have been more successful had Congress carried out his full national bank system in 1862 instead of 1865, and had he avoided the serious mistake of refusing to make long loans at par at high rates of interest. Here again the defective currency system came in to check his best laid plans, for he was justified in the hope to strengthen his legal tenders by making them convertible into bonds, and can hardly be held to account for failing to foresee that the bonds were weakened by the bringing of their price down to the level of the greenbacks.

The legal tenders came upon him unexpectedly and like a flood. Here his fault, if there were one, lay in supposing that he could immediately stop the state bank issues and thus prevent inflation; and in failing to see that Congress, and even the secretary, would inevitably fall back upon the printing-press whenever there was a crisis in the Treasury. Having once yielded to the pressure of many of his financial advisers, as well as to the popular feeling reflected in Congress, Chase could never recover his ground, and later said that the only thing he regretted in his treasury experience was his giving way on that point. As for the national banks, Chase, with all his energy, could succeed only in laying the foundations upon which his successors built; but he laid them deeply and firmly.

The errors in Chase's finance were, then, due partly to inexperience, partly to want of apprehension of the tremendous task thrust upon him, and partly to the hurry and rush of a desperate time. His positive measures were on the whole successful, and it must never be forgotten that he had two qualities which were more valuable to the country and the Treasury than financial genius: he had indomitable persistence, and he had the honesty which needed not his own too frequent approval. However much he groaned over the difficulties of his place, he met those difficulties firmly day by day, and he did not deceive or cajole. Nor did he protect dishonest men: his immediate subordinates were trustworthy and efficient, and justified his confidence; indeed, the average character of the treasury official was higher than in any other department of the public service except perhaps the Navy. Chase deserves to be called a great Secretary of the Treasury.

CHAPTER XII

CHASE AND LINCOLN

THE relations of the Secretary of the Treasury with the President during the Civil War have been much discussed and much misunderstood. Though each at times found his patience sorely tried by the other, the two men had always a genuine respect and esteem for each other, and they were perhaps more nearly in accord in their judgment on political questions than were any others in the cabinet council.

It was a misfortune that the two men had known each other but little before their association in the same administration. When Chase came to Washington, he expected a more intimate friendship with the President than he ever gained; in after years he felt that perhaps he had made a mistake in choosing a house more than a mile from the White House; for Seward, he thought, lived so near by that he had an opportunity to know Lincoln in an informal good fellowship which was denied to him. But the real cause that kept Lincoln and Chase from coming close together lay much deeper than a separation by a few furlongs. While kindly, genial, and agreeable among his friends, Chase had the misfortune to lack a sense of humor; and a Puritan conception of the gravity and seriousness of his work kept him from really understanding the easier and less strenuous attitude of the born Kentuckian. Chase was also apt to feel that his good counsels were slighted or disregarded, and he was touchy about the conduct of his office; while Lincoln was willing to go great lengths in order to preserve the peace and keep the machinery of government moving.

In the duties of his office Chase experienced from Lincoln such consideration and such willingness to leave department matters to his secretary's judgment as fall to the lot of few cabinet officers. Lincoln was satisfied to throw the responsibility of the Treasury upon his secretary's shoulders, though he sometimes helped him out by a special message to Congress. In the great questions of the Civil War, the two men had the same high sense of their duty to preserve the country from dissolution and the people from injustice, but by their natural habits of thought they felt in very different proportions an interest in the main issues; for instance, Lincoln had a much stronger sense of the political and military necessity of placating the border States than was possible to the Ohio anti-slavery man. On the question of slavery also the two men had different points of view, for Chase hoped and expected that slavery would receive its death-blow, while Lincoln a few days before his Emancipation Proclamation announced that he was willing to save the Union without freeing a slave. The hostility of the two men to the institution itself was very similar; but in Chase's mind the war was a means to emancipation, in Lincoln's mind emancipation was a means to successful war. In political matters also the two men never pulled together. Chase sought to build up the Republican party because he thought it the safeguard of freedom; Lincoln hoped to get the support of the people in order that he might restore the Union. To sum up the whole matter in a sentence, union and freedom were dear to both men, but to Chase freedom was the necessary foundation of union, and to Lincoln union was the prerequisite of freedom.

Considering the free scope which Chase had in his own department, it must have been trying to the President that the Secretary of the Treasury should so often attempt to put pressure upon him in military matters. Chase reasoned that he was witness to a military expenditure which he could not control, and yet which he must meet, at the risk of his reputation as a financier, and even at the peril of the national credit. He found it possible to concentrate the capital of the country behind him and to impress upon Congress the need of financial vigor, and hence he thought that similar energy in other departments would bring the war to a speedy end. Maunsell Field, one of Chase's subordinates in the treasury, says that on one occasion Chase was so wrought up by the reports of scandalous waste in the quartermaster's department that he personally upbraided Stanton. From time to time his letters and his diary express wrath and grief over unnecessary expenditure, which seemed to produce no military advantage, in such terms as this entry in his diary for September, 1862: "Warrants to-day enormous, over $4,000,000, and unpaid requisitions still accumulating — now over $40,000,000. Where will this end?" All the world now knows that Chase was right in feeling that the men and money were not so applied as to get the greatest result; his error was in failing to realize the political difficulty of managing so complex a machinery as the volunteer army.

Another cause of friction with the President was a different conception of the functions of heads of departments. From time to time Chase complained in his private diary and in conversations and letters that there was no cabinet. On one occasion he "told Weed that we must have decided action and that he [Weed] could insure it; was going to meeting of heads of departments, not to cabinet." A few days later he wrote to Greeley: "It seems to me that in this government the President and his cabinet ought to be well advised of all matters vital to the military and civil administration; but each one of us, to use a presidential expression, turns his own machine, with almost no comparison of views or consultation of any kind. It seems to me all wrong and I have tried very hard to have it otherwise — unavailingly." About the same time he complained to Senator John Sherman of the lack of discussion on the campaign. "We have as little to do with it as if we were heads of factories, supplying shoes or clothing. No regular and systematic reports of what is done are made, I believe, even to the President; certainly none are made to the cabinet." That there ought to have been some sort of clearing-house in which the several heads of departments might understand each other's purposes is undeniable, but Chase appears to have reached out farther: even when the cabinet was summoned to discuss great military crises he felt aggrieved if the President went on his way, disregarding the plentiful good advice of the Secretary of the Treasury.

Occasionally Chase tried giving unasked counsel. In June, 1862, when McClellan was engaged in the Peninsula, Chase strongly urged the President to direct a column of troops to Charlottesville, and was much pained that his judgment was not followed. A little later he was writing to General Pope and General Butler on the slavery question, and was trying to impress the President with the necessity of a campaign against Vicksburg. In August, 1862, he joined Seward in an attempt to coerce the President into dismissing McClellan from command of the troops before Washington; the two got Bates and Smith to join them in a protest, and secured Stanton's neutrality. Lincoln expressed his distress to "find himself differing on such a point from the Secretary of War and the Secretary of the Treasury; that he would gladly resign his place, but he could not see who could do the work wanted so well as McClellan."

Chase's military interest was not confined to the cabinet; his active correspondence with army officers in the field, and his exchange of views with them about the military policy of the President, have been brought out clearly by letters printed by Warden, Schuckers, and Hay and Nicolay; which might be enlarged from the files of his correspondence. Upon these letters, biographers of Lincoln have even founded an indictment against Chase, as a man trying to undermine his superiors and counseling disobedience to the President's orders.

From December, 1861, to the final failure of the campaign of 1862, Chase did attempt to infuse vigor into the commanders by direct incentive. In December, 1861, he asked McClellan to confer with him, and the next day he sent a direct communication to the general asking him to protect the Baltimore and Ohio Railroad. In 1862 he began a correspondence with Colonel James A. Garfield, with whom he maintained intimate relations throughout the war. General Morgan asked him for regular troops; General Shields wanted him to confer in his behalf with the President; he was in direct and confidential correspondence with General Butler in New Orleans; General Banks sent him a message saying that he should like to join forces with Chase, the two to be "head and arm;" to General McDowell, in March, 1862, he sent an article from the "Cincinnati Commercial" criticising McClellan, who was then superior in rank to McDowell; to Colonel Key he expressed his reasons for approving Lincoln's orders to McDowell before McClellan's campaign of 1862. When his confidence in McClellan at last broke down, he wrote again to McDowell, saying: "With 50,000 men and you for a general I would undertake to go from Fortress Monroe to Richmond in two days." A note to Greeley on May 21, 1862, sums up his opinion in a few words: "McClellan is a dear luxury — fifty days — fifty miles — fifty millions of dollars — easy arithmetic, but not satisfactory. If one could have some faith in his competency in battle, should his army ever fight one, if not in his competency for movement, it would be a comfort."

After the failure of the Peninsular campaign, Chase was very anxious to be rid of McClellan. Nevertheless when a few days later he called on General Halleck he "judged it prudent not to say much of the war." For McDowell and for Pope he had a special sympathy, and he did what he could to make their retiring easier. On September 23, 1862, he called on Hooker, and gave that general to understand that he had favored his appointment immediately after the Peninsular campaign. As new officers came forward in 1862 and 1863, Chase made it a point to get into relations with them. He congratulated Rousseau; he wrote to Rosecrans, regretting that his only connection with the general's fortune had been an effective influence in obtaining his brigadiership; and urging him to seize East Tennessee. Just before the battle of Gettysburg he wrote to the President, urging that Hooker should not be relieved. He also wrote a personal letter to Grant, intimating that the treasury agents had done the general a service by favorable reports upon his campaigns. No one can blame a man, who had such opportunities of seeing actual difficulties, for suggesting and remonstrating. The reprehensible thing in Chase's system was that he entered into relations with military men and gave them advice which did not come from the consent of the other members of the cabinet or from an understanding with the President. Hence he could never escape the suspicion that he was trying to make friends who would be useful to him in politics.

Secretary Chase did not mean to reverse, but rather to supplement, the direct orders of the President and of the Secretary of War, — he meant to enforce energy and not to divide counsels. He had a natural breadth and definiteness of view, and his military instincts though untrained were good. Unfortunately, when things went wrong he could not refrain from expressing his disapprobation, even to the point of direct criticism on the President. For instance, on May 30, 1861, he protested against a proposition to call out more three-months men, complaining that in the cabinet meeting "the President did not give me a chance to express my views." He also advocated the seizure and fortification of Manassas two months before the battle of Bull Run; but, said he, "I have not been able to make our friends in the administration see as I have seen; when, therefore, I am overruled, I have quietly submitted."

These discussions were of course within the circle of the administration, but at various times Chase wrote letters to other persons — who doubtless circulated them — in which he expressed his distrust of the President. "We have not accomplished what we ought to have accomplished," he writes, September 8, 1862: "we have put small forces where large forces were needed, and have failed to improve advantages and successes when obtained." September 12 he notes: "Expenses are enormous, increasing instead of diminishing; and the ill success in the field has so affected government stocks that it is impossible to obtain money except on temporary deposit. . . . It is a bad state of things; but neither the President, his councilors, nor his commanding generals seem to care. They rush on from expense to expense, and from defeat to defeat, heedless of the abyss of bankruptcy and ruin which yawns before us. May God open the eyes of those who control us before it is too late!"

To John Sherman he wrote, September 20,

1862; "It is painful, however, to hear complaints of remissness, delays, discords, dangers, and to feel that there must be ground for such complaints, and to know that one has no power to remedy the evils, and yet is thought to have." And on the same day to John Owen: "Oh! that the President and those who control military movements may see the necessity of following up vigorously and indefatigably the success now achieved." To an intimate friend he wrote, four days later, that if his advice had been taken the war would have been already finished. "What could I do beyond what I have done," he added, "except resign and come home?" And a few weeks later he was sure that, if McClellan had conferred with him, the rebellion would have been ended before that time. To another correspondent he complains: "The President, from the purest motives, committed the management of the war almost exclusively to his political opponents; it is sad to think of the delay and anxiety which have marked the past, but I am confident that it will not characterize the future."

From these examples it is evident that Chase expostulated and sometimes wrangled with the President about military matters, and that he many times expressed his dissatisfaction to his friends. This is the greatest weakness in his political life, and must be contrasted with the President's own forbearance and his care not to throw the responsibility of the national defense upon other people. The explanation is that Chase understood neither the President's difficulties nor the temperament of the people, nor the efficiency of Secretary Stanton, a man as vigorous and determined as Chase himself. What the country really needed was not simply commanders of great military genius, but commanders of experience in handling armies, and of reputation such as would gain the confidence of the country; and nothing could be more certain than that a military administration such as Chase desired — a coalition of cabinet officers with a few military men — would have been far less likely to discover and support such commanders than was the administration of a single person.

Another cause of disagreement between Lincoln and Chase was the latter's uneasiness at the application of military government to regions where no war was going on. Chase disapproved of the military court-martial of Vallandigham in 1862, on which the Supreme Court later passed an unfavorable judgment; "not," he said, "that I am averse to arrests for sufficient cause and in the proper time and place, . . . but I think the exercise of such power ought to be reserved for grave and clear occasions." In cabinet discussions of the *habeas corpus*, Chase stood out for the right of state courts to issue the writ in order to discharge persons wrongfully detained as enlisted men; but after consideration the secretary admitted that the President had the constitutional power to suspend the writ as to both state and federal judges, without authority of Congress, though he insisted that the authority of the President was based distinctly on the *habeas corpus* clause of the Constitution (to some degree defined by statutes) and not upon any general military power. With the military trials of civilians Chase had little sympathy; and later as chief justice he had the opportunity for asserting the supremacy of the judiciary over military government outside the theatre of war.

On the whole, Chase's interference in military matters did not lead to friction in the cabinet, both because he was disregarded and because he kept on good terms alike with the too facile Cameron and with the testy and violent Stanton. When Cameron was compelled to resign, Chase asked and secured from the President a letter of polite regret. Of Stanton Chase wrote, eight years later: "I do not know that we ever agreed fully either as to theory or practice in respect to the rights of colored citizens or as to the duties of the government and the nation to them, . . . though he came into the cabinet adopting practical principles more akin to mine, especially on the subject of enlisting colored men as soldiers." The two men respected each other's energy, and Chase rebuked his correspondents for holding Stanton responsible for failures in the field.

With Seward, Chase's relations were peculiar. Coming in with a strong sense of rivalry, each man hoping and perhaps expecting to obtain the ascendency over the President, the two secretaries found it difficult to harmonize. They could coöperate in the appointment of Stanton, and during 1862 their relations were more cordial. Chase wrote to Seward frankly and confidentially, asking that Cameron be allowed to come home from Russia, and to mutual friends he expressed his "wishes for harmony." In September, 1862, a strong current began to set against Seward, because he was supposed to be resisting the radical views on the slavery question; Thurlow Weed even came to Chase with stories of dissatisfaction in New York toward Seward. If this were a trap, Chase avoided it, but he seemed struck by Weed's suggestion that he and Seward "must agree on a definite line, especially on the slavery question, which we must recommend to the President." Matters came to a head on December 17, 1862, when a caucus of the Republican senators agreed, with one dissentient, that the President must "reconstruct his cabinet."

In this crisis Chase and Seward came to an understanding by which each sent in his resignation. Major Dwight Bannister, in reminiscences written many years later, records Chase's explanation to a congressman as follows: "He told the gentleman that he resigned from the cabinet much through disgust at Mr. Lincoln's weakening and consenting that, at the dictation and demand of the disaffected senators, he should be willing to let his chief friend in the cabinet be driven out. That six months after the whole country had lost all confidence in the ability or fitness of General McClellan, Mr.

Seward almost solely and alone of the cabinet officers had supported the President in still retaining McClellan in command of the Army of the Potomac; and now, to let him be driven out simply because he has faithfully stood by him in his policy seems to me almost pusillanimous. And, besides, Seward is the only distinctive and original anti-slavery man besides myself in the cabinet; and when he is allowed to go out, I stand as such almost solitary and alone. There is no cabinet; there are certain heads of departments, but no real cabinet. I tell you I am sick of it and I am glad to get out of it."

Chase's three letters written to Lincoln on the three successive days of the crisis clearly show that he expected that more attention would thenceforward be paid to his own opinions, and those of his colleagues. In the first letter, December 20, he resigned without any suggestion of reasons. When the President at once replied to Seward and Chase that the public interest did not allow him to accept their resignations, Seward promptly and cheerfully resumed his office, but Chase still held out on the ground that, "being once honorably out of the Cabinet, no important public interest now requires my return to it." On December 22 he sent a second letter to the President to the effect that he had been led "to the conclusion that I ought in this matter to conform my action to your judgment and wishes;" but he could not forbear sending also a third letter prepared two days beforehand, setting forth that, "I could not, if I would, conceal from myself that recent events have too rudely jostled the unity of your Cabinet, and disclosed an opinion too deeply seated and too generally received in Congress and in the country, to be disregarded, that the concord in judgment and action, essential for successful administration, does not prevail among its members."

Although it cannot be actually proven, it is probable that Chase had expected Seward to join him in making some definite terms with the President. If it be so, the scheme was broken up by Seward's eagerness to have the President's protection, and Lincoln came out of the controversy with much greater prestige than either of the two secretaries. For a few days there were threats of military conspiracies to depose both the President and cabinet, but the issuance of the final Proclamation of Emancipation swept the affair out of sight. On January 26, 1863, Chase wrote to Greeley: "Let us get the measures necessary to the success of any Republican administration adopted, and then let the cabinet be reconstructed if you will. For one I am quite willing to be reconstructed."

Two months later, however, the Secretary of the Treasury could not forbear again measuring his powers against those of the President. The issue was the rejection by the Senate of the nomination of Mark Howard to be the collector of internal revenue in Connecticut. Chase believed that the rebuff was due to the personal influence of Senator

Dixon, and he demanded categorically that no person proposed by Dixon should be appointed, and that he himself should nominate to the vacancy. When the President decided to select a name on Dixon's list, Chase protested; and though the difficulty was removed by personal conference between Dixon and Chase, the secretary could not forbear laying down a new ultimatum: "To secure fit men for responsible place, without admitting the rights of senators or representatives to control appointments, for which the President and the Secretary, as his presumed adviser, must be responsible. Unless these points can be practically established, I feel that I can not be useful to you or the country in my present position." As the President still stood by the prerogatives of his office, Chase prepared a note of resignation, but the dangerous paper was withdrawn, and a second time the secretary reassumed his functions.

Three months later, in May, 1863, trouble came up again over one of Chase's subordinates. One of the early appointments made by the President, at Chase's express desire, was that of Victor Smith of Cincinnati to be collector of Puget Sound. Smith had been a personal friend of Chase, and went away owing him money, perhaps remnants of old transactions, perhaps sums borrowed in order to pay his passage to his new post of duty. Smith went out to his office full of zeal, and wrote frequent and confidential letters to the secretary. He very soon became engaged in land speculations and made strenuous efforts to have the Custom House removed to a little place which he was trying to build up. By temperament and reputation he was not fitted for the important post given to him, and eventually charges of corruption were brought against him, and strong pressure against him was put upon the President by members of Congress from the Pacific coast. For the charges there seems to have been no sufficient ground, but Lincoln notified Chase that his mind was made up to remove Smith on the ground that "the degree of dissatisfaction with him there is too great for him to be retained." Finally, in Chase's absence the President did remove him, whereupon Chase wrote a solemn letter claiming the right to be consulted on the appointment of persons "for whose action I must be largely responsible." He protested against the appointment of the successor of Smith, and ended with saying: "If you find anything in my views to which your own sense of duty will not permit you to assent, I will unhesitatingly relieve you from all embarrassment, so far as I am concerned, by tendering you my resignation." The President felt the matter to be so serious that he went himself to Chase's house; as he told a friend afterwards: "I went directly up to him with the resignation in my hand, and, putting my arm around his neck, said to him, 'Chase, here is a paper with which I wish to have nothing to do; take it back and be reasonable.' I told him that I could n't replace the person whom I had removed — that was impossible — but that I would appoint any one else whom he should select for the place. It was difficult to bring him to terms; I had to plead with him a long time, but I finally succeeded, and heard nothing more of that resignation." Smith took the matter better than did his superior, and accepted his removal with good nature; but the continued strain of these differences between the President and secretary was beginning to tell upon the good humor of both, and the question of the nomination of 1864 now came in to sow still greater dissensions.

To understand the point of view of Secretary Chase in the preliminary canvass of 1863 and 1864, we must remember that to his mind and that of most of the old Republicans Mr. Lincoln was an accidental President. Congress pulled against him, and Seward, Stanton, and Chase, each in his own way, tested the President's mastery. Stanton's practice was occasionally to defy the President in minor matters by refusing to carry out his orders, or by returning a commission with the curt indorsement: "The President may get another Secretary of War, but this Secretary of War will not sign that paper." Aware of Stanton's infirmity of temper, and sincerely prizing his administrative power and his undeniable abilities and patriotism, the President gave way in many small matters, but was tenacious on questions of principle. Seward yielded easily in details, but occasionally ventured to take upon himself a responsibility which belonged to the President, as for instance in his promise to the British ambassador that the mails of prizes should be sent to England unbroken, a promise which enraged the Secretary of the Navy. Chase's habit was that of direct obedience where the President gave a disagreeable order, accompanied, in what he thought critical affairs, by a threat of resignation. His method had its foundation in the assurances of Chase's correspondents all over the country that he was the mainstay of the administration. He could not help knowing that his was the most effective and successful of the great departments of the government, and his position as a leader in anti-slavery movements gave him weight in the cabinet. However wearisome it may have been for the President to be called on so often to dispel the clouds in his secretary's mind, he had at least the assurance that Chase would not disregard his directions, nor usurp presidential powers.

The war was but a part of the President's anxieties. He understood that he was dependent on the support of a majority in Congress, and he felt that upon him fell the duty of maintaining such influence in the country at large as would give him the support of state governors and administrations, and would keep Congress in line. This political function was always before his mind; and when the question of the Republican nomination of 1864 arose, there was a rivalry between him and Chase which accentuated minor differences. Chase, too, felt the keenest interest in keeping up the Republican majority in Congress; but one of the effects, foreseen but inevitable, of the first proclamation of emancipation was an increase of the Democratic vote in Ohio and Indiana, and the consequent election of many Democratic members of Congress; and Chase's influence could not stay the tide.

From the early part of 1862 Chase had also in mind the presidential nomination of 1864; but for some time his only share in the agitation was to try to heal dissensions in his own party, and especially to come into pleasanter relations with Senator Wade. In the spring of 1863 the canvass began to take more distinct form, and Chase allowed it to be known that he was willing to accept any responsibility that the country might think proper to impose on him. In August, 1863, his friends were openly suggesting him for the presidency; and although he repeatedly expressed a preference for "a judicial position," he felt sure that "he could administer the government of this country so as to secure . . . our institutions." In October he went out to Ohio and took part in the state election by making a series of excellent speeches. Greeley took up his cause, and in private correspondence expressed the hope that he would be nominated.

The motives in Chase's mind are well expressed in an intimate letter of November 26, 1863. "I doubt the expediency of reëlecting anybody, and I think a man of different qualities from those the President has will be needed for the next four years. . . . I can never permit myself to be driven into any hostility or unfriendly position as to Mr. Lincoln. His course toward me has always been so fair and kind; his progress toward entire agreement with me on the great question of slavery has been so constant, though rather slower than I wished for, and his general character is so marked by traits which command respect and affection, that I can never consent to anything which he himself could or would consider as incompatible with perfect honor and good faith, if I were capable — which I hope I am not — of a departure from either, even where an enemy might be concerned." The interpretation of this sincere and creditable letter is very clear: Chase saw no reason why he should not seek the nomination of the convention, and prepared the way for it by the organization of his friends; but he would not take part in any effort to divide the Republican party. At the same time his old delusion as to the free principles of the regular Democracy came up to plague him. He had some dim idea of making a combination of Republicans and war Democrats, on the platform of freedom; of such a combination he would have been the logical candidate.

That his canvass showed disloyalty to Lincoln did not enter his mind; for in 1863 the real strength of Lincoln before the people was not evident to Congress nor to some of the greatest Republican newspapers, and there was a disposition to hold him responsible for every military defeat, and to give credit to the generals for all the victories; nobody could then predict that Lincoln would be renominated, and to Chase's mind the field was fair and open.

A great pressure was now put upon the secretary to make political use of his enormous patronage throughout the Union. Some of his nominees, especially in southern Ohio and the Pacific coast, were anxious to press him for the presidency; but the executive journals of the Senate bear indubitable testimony to the fact that, after the first series of appointments in 1861, removals in the Treasury Department were very few, probably no more than were justified by incompetency and fraud; and that, so far from building up a treasury machine, he resisted the piteous appeals of his friends to reorganize the Custom House in New York and other important offices. Collector Barney had many enemies, who worked upon the President to remove him; yet, in a place where the temptation was strong and the power unquestioned, Chase forbore to use his patronage for his own advantage, and thereby he incurred the reproaches and even the scorn of some would-be supporters. All the evidence bears him out in his own statement of January, 1864: "I should despise myself if I were capable of appointing or removing a man for the sake of the presidency."

Early in Chase's canvass it appeared that he had not the open support of a single great party leader, and his smaller friends brought upon him a needless humiliation and took away every chance of his nomination by the so-called Pomeroy Circular, issued in February, 1864, by a committee purporting to be in charge of Chase's canvass, headed by Senator Pomeroy of Kansas, who was known to be a friend of the secretary. The circular asserted that Chase had "more of the qualities needed in a President, during the next four years, than are combined in any other available candidate;" but it also declared that "the cause of human liberty and the dignity of the nation" suffered from Lincoln's tendency toward compromise; and that the growth of the patronage of the government demanded a one-term principle. The circular therefore distinctly measured the two men against each other, and attempted to build up Chase's fortunes by depressing the President's.

This premature and unwise action put Chase in a very serious dilemma. He wrote one of his long letters to the President, explaining that he had indeed conferred with the committee, but had no part in their circular, and for at least the fourth time he intimated that he was ready to withdraw from the Treasury if the President thought best. Chase's mortification was made plain in a letter to Greeley a few days later, with an account of Lincoln's answer: "To this he replied, closing with the statement that there was nothing in the condition of the public interests which called for a change in the headship of my department; but there was no response in his letter to the sentiments of respect and esteem which mine contained. But this is not remarkable. Whatever appreciation he may feel for the public service he never expresses any. So I have worked on."

Under such conditions Chase's continuance in the treasury was only possible if no new accident came up to disturb the truce. From various causes, but chiefly from the necessary restrictions on trade in the Southwest, Chase had the ill-will of many of the Republican politicians of Missouri, and especially of the two Blair brothers, who together formed a considerable political power; and Chase considered their relations to him "all the more embarrassing by their uncontradicted claim to be the special representative of the policy and views of Mr. Lincoln." On the 27th of April, 1864, Frank P. Blair made a scurrilous attack on Chase in the House, asserting that certain statements with regard to himself were a forgery prepared by a person in the Treasury, "uttered and put in circulation by a special agent of the Treasury, and put in a newspaper which was pensioned by the Secretary of the Treasury." Against Chase he personally brought charges of weakness in resisting secession, based upon information as to a private cabinet meeting communicated by his brother, Montgomery; Blair at last worked himself up to the charge that Chase was using his authority to control border intercourse and to collect abandoned property "as a fund to carry on his war against the administration which gave him place."

No wonder Chase was that night found in a condition of violent rage; and that, when he learned that after this speech the President had carried out a long standing promise of reviving Blair's commission as major-general in the army, he was on the point of resigning. It was not a question on which Lincoln cared to make an issue. To him the Blairs had become disagreeable annoyances, to be palliated as much as possible. The President told Chase's friends that he had restored Blair to the army before his speech. "Within three hours I heard that this speech had been made, when I knew that another bee-hive was knocked over. My first thought was to have canceled the orders restoring him to the army, and assigning him to command. Perhaps this would have been best. On such information as I was able to gain about the matter, however, I concluded to let them stand." The matter was thus patched up for the time being, and in the course of the next few weeks it became evident that Lincoln was certain to be renominated. Even in Ohio, despite the strong efforts of Chase's friends, the Republican members of the state legislature passed a resolution in favor of Lincoln; and on April 26 Chase wrote a public letter of withdrawal.

When on June 7 the Baltimore Convention renominated Lincoln, Chase's friendly relations with the President ought once for all to have been reestablished: thereafter, no longer a rival, he might have gone steadily forward with his own important duties. It was, however, a dark period in the financial history of the war: the credit of the government measured by its legal tender notes was steadily declining, and the strain on Chase's mind and temper was growing more and more severe, till it culminated in the Gold Bill of June 17. An unusual self-abnegation on Chase's part might have prevented a rupture, but that self-abnegation he did not show, for even after the nomination he felt injured and sore. Another cloud now arose in the New York Custom House. On June 6, the President called on Chase, and pressed for the removal of Barney, to whom he had previously offered a diplomatic position. This personal conference removed the difficulty for the time being; there is some reason to suppose that Chase again threatened to resign, and that the President again gave way.

A few days later, another question of patronage in New York came up, by the action of John J. Cisco, in resigning his post of assistant treasurer, because the office, one of great fiduciary importance, was underpaid. Mr. Chase at once notified Lincoln that he would himself shortly designate a successor. After several failures to secure an eminent New York financier, he offered the place to Maunsell B. Field, then assistant secretary of the Treasury. Senator Morgan, of New York, insisted that it was necessary to appoint a man who would reorganize the assistant treasurer's office, and turn out a lot of the clerks. The issue was decidedly offensive to Chase, who felt himself assaulted in his prerogative of appointing his immediate and confidential subordinates, and who was himself called upon to assent to the political dismissal of experienced subordinates.

Field's remembrance of the President's account to him of the whole transaction is characteristic and probably not far from correct. "The Republican party in your State is divided into two factions, and I can't afford to quarrel with them. By accident rather than by any design of mine, the radicals have got possession of the most important Federal offices in New York. . . . Had I under these circumstances consented to your appointment, it would have been another radical triumph, and I could n't afford one."

Nevertheless the President bent himself to a peaceful settlement of the perplexing question: he promoted a conference between Senator Morgan and Chase, and promised to appoint any man upon whom Chase and the New York senators could agree. But when Chase asked for a personal conference, the President replied that he hesitated, "because the difficulty does not, in the main part, lie within the range of a conversation with you. As the proverb goes, 'No man knows so well where the shoe pinches as he who wears it.'"

On June 29, Chase solved the difficulty by persuading Cisco to withdraw his resignation; and there the matter might have ended, had he so chosen; but he had already written a letter of resignation, which he could not deny himself the satisfaction of sending, as a suggestion of the danger which had been escaped. "I can not help feeling," said he, "that my position here is not altogether agreeable to you; and it is certainly too full of embarrassment and difficulty and painful responsibility, to allow in me the least desire to retain it. I think it my duty, therefore, to inclose to you my resignation. I shall regard it as a real relief if you think proper to accept it, and will most cheerfully render to my successor any aid he may find useful in entering upon his duties."

This fourth or perhaps fifth formal resignation of Secretary Chase ended his official life. The President unexpectedly accepted it, and though the next day Chase hinted to Stanton, "I feared you might be prompted by your generous sentiment to take some step injurious to the country," no other member of the Cabinet stirred. In truth, Chase was taken by surprise that the President had not put the resignation through the usual course of remonstrance, argument, and recall; and his anger and disappointment are too frankly recorded in his own diary: "There I found a letter from the President, accepting my resignation, and putting the acceptance on the ground of the difference between us indicating a degree of embarrassment in our official relations which could not be continued or sustained consistently with the public service. I had found a good deal of embarrassment from him; but what he had found from me I could not imagine, unless it has been caused by my unwillingness to have offices distributed as spoils or benefits, with more regard to the claims of divisions, factions, cliques, and individuals, than to fitness of selection. He had never given me the active and earnest support I was entitled to; and even now Congress was about to adjourn without passing sufficient tax bills, though making appropriations with lavish profusion, and he was, notwithstanding my appeals, taking no pains to insure a different result."

The real reason for the resignation was expressed by Chase in a private conference with Whitelaw Reid: "He supposed that the root of the matter was a difficulty of temperament. The truth is that I have never been able to make a joke out of this war." At first he could not believe that he was actually out of the administration. When his successor, Fessenden, informed him that the President had asked him not to remove Chase's friends, Chase entered in his diary: "Had the President in the reply to my note tendering my resignation expressed himself as he did now to Mr. Fessenden, I should have cheerfully withdrawn it." And when Sumner suggested that he might be recalled as Necker had been in France a century earlier, he replied that Lincoln was no Louis the Sixteenth.

CHAPTER XIII

THE JUDICIAL PROBLEM OF RECONSTRUCTION

In an article written in early life, Chase eulogized Chief Justice Marshall, "whose decisions upon the delicate and important questions at this period perpetually arising, by their wisdom, their justice, and their explicitness, commend themselves equally to the understanding, the conscience, and the heart of all our citizens." An interest in the position of chief justice never ceased to influence him. While still a senator he said to a friend that there were two offices which he should like to hold: "I should like to be chief justice of the Supreme Court and overrule all the pro-slavery decisions; I should like to be President of the United States and reverse the policy of the administration as Jefferson reversed it." When, in the third year of the secretaryship, Taney was known to be failing, the thought was evidently in Chase's mind that he himself might be the successor. He had already dropped the remark to the President, that he "would rather be Chief Justice than hold any other position that could be given;" and in July, 1864, Lincoln told the Senate Committee on Finance that he should appoint him to the office if there were a vacancy. He afterward said to Carpenter that "there had never been a time during his presidency when, in the event of the death of Judge Taney, he had not fully intended and expected to nominate Salmon P. Chase for chief justice." Hence it is probable that if the death of Taney had occurred in the spring of 1864 instead of in October, Chase would have been at once transferred, in time to prevent the pain and humiliation of his retirement from the treasury. Meanwhile after his withdrawal he said many bitter things of Lincoln, and for three months he hung back in the presidential campaign; not until September did he begin to work on the stump in behalf of the Republican ticket. That he was unaware of Lincoln's magnanimous purpose seems clear from the strong but unsuccessful attempt of his friends, in August, to secure for him a nomination from the Cincinnati district to the lower house of Congress.

As soon as the presidential election was over, the President set himself seriously to the selection of a successor to Taney. Candidates were numerous: Justice Swayne of Ohio desired and manœuvred for promotion, and had the powerful support of Justice David Davis, a personal friend of Lincoln; Montgomery Blair, who had been cast out of the cabinet, sought for the nomination; Chase at one time believed that Stanton was the person to be designated; of another candidate put forward by Massachusetts men, Chase said: "Evarts is a man of sterling abilities and excellent learning and a much greater lawyer than I ever pretended to be. The truth is, I always thought myself much overestimated. And yet I think I have more judgment than Evarts, and that tried by the Marshall standard [I] should make a better judge; while he might, tried by the Story standard." Chase's warmest friend and most effective supporter was Sumner, who thought that months earlier he had secured a promise for his friend from Lincoln; and he did not cease to press his candidate.

On the other side there was a strong objection to Chase from leading Republicans the country over; delegations appeared from Ohio, and protests were filed. Lincoln had no longer any personal rivalry to fear, but those who were nearest to him were at the time convinced that he hesitated because he feared that Chase would make the bench a stepping-stone to the White House; when Riddle, at Chase's urgent request, waited on Lincoln to urge his claims, the President asked him whether Chase would be satisfied to remain chief justice. His own recent differences with his imperious secretary, and even the reports of Chase's exasperated comments, made so little impression on Lincoln that on December 6 Chase was nominated for the chief justiceship and forthwith confirmed by the Senate without reference to committee. He accepted the appointment in a very warm note, assuring Lincoln that he prized his confidence and good-will more than any nomination to office.

Upon the whole the appointment seemed judicious and was well received. It was true that Chase's experience had been chiefly legislative; but it was also true that both Marshall and Taney had been appointed from cabinet offices and not from active practice or the bench; and that the immediate questions which confronted the court required less a consummate knowledge of law than a broad statesmanship, which could take into account the significant legal and political changes brought about by the Civil War, together with such a sense of the dignity of the court as might restore its weakened prestige.

Although Chase had never sat upon the bench, he fell easily into the routine of the court, and interested himself in improving its library and other facilities. He was thought by some of the subordinate judicial officers to be unduly severe; and sometimes freely criticised the reporter or even associate justices for what he thought inaccurate statements of his opinions. He had in his hands a considerable patronage, of which the most valuable was the designation of the marshalship of the Supreme Court. The incumbent when Chase assumed his office was Ward H. Lamon, a personal friend of Lincoln; but Chase complained of his accounts; he retired in June, 1865. The chief justice took an opportunity in April, 1867, to secure the appointment of his intimate friend, Richard C. Parsons, of Cleveland. Unfortunately, in 1872, Parsons became involved in a lobbying enterprise with Judge Charles Sherman, the result of which was that both were compelled to resign, and John G. Nicolay was appointed in Parsons's place.

In 1867 the new bankruptcy act required the commissioning of a large number of registers in bankruptcy. Since Congress was unwilling to give additional patronage to the President, it made the unusual provision that the registers should be appointed by the district courts, but only on recommendations by the chief justice. Barney wrote to Chase from New York: "At least three hundred members of the bar have asked me for letters recommending them or their friends for register." The distribution of this patronage gave the chief justice much annoyance, but also a power, which he highly enjoyed, of pleasing his friends and of exercising his discrimination.

No man in the history of the country, except perhaps John Jay, has ever had such opportunities for experience in all three of the great departments of the government. Chase had been senator and had seen much of the working of Congress during the Civil War, had been the most important figure in a cabinet, and was now to learn the inner workings of the federal judiciary department. He found it in a depressed and humiliated condition, its jurisdiction limited by the creation of extra-judicial tribunals, its machinery embarrassed by an outgrown, clumsy, and laborious system of circuits. The Supreme Court, although it still continued its decisions in cases of private law, showed little vitality during the Civil War, and avoided decisions which bore on the great questions then before the country.

In 1864 the court was undergoing the process of rapid renewal, which it had experienced twice before in the history of the country: between 1804 and 1811 five of the seven justices were newly appointed; and again, between 1829 and 1837, Jackson had the nomination of six of the nine judges; and the court which he thus reconstituted at once took more conservative ground on the powers of Congress and the limitations on the States. Lincoln found among the nine justiceships one vacancy which had not been filled by Buchanan; and the death of McLean in April, 1861, and the resignation of Campbell in May, 1861, together with a tenth justiceship created by the act of March 3, 1863, and the death of Taney in 1864, gave the opportunity of replacing five conservative judges with Republicans and anti-slavery men. For some time Lincoln hesitated to use his power. In his annual message of 1861, he pointed out the difficulties due to the existence of civil war in two of the vacant districts, and said: "I have been unwilling to throw all the appointments northward, thus disabling myself from doing justice to the South on the return of peace." He proposed the creation of additional circuit judges, to relieve the supreme justices from the increasing labor of service on circuit.

In 1862 Lincoln overcame these scruples, and

appointed in quick succession Swayne of Ohio, Miller of Iowa, and Davis of Illinois; in 1863 he added Field of California as tenth justice; and in 1864 he appointed Chase. Though Catron died in May, 1865, and Wayne in 1867, no successors to them were appointed, and no further change occurred till after the first legal-tender decision in 1870. From 1865 to 1870 the court remained made up of Lincoln's five appointees, together with Nelson, Grier, Clifford, and (till 1867) Wayne.

It had thus unexpectedly been put into the power of Lincoln to carry out a plan which he himself suggested in 1858, the plan of reorganizing the Supreme Court till it should reverse the Dred Scott decision; but before a majority of the judges had been obtained, the spirit of the Dred Scott decision was effectually reversed by the Thirteenth Amendment; and precisely as had happened under Jefferson and Madison, it was found that the reconstructed court inherited the conservative spirit of its predecessors. The Supreme Court continued to hold fast to its time-honored principles on public law and private rights rather than to set up a new régime; and Chase's influence bore for caution and restraint, and not for radical changes.

Notwithstanding the violent legislation of the Civil War, and the disturbance of property rights caused by military movements, the Supreme Court from 1861 to 1864 pronounced but three decisions on what could fairly be considered political cases; and in neither of the three did it stand against authority claimed by Congress or the President. In the first of these cases (*State of New York* v. *Commissioners of Taxes*, 1862–63) the court held that a State could not tax bank capital which stood in the form of United States securities. The decision in the *Prize Cases* of 1863 gave the Supreme Court an opportunity to acknowledge the existence of "civil war," and the right of the President to declare a blockade, while it held also that the war "may be called an 'insurrection' by one side, and the insurgents be considered as rebels or traitors;" and all persons residing within the Southern lines were "liable to be treated as enemies." The decision plainly applied the principles of international law to the struggle, without denying that in the end the participants might also be subjected to the penalties of the municipal law.

Various attempts were made to secure from the Supreme Court a decision against the arbitrary powers assumed by Congress and the President; but, though the court held back, Chief Justice Taney delivered an opinion in the case of *Ex parte Merryman*, which was intended to be a protest against the suspension of *habeas corpus* by executive regulation. In May, 1861, Merryman was arrested in Maryland on a charge of treason, and confined in Fort McHenry. Taney sitting alone on the Circuit bench issued a writ of *habeas corpus*, to which the military officer — though no public notice of any executive orders had been given — replied that he was authorized by the President to suspend the writ of *habeas corpus* for the public safety. Taney thereupon ordered the arrest of the officer, on the ground that there was no process short of an act of Congress which could justify military detention of a civilian, and that the President had no constitutional authority to suspend the *habeas corpus*, and of course none to delegate such suspension. The marshal was, however, by military force prevented from serving the writ, and Taney, with a clear understanding of his helplessness, certified his decision to the President, in order that, as he said, that officer might "perform his constitutional duty to enforce the laws; or at least to enforce a process of this kind." The President simply ignored Taney's decision, and throughout the war continued to hold suspected persons under arrest, at first by his own authority and then under legislation obtained from Congress.

March 3, 1863, Congress passed an act authorizing the suspension of *habeas corpus* by the President, and this was subsequently construed to authorize military commissions even within the limits of Northern States removed from the theatre of war. The only legal authority for such action was to be sought in a broad and dangerous extension of the power to make war, and it ignored the ordinary judiciary. In the *Vallandigham Case*, in February, 1864 (the third of the political cases brought before the court) an attempt was made to reverse the decision of a military commission held in Ohio, which condemned Vallandigham for offensive and treasonable utterances in public speeches. The Supreme Court, however, refused to interfere, basing its decision on the technical ground that, whatever the merits of the case, it had no jurisdiction, because there was no legal method of appealing from a military commission to the Supreme Court.

On slavery, on the validity of the acts of the seceded States under the Confederacy, and on the relation of those States to the Union, the Supreme Court expressed no opinion; and, so far as possible, it staved off cases which involved such questions. At the end of 1865, Chase informed the President: "The Supreme Court has hitherto declined to consider cases brought before it by bill or writs of error from circuit or district courts in the rebellious portion of the country." This principle applied even in those parts of Virginia within the Union lines, in which the federal courts had maintained a formal existence. Chase himself, when he first faced the problems likely to come before the court, intimated to a friend that he might be more useful off the bench than on it "when the reorganization comes about;" but his correspondent replied: "The Supreme Court may be the great power yet that is to settle the great questions upon which perhaps may depend the perpetuity of our government."

This prophecy was soon to be justified, for within two years after Chase's appointment the court had begun to render a series of brilliant and far-reaching decisions, which at the same time restored its own prestige, crystallized the body of law arising out of the Civil War, and moderated the excesses of Congress. All the questions which finally stood forth for judicial decision had been presented to Chase while he was still Secretary of the Treasury, and upon most of them he had then made up his mind. The first and most difficult inquiry was, What is the legal status of the seceded States? The second was, By whose authority shall they be allowed to resume their place in the Union after the war? A third was, What shall be the status and punishment of the individuals who have joined in the rebellion? The fourth question, which grew more important throughout the war and was the last of all to be completely decided was, What legal and political status shall be given to the negro?

On all these points Lincoln early took ground, and on nearly all Chase opposed him. Lincoln's theory of the status of the States was set forth in his own fashion in an argument which he made in July, 1862: "Broken eggs cannot be mended; but Louisiana has nothing to do now but to take her place in the Union as it was, barring the already broken eggs. The sooner she does so, the smaller will be the amount of that which will be past mending. This government cannot much longer play a game in which it stakes all, and its enemies stake nothing. Those enemies must understand that they cannot experiment for ten years trying to destroy the government, and if they fail still come back into the Union unhurt." This pungent statement indicated Lincoln's purpose to restore the States as soon as they were sufficiently cleared of the Confederate troops, and he carried out his policy in 1862 by favoring the admission of West Virginia with a separate state government, and by securing through his military commanders a choice of two congressmen from Louisiana; and the House of Representatives admitted the principle by admitting those two as members. Chase was from the first opposed both to the principle of presidential reconstruction, and to the method; for he could not accept the idea that the States were to come back into the Union whenever they withdrew from the Confederacy. In March, 1862, he gave his adhesion to the theory that "the government in suppression of rebellion, in view of the destruction by suicide of the State governments with the actual or strongly implied consent of the majority of the citizens of the several rebel States [which] have so far forfeited all right to be regarded as States, might justly treat them as territories," and he preferred to have Congress assert authority to set up provisional governments in place of those supported by the President.

On the question of the Southern whites, Lincoln took ground by his proclamation of December 8, 1863, in which he prescribed a test oath, which committed the taker to support all acts of Congress and proclamations of the President with regard to slavery, "so long and so far as not repealed, modified, or held void by Congress or by decision of the Supreme Court." He promised to recognize such state government in each of the seceded States as might be set up by persons who could and would take the oath and were in number not less than one tenth of the vote cast at the election of 1860. This meant that the authority in the reconstructed States should be committed to such of the whites as had not held conspicuous stations in the service of the Confederacy and were willing to accept the emancipation proclamation. Chase criticised this proposition, which indeed had many elements of weakness. "I don't like the qualification in the oath required," said he, "nor the limitation of the right of suffrage to those who take the oath, and *are otherwise qualified* according to the state laws in force before rebellion. I fear these are fatal concessions. Why should not *all* soldiers who fight for their country vote in it?"

On the question of the negroes Chase held the strongest convictions of his life, and he protested against excluding them from a share in the reconstructed governments. During 1863 Chase put forth a strong pressure for the reorganization of Florida, of which a small tract in the neighborhood of Fernandina and Jacksonville was occupied by Federal troops. His interest in this enterprise led him to analyze more carefully the conditions of the problem. As a result he came to see how important was the future of the negro, and how hard it would be to protect him. He proposed arming the "loyal native population, white and black," and holding back the States from reconstruction till they should abolish slavery. By the beginning of 1864 he was writing of "the free labor and free suffrage basis," and had proposed to his agents in Louisiana to secure negro suffrage with an educational clause.

Meanwhile Congress had become aroused to the gravity of the problem, and to the immense power which the President proposed to exercise, by himself deciding the conditions of reëntrance to the Union; and in July, 1864, the so-called "Davis-Wade Bill" brought the President and Congress into sharp collision over the fundamental question as to which of the two authorities was to determine when the States were ready to reassume their place in the Union. Though the bill authorized the President to set up provisional state governments, it provided that these were to be transformed into permanent governments only through action of Congress. Accordingly Lincoln refused to sign it, and took the unusual step of issuing a proclamation, declaring his purpose to decide that question himself. During the adjournment of Congress and the campaign of 1864, Lincoln on his own responsibility caused the reorganization of state governments in Louisiana, Arkansas, and Tennessee; and had he lived to the session of 1865–1866, the conflict of his authority with that of Congress must have again come up in a more serious form.

The assassination of Lincoln, and the accession of a man who hated the dominant white element in the South, threw the whole scheme of reconstruction into confusion; and during the year 1865 the conditions of the South and the dimensions of the problem began to be more clearly appreciated in the North. The most important question at the outset was the status of the Southern whites. Events had long since destroyed the belief, held at the beginning of the war, that a large majority in most of the Southern States was really opposed to secession; nearly all the able-bodied men in the South went into the Confederate Army, or at least into the civil service of the Confederacy or the state governments. If secession were treason, almost all Southerners had involved themselves in the penalties for the act; and general convictions and executions would be very like massacres.

Economically the South was prostrate. The great slaveholders, who had held the most important stations before the war and the most dangerous responsibilities during it, had met financial ruin. Their invested funds had gone directly or indirectly into Confederate loans; their accumulations had been swept away by the demands of the war; large numbers of their negroes either were wanderers or had disappeared altogether. Only the soil was left, and even that in many cases had been devastated by campaigns. Politically the old leaders were for the time overborne; some were in exile, and many were glad to seek obscurity; a few, including Jefferson Davis, were in the hands of the federal government, and it was expected that an example would be made of them by trials for treason.

In May, 1865, practically under commission of the President, Chase made a visit to the Southern ports of South Carolina, Florida, and Louisiana, returning by the Mississippi River. He reported to the President a belief that many of the white men who had engaged in the rebellion would be glad to take a loyal part in the reconstructed government: but before he returned Johnson had issued his proclamation of May 29, 1865, granting general amnesty and pardon to such as would take an oath to support all laws and proclamations made, during the rebellion, with reference to the emancipation of slaves. From the privileges of this amnesty, however, he excluded fourteen classes of persons, including nearly all those who had shown energy and character during the Civil War. It was therefore apparent that the President intended to let the poor whites organize and carry on the Southern state governments with the assistance of such of the more distinguished persons as he might individually pardon. The class upon which Johnson depended was not equal to the responsibility which he thrust upon it. The former small slaveholders stood not far from where they had been at the beginning of the war, for they could easily replace their lost slaves with hired laborers, and they were not on the lists of proscriptions. The poor whites, notwithstanding their great sacrifice of life during the war, found their condition hardly altered. Throughout the South was also a sprinkling of Northerners, in many cases former federal officers, who had taken part in the founding of the new governments in 1865. These "carpet-baggers" were already hated, and now, as centres of organization for the negroes, they became the point of attack by the native Southerners.

Of all the questions of reconstruction, that in which Chase was most interested from beginning to end was the status of the negroes. As far back as September, 1862, he notes that he "called on attorney general about citizenship of colored men. Found him adverse to expressing official opinion;" and in an earlier chapter we have seen how faithfully he followed up the interests of the freedman. So far as the existence of slavery went, the Thirteenth Amendment, declared to be in force in December, 1865, was a constitutional guarantee which superseded the revocable abolition acts of the States reconstructed during that year; and it took out of the list of conditions which might be imposed upon the States an acknowledgment of the freedom of the former slaves; it superseded also the special conditions of the amnesty proclamations of Lincoln and Johnson. There still remained a necessity for statutes or constitutional amendments to define the judicial and other civil rights of the negroes; and Chase was one of the earliest among public men to insist that negro suffrage must be made a general system, and must be imposed as a condition of reconstruction. This conviction found voice in his last letter to Lincoln, April 12, 1865: "Once I should have been, if not satisfied, partially, at least, contented with suffrage for the intelligent and for those who had been soldiers; now I am convinced that universal suffrage is demanded by sound policy and impartial justice."

During 1865 both the legal and the economic status of the negroes were confused and unsatisfactory. President Johnson's favored state governments in the South showed little sympathy with the blacks, and in several of the States, according to Chase's own observation, they seemed likely to return to a legal restraint very like their former bondage. In some cases vagrant laws were passed, so stringent that the negroes would practically have been again subjected to the forcible control of their former masters.

The war had brought about, not only freedom, but great changes in economic conditions. Many thousands of the freedmen had abandoned their plantations and were still under government supervision; hence at the end of the war it was found necessary to continue the control and support which had for several years been carried on under military authority. This was done through the so-called "Bureau of Refugees, Freedmen, and Abandoned Lands," which was created by an act of March 3, 1865, and put under the control of a special commissioner. This institution was continued by an act of July, 1866, passed over the President's veto; and the United States was thus committed to the position of guardian to thousands of negroes. The system had Chase's warm sympathy, and in 1866 he accepted the presidency of the "American Freedman's Union Commission," one of the benevolent societies intended to carry on the work of civilization. Both under government supervision and through the missionary associations, schools were started, and the negroes showed a great desire to learn; but they were unorganized, very ignorant, poor, and dependent upon day wages; and moreover the efforts to relieve them were viewed by the Southern people as an attempt to give them social equality with white people.

The conditions of the problem were difficult in themselves, and its solution was delayed by the unfortunate controversy between President Johnson and Congress, which began as soon as Congress assembled in December, 1865. In the details of that controversy and in the discussion of the fundamental basis on which it rested, Chase took little part, except so far as the special interests of the negroes were concerned. He saw as clearly as anybody that peace had brought about a logical dilemma from which there was no escape: the war, begun in 1861 on the theory that it was impossible for a State to withdraw from the Union, ended in the plain fact that the seceded States were practically out of the Union; and the President, Congress, and the Northern people all took for granted that the Southern States should be subjected to some kind of expiatory process before individuals returned to their former public rights, and before communities recovered their privileges as a part of the federal government. Significant differences of opinion arose over the question as to what the expiatory process should be. The Southern people supposed that an oath of allegiance to the United States would readmit them into its fellowship; Johnson took the ground that all the important participants in the rebellion would be punished by loss of the suffrage, until he should restore the privilege by individual pardons; Congress intended that it was to decide what persons might take part in reviving the state governments, and was determined that the States as communities should be punished by the imposition of humiliating conditions of restoration. The only logical and consistent theory was that of the Southerners, and that was impracticable because it did not secure to the country the objects for which the war had been fought. Restoration by amnesty was not popular in Congress under Lincoln, and was impossible under Johnson. It proved in the end that the only force capable of settling the controversy was the two-thirds majority in both houses of Congress, through which the President's veto could be, and was, relentlessly overridden. But the process was long and heated: the first stage ended in the appointment of a joint committee on reconstruction, and a joint resolution of March 2, 1866, providing that "no senator or representative should be admitted into either branch of Congress from any of the said States until Congress should have declared such State entitled to such representation."

In the discussion of 1865–66 Chase was rather a spectator than an actor, but he did not hesitate to express his personal opinions on that part of the controversy which most interested him, — the status of the freedmen; and he was one of the first to insist that no seceded State ought to be admitted back into the Union until it had given suffrage to negroes. He said: "It would really not be a greater crime to continue slavery itself than to leave the only class which, as a class, had been loyal, unprotected by the ballot."

As soon as it became evident that Johnson had no interest in negro suffrage, and was willing to reinstate by his pardoning power a large proportion of those who had been concerned in the rebellion, Chase found himself separated from the President, who no longer invited an expression of his opinion. At the same time his friends in the South assured him that, without protection from the United States, the Union men would be completely overborne and the freedmen in danger. For instance, a correspondent wrote: "Criminal law is a dead law in Texas, and but few troops are stationed among us. As matters stand, Congress might declare every rebel to be disfranchised, and all would vote at the first election. Congress might by law enfranchise every freedman, and not a single freedman would be permitted to vote."

Chase's sympathy now began to turn toward the congressional plan, and he especially approved the Civil Rights Act, passed over the President's veto, April 9, 1866, which declared "all persons born in the United States and not subject to any foreign power to be citizens of the United States," and provided for equality of civil rights. This was a legislative reversal of whatever was left of the Dred Scott decision; and the special machinery provided to carry out the act was a satirical adaptation of the clauses of the Fugitive Slave Act of 1850, which had aroused such an uproar among anti-slavery men.

The act was certain to rouse the opposition of the South, and was itself liable to repeal. It seemed therefore desirable to put its provisions into a constitutional amendment, which would forever protect the rights of the negroes and which at the same time would take out of the hands of the President the restoration of former rebels to their political status. This suggestion of another amendment aroused Chase. On April 30, 1866, he wrote to Associate Justice Field that the proposed plan of congressional reconstruction "seems very well, provided it could be carried out; but I am afraid that it is, as people say, rather too big a contract." He thereupon drew up a brief amendment, to be "Article Fourteen of the Constitution," which provided that, in case the suffrage were reduced by any State, the basis of representation should be correspondingly reduced, and that no debts should ever be paid that had been incurred in behalf of the rebellion; and he proposed that the ratification of this amendment should be made a condition of reconstruction. Congress finally adopted these two clauses substantially as Chase wrote them; but it adhered to its own clauses asserting the citizenship and civil rights of the negroes and granting Congress the power to enforce them; that is, it put the Civil Rights Act into the Constitution. To Chase's mind these additional propositions were inexpedient, because, as he said, "it seems to me that nothing is gained sufficiently important, and unattainable by legislation, to warrant our friends in overloading the ship with amendment freight." Nevertheless, he later applied the amendment in its most sweeping form in his dissent from the decision of the Supreme Court in the *Slaughter-house Cases.*

The continued holding of troops in the South had caused several vexed questions as to the relations between civil and military authority; hence, on April 2, 1866, Johnson issued a proclamation announcing that the war had ceased in ten of the seceded States, and on August 30, another proclamation setting forth that it had ceased also in Texas. The process of reconstruction was, however, delayed until the next year, when the elaborate statutes of March 2 and March 23, 1867, established the legal basis of reconstruction, and also prescribed the conditions of the reëntrance of the States into the Union. The existing state governments were declared to be provisional, and no State was to be received back until it had established negro suffrage; in order to have assurance that the States should actually fulfill these conditions, they were for the time being put into the hands of military commanders.

Down to the end of 1866, as we have seen, Chase's connection with reconstruction was that of a statesman and not that of a judge. The strife between President and Congress had, however, an indirect influence on the Supreme Court. There was an apprehension that the court would take sides; and hence when Justice Catron died in May, 1865, and President Johnson nominated as his successor his Attorney-General, Mr. Stanbery, the Senate declined to confirm the nomination. The federal courts were just then distressed by the serious crowding of the circuits, and nearly all the justices favored a pending bill for reorganization by adding new circuit judges. Upon this bill was tacked a provision to reduce the number of associates to eight, which of course took away the necessity for an immediate appointment by Johnson. The Senate went even farther by an amendment through which, as vacancies should occur, the number of associates was to be reduced to six; the purpose was to put it out of the power of the President, during his whole term, to appoint any justices who might be favorable to his side of the controversy.

On this proposition Johnson did not choose to take issue, and it became law July 29, 1866.

About the same time the long-suspended federal courts began to resume their sittings in the Southern States. During 1866 the federal district judges, Underwood and Brooks of Virginia, Hill of Mississippi, and Busteed of Alabama, all undertook to hold courts. As successor to Taney, Chase's circuit included Maryland, Virginia, and North Carolina; but even after the President's proclamations declaring the Civil War at an end, he steadfastly refused to hold any court in Virginia or North Carolina "until all possibility of claim that the judicial is subordinate to the military power is removed by express declaration by the President."

Chase's attitude was practically an opinion that the military governments established by the President were abnormal; and also an indirect assertion of the supremacy of ordinary tribunals in time of peace; and it reinforced the decision of the Supreme Court in the *Vallandigham Case* of 1864. But in the other Southern circuits decisions were made, and soon after appeals began to be taken to the Supreme Court. Under the judiciary act of 1866, the Supreme Court justices had no circuit jurisdiction in the South; but in March, 1867, that jurisdiction was restored, and Chase soon after assumed his functions at Raleigh, and delivered an opinion on June 16, 1867. The service of process under his decisions was resisted by the military authority, acting under orders from General Sickles, the commander of the department. Chase was willing to force the issue by direct prosecution of the military officer concerned; but the President speedily removed Sickles, and appointed a successor with instructions not to interfere with the processes of the court: and the jurisdiction of the federal courts within the States lately in rebellion was not again brought into question.

While the contest between Johnson and Congress was reaching its height, during 1866 and 1867, the Supreme Court at last began to prove its vitality in a series of decisions which involved questions arising out of the Civil War. Within four months six cases were decided, in four of which the court took jurisdiction, and stood forth once more as an arbiter between the States and the nation, if not between the other two departments of the federal government. The first of these cases, *Ex parte Milligan*, in the term of December, 1866, gave the desired opportunity to reassert the right of the court to be the expounder of the Constitution, for it traversed the authority of the unpopular military commissions at a time when their necessity was past. L. P. Milligan was arrested in Indiana in October, 1864, under color of the act of March 3, 1863, authorizing the suspension of *habeas corpus*, an act which had already been held void by the Supreme Court in the case of *Gerder* v. *the U. S.* (1864–65) so far as appeals from the Court of Claims were concerned. He was duly tried by a military commission, and sentenced to be hanged. Lincoln approved the finding, but execution was delayed, and hostilities soon after ceased. In May, 1865, Milligan appealed to the Circuit Court for a writ of *habeas corpus*, which would raise the question of jurisdiction. The circuit judges disagreed and referred the case to the Supreme Court; but the case was long held under advisement, and the decision was not announced till December, 1866. The fact that James A. Garfield took up Milligan's cause with spirit and force, and argued the case as his counsel before the Supreme Court, was a sufficient proof that the whole system of military courts was unpopular; and the behavior of the commission appointed to try Lincoln's murderers in May, 1865, had not increased public confidence in that arbitrary kind of justice.

In the decision of the appeal by the Supreme Court, all the nine justices agreed that the commission which had tried Milligan had no jurisdiction under the terms of the statute, and therefore ordered him to be discharged and the proceedings of the military court to be nullified. But a fundamental and nearly evenly balanced difference of opinion was revealed on an important principle; for five judges held that Congress could not authorize such tribunals in regions where the civil courts were open, while Chase and three of his fellows held the contrary. Though Chase at that time gave no evidence of a desire that the court exercise restraint over the legislative power of Congress, the decision was everywhere accepted as the triumph of the civil over the military power, even during war. The reign of military law within the Northern States was at last over.

This famous decision has so long been recognized as a public service that it is difficult to realize the storm of unpopularity which fell upon the court. According to the New York "Independent," the decision restored the court "to the proud eminence it occupied when Taney directed its decrees." The "National Anti-Slavery Standard" declared that "an alliance, offensive and defensive, has at length been favorably concluded between the Supreme Court and the President;" and Wendell Phillips proposed that the court be abolished out of hand, for "the nation must be saved, no matter what or how venerable the foe whose existence goes down before that necessity."

A few days later, January 14, 1867, the court held void a clause of a state constitution, in the so-called "Test oath" cases (*Cummings* v. *Missouri* and *In re Garland*). Arguments had been heard many months earlier, and Chase appears to have interested himself in postponing the decision for the time being. Nevertheless, somehow Johnson learned or supposed that the court had come to a decision against the validity of the oaths, for he publicly stated in the campaign of 1866 that his own opinion on that subject had their concurrence.

The point in the *Cummings Case* was the validity

of a retrospective oath of loyalty imposed by the radical Missouri Constitution of 1864, under which any person, who had "by act or word" manifested sympathy with those engaged in rebellion, was disfranchised and excluded from public office, from office in any corporation, and from the practice of any profession. This enactment was applied to Cummings to prevent him from officiating as a Catholic priest. It was defended as the act of a State possessing "attributes of sovereignty," and it was a problem to find constitutional limitations which would annul this disagreeable clause in the Missouri Constitution, and yet leave no loophole of escape from the philanthropic articles of the constitutions of the reconstructed States. Five judges, the bare majority of the court, found the desired limitations in the constitutional prohibitions of *ex post facto* laws and bills of attainder. From this conclusion Chase dissented, together with Swayne, Miller, and Davis, all four appointees of Lincoln; their ground was mainly that the *ex post facto* clause applied only to criminal cases and not to civil disabilities.

The *Garland Case* turned on the validity of an act of Congress of January 14, 1865, which imposed a test oath for attorneys before the Supreme Court. Garland had been admitted as a counselor before the war, but now found himself excluded, although he had fortified himself with a pardon from the President. The majority of the court held that it was not in the power of Congress to stretch its power of prescribing qualifications for attorneys so as to make it "a means for the infliction of punishment, against the prohibition of the Constitution," or "to inflict punishment beyond the reach of executive clemency." Again Chase and his three fellows dissented, partly on legal grounds, and partly from the political reason that "to suffer treasonable sentiments to spread here unchecked is to permit the stream on which the life of the nation depends to be poisoned at its source." They held also that the President's pardon could not relieve from a qualification, though it might from a punishment.

The significance of these cases is not only that all the older judges united in annulling, on narrow and technical grounds, provisions of a state Constitution and of a federal statute, but also that the decision suggested to Congress what might be expected when the pending reconstruction acts came up for judicial examination. Within a few weeks efforts were made to stop the execution of those acts, which had passed Congress by two-thirds majorities, in the face of hostile veto messages, in which Johnson had freely declared them unconstitutional. The statutes by which existing state governments were placed under military control were assailed by Governor Humphrey of Mississippi, who through his attorney, Robert J. Walker, asked for an injunction to restrain President Johnson from carrying out the statutes in Mississippi; by this proceeding troublesome preliminaries of cases brought slowly from the lower courts might be avoided, and a decision might almost be forced from the Supreme Court. The petitioner argued that no penalties or disabilities could be laid upon the State as such, but only upon individuals who might have violated the laws of the United States; and he thus brought up the whole question of the status of the seceded States. The President had no wish to raise a contest on that issue, and therefore the Attorney-General objected to the injunction; indeed, the case was without precedent, since this was the first attempt in the history of the court to make the President party of record to a suit before the Supreme Court. The brief decision rendered April 15, 1867, took the sagacious ground that the duties imposed by the act were "purely executive and political;" and, without a dissent, the court declined to assume jurisdiction, and left the President and Congress to settle their own differences.

Another suit was pending, however, in which the authorities of the State of Georgia asked for an injunction, not against the President, but against the Secretary of War, and for this form of action there were precedents. President Johnson had his own reasons for unwillingness to protect Stanton, and interposed no objection. The court, therefore, gave renewed consideration to the issue, but adhered to the principle of the first case. Notwithstanding the excitement of the secretary, and the widespread belief that the remedy sought would be granted by a majority of five to four as in the Milligan case, the case was dismissed on May 15, 1867, upon the ground that it was a political question which could not be settled by a court. Some thoughtful men, who had expected to see a check applied to the rising power of Congress, exclaimed in despair that "no State in the Union could rely upon the protection of the Supreme Court."

The end had not yet been reached; another case was now presented, in which the parties were not executives of State or nation, in which the point involved was supposed to be the same as that in the Milligan case, and yet which brought up the validity of the reconstruction acts. Colonel McCardle, the editor of a Vicksburg paper, was brought by the military commander of the district before a military commission on the charge of publishing insurrectionary articles. Application was made to Judge Hill of the United States Circuit Court to grant a writ of *habeas corpus*, by which the authority of this extra-judicial tribunal might be tested. Hill asserted the constitutionality of the commission, but appeal was taken to the Supreme Court, and speedily argued before it. In December, 1867, that body, in preliminary proceedings, asserted its jurisdiction, but argument on the principle involved was postponed till the next term. The question was now distinctly presented of the power to pass statutes authorizing trials by military commissions after the official announcement that no war was going on; and no one could predict the decision.

Until after the impeachment of Johnson in 1868, the court made no more great constitutional decisions; it never had to decide a fundamental case of freedom under the Emancipation Proclamation, or even under the Thirteenth Amendment; and none of the legal questions of treason reached it. But to Chase, as judge in a Southern circuit, came the opportunity by a judicial decree to strike the bonds from a large number of helpless Africans. At the time of the abolition of slavery in Maryland, in 1864, Elizabeth Turner was immediately bound as apprentice to her former master. This indenture, servile in terms, and forced on a defenseless child, Chase had the satisfaction to declare void, on two grounds: because it established a modified form of slavery, contrary to the Thirteenth Amendment; and also because it violated the Civil Rights Act of 1866, which assured equal legal privileges to negroes and whites. The apprentice decision attracted wide discussion, and General Howard reported that it brought about the release of a large number of children held in virtual slavery. It was also a notice to the Southern States that their offensive vagrant laws of 1865 and 1866 would not stand before the federal courts.

The fact that Chase's circuit included the former seat of the Confederate government brought within his jurisdiction the prosecutions for treason against former officials of that government. At the end of the war, under Stanton's authority, writs were issued for the arrest of the principal military and civil leaders, including both Lee and Davis; and though General Grant interfered effectively to prevent the arrest of the military commanders, Jefferson Davis was confined in Fortress Monroe from 1865 to 1867, and remained under indictment till 1869. If the war was to be followed by criminal trials for treason, a clearer case than his could not be made out, and President Johnson was at first anxious that Davis be put on his trial; so that Chase seemed likely to have an opportunity to expound the law of treason, such as Marshall had in the *Burr Case*.

From the first, Chase disliked the prospect: that Davis's acts were treasonable he never doubted, and he must have so ruled had there ever been a trial; but he thought that a military commission was the suitable tribunal; and by 1867 he was out of harmony with Johnson, whose Attorney-General must direct the preliminaries of a prosecution. So long, therefore, as military rule continued in the South, Chase declined to hold any court for the trial of Davis on indictments found in Virginia. Another indictment found in the District of Columbia was inadequate; and the trial hung fire, even after the President's proclamation of 1866, declaring the war at an end, and notwithstanding resolutions in Congress demanding prosecution. In May, 1867, the President definitely threw the responsibility on the judiciary, by allowing the military custodian to surrender Davis to the custody of the federal court under a *habeas corpus* issued by Chase. At last there seemed a prospect of a trial; but when Davis appeared in court for the first time, Chase refused to sit, and Davis was admitted to bail by Judge Underwood.

By this time it was plain that the chief justice had no heart in the prosecution, that the administration would not urge it, and that Northern men saw no advantage in making a martyr of the President of the Confederacy. The trial was, by agreement, postponed from term to term, till November, 1868. Then for the first time Chase sat as judge in the court; but Davis's counsel set up the plea that their client was one of those included in the Fourteenth Amendment (which had just gone into effect), and that the penalties there enumerated took the place of any previously incurred penalties for treason. The plea seems far-fetched, but Chase approved it. The regular circuit judge, probably by arrangement, took the other side, and the court certified its divergence up to the Supreme Court for settlement there. A few days later, however, December 25, 1868, President Johnson issued a proclamation of general amnesty, and at the next term the circuit judge discharged Davis on the ground that he was included in that pardon. The Supreme Court did not interfere, and thus ended the great treason case, with no trial on its merits.

Though fiercely assailed at the time for his lukewarmness, and though accused of favoring

Davis as a means of making friends with the Southern Democrats, Chase performed a public service by delaying a trial; the release of Davis made the Confederate leader harmless, and he could never have been convicted in Virginia without packing the jury. By this time all the country was adjusted to the principle of the reconstruction acts, — that the South was to be punished by penalties on the States as communities, and not by executing individuals "*pour encourager les autres.*"

The year 1867 was not a favorable time for the Supreme Court to emphasize its authority to review acts of Congress. The two-thirds majority of that body relentlessly overrode the President's vetoes, and was in no temper to be restrained by a court. It was remembered that in 1802 Congress had disposed of a hostile judiciary by a statute dissolving some of the courts, and thus depriving the judges of their places; and that the whole machinery of appeals was fixed by revocable acts of Congress. Suggestions were promptly made in Congress that unfavorable decisions by the Supreme Court might be prevented by resolute legislation, and members complained that the judges were "too apt to turn their attention back in search of some stale precedent of the dark ages." It was supposed that Justice Wayne of Georgia was arbiter between two factions of four judges each, and that his sympathies were with the presidential policy; still he had shown remarkable impartiality during the Civil War, and but for his death in 1867 he would probably have backed up the congressional theory.

When Congress assembled in December, 1867, one of the first questions to come before it was that of the Supreme Court. An early bill proposed that two thirds of the entire court must concur in deciding adversely on the constitutionality of any law of the United States; another plan required unanimous agreement in such cases. Although men like Sumner supported this extravagant proposition, it finally gave way to a bill taking away part of the appellate jurisdiction, the purpose being to prevent the further consideration of the McCardle case. Schenck of Ohio supported the measure, because, as he said, "I have lost confidence in the majority of the Supreme Court. I believe that they usurp power whenever they dare to undertake to settle questions purely political." It passed both Houses, and though the President at once interposed his veto, in March, 1868, it was carried over his head. When at the next term of the court, McCardle's case came up, the court wisely held that its jurisdiction had been removed: as Chase expressed it in his opinion, "Judicial duty is not less fully performed by declining ungranted jurisdiction than by exercising firmly that which the Constitution and the laws conferred."

Notwithstanding the panic in Congress, there seems little reason to suppose that the court would have thrown the process of reconstruction into confusion by holding the main acts unconstitutional.

It is alleged that Justice Field told his friends that in the court's opinion the acts were unconstitutional; if it were so, Chase took care that no such opinion should be pronounced. On August 7, 1867, he wrote to General Garfield: "The country is well satisfied with the action of Congress, not, I think, that the people want a continuance of military authority, but because they want restoration on solid and just foundation as soon as possible — the President must yield to the People; or the People will take up and put through impeachment."

CHAPTER XIV

THE SECOND STAGE OF RECONSTRUCTION

THROUGHOUT the first stage of reconstruction, Chase's attitude had been dignified and his influence conservative and conciliatory: he had done his best to restrain Johnson from excess; he had as circuit judge, and as judge in the Supreme Court, thrown his influence against technical decisions; he had allowed the method of congressional reconstruction to go on untroubled to the end. The Southern States duly paid the price of their readmission by ratifying the Fourteenth Amendment, and from 1868 they were gradually allowed to reoccupy seats in Congress. But the struggle between the President and Congress had grown so bitter that it was determined to remove Johnson from his office, though his term had but a few months longer to run, and though there was not the slightest danger of his reëlection. His violence, even when he was in the right, had weakened him beyond any power of harm, and the relentless two-thirds majority in Congress could override him at will; impeachment was unnecessary, and therefore tactless. The issue finally selected was that he should be impeached for a violation of the Tenure of Office Act, passed to curb him in March, 1867. In August, 1867, Johnson removed Secretary Stanton, and designated General Grant as secretary *ad interim.* When at the next session of Congress in December, 1867, the Senate refused to assent to the removal, Stanton, according to the terms of the statute, was restored to his office; but Johnson refused to acknowledge him, and took some steps to make up a test case for the Supreme Court. Within two days a resolution of impeachment passed the House, and in March, 1868, the Senate began to sit as a court of impeachment.

For the first time in the nation's history had come about the impeachment of a president, a proceeding in which the Constitution designates the chief justice to preside over the Senate. Notwithstanding his judicial office and his special function as presiding officer, Chase did not conceal his strong opinion that the trial was impolitic and unjust. Although his friend Ashley had been the first to urge impeachment, Chase could not share in the violent antipathies of Congress; for his personal relations with Johnson had not been unfriendly, and he could see clearly the danger of the supremacy of Congress if it succeeded in removing a President. Nor is it likely that he looked forward with pleasure to the prospects of his old rival, Benjamin F. Wade, then president of the Senate, and hence next in succession to the vice-president. A few days after the end of the trial, he expressed in a letter to Greeley sentiments which had been sufficiently evident throughout the proceedings: "I was against impeachment as a policy — so were you; my strong impressions were against the sufficiency of the article and the proof to warrant conviction and these impressions have gradually ripened into beliefs."

From the first, the Senate felt uneasy at his participation, and, before organizing under his presidency, drew up a set of rules to govern the trial. When, on March 6, Chase was notified to attend, he properly protested against any official action of the Senate upon the impeachment without his presence; and he insisted that the rules should be adopted by the Senate as a court, before going farther. As soon as the trial had fairly begun, it became evident that it was the intention of the leaders to deny the chief justice any real part in the proceedings; they therefore maintained that the Senate did not sit as a court, and hence was not bound by legal procedure and principles of evidence. Against this assertion Chase set himself with effect; and he successfully used his right to act, not simply as a moderator, but as the presiding judge in the tribunal. When the question of the admissibility of evidence came up, he decided upon his own motion, subject to the revision of the Senate if a vote were demanded; and the Senate did not know how to avoid his action. An understanding had been reached among the radical Republicans that, on the first attempt of Chase to vote upon a tie, a rule should be passed against him; but the first tie arose unexpectedly on a question of the retirement of the Senate for consultation, and instantly Chase added his vote in favor of adjournment, and declared the session closed.

From this time it was evident that Chase could not be set aside. His moderating influence aroused the wrath of Thaddeus Stevens, who said in the course of the trial: "It is the meanest case, before the meanest tribunal, and on the meanest subject of human history." Party feeling ran high. It was known that some of the Republican senators would not support the impeachment, and Chase drew upon himself the anger of the disappointed radicals. He was even accused, notwithstanding his positive denial, of personally soliciting votes for acquittal. On the contrary, he failed to gauge the play of feeling, and was surprised, on the test vote of May 16, to see that seven Republican senators voted for acquittal, and that the opponents of Johnson thus lacked one vote of the necessary two thirds. At no time in his life did he show more calmness, good judgment, and foresight than in the impeachment trial; and for his effort to raise the proceedings above a partisan investigation, and to hold them to their proper character of a judicial process, he deserves the credit of averting a great public danger. Though he had no vote, and little opportunity for direct interference, the weight of his character, his reputation as an anti-slavery man, and his great office were thrown into the conservative side of the nearly evenly balanced scale.

It was unfortunate for Chase, that, even while the trial was going on, he permitted his friends again to urge him for the presidency. In his service as chief justice he had an excellent opportunity to show his powers as a constitutional lawyer; and the decisions of the court during that period, on both public and private law, were not inferior to those of the previous decade. Had he withdrawn altogether from political strife, his motives on the bench would have been unassailable; but from the moment he sought the presidency he could not escape the suspicion that his decisions had been influenced by his conception of their effect upon his political chances.

In the four years of his chief-justiceship, Chase had never lost sight of the Republican nomination of 1868. One reason was, that he did not feel an absorbing interest in the work of a judge. "The office is dignified," said he in 1868; "I enjoy many things in the work, but I confess that my own mind is executive rather than judicial. I should prefer to conduct affairs in the way that seems to me wisest, rather than to decide on matters that are past;" and very soon after his induction he wrote: "Working from morning till midnight, and no result, except that John Smith owned this parcel of land or other property instead of Jacob Robinson; I caring nothing, and nobody caring much more, about the matter." For several years it seemed doubtful whether the Supreme Court under Chase would recover its great position as a national arbiter; while the opportunities for distinction to a vigorous and commanding President were never more alluring.

To blame Chase for desiring to be President is to blame him for being what he was: conscious of his own great abilities, he felt that he had never had a full opportunity to show his powers; and he was extremely sensitive to the opinion of those about him, and desired the highest approval that could be given. He would have been a greater judge and a happier man without this unsatisfied ambition; he would have left a greater reputation had he set Marshall before his mind as a model rather than Washington; and all our national experience had shown how unsettling to the man and to the court is the ambition of a judge for political office. But Chase was a great man who had played a great part, and the quality of his ambition can only be settled by an ethical inquiry into his motives. As one of the founders of the Republican party, which, in his own judgment, owed him loyal support, Chase felt that he was the legitimate candidate for its nomination in 1868; and no other civilian of equal abilities and reputation was suggested. Seward had lost reputation in the cabinets of both Lincoln and Johnson, and none of the senators stood forth preëminent. By 1867, however, it became evident that the party might look for a military candidate, and against such a nomination Chase threw himself with all his strength, not only because he desired to be President, but because he felt the danger of electing military heroes.

He did not hesitate to put himself forward in the presidential struggle, and to follow the same methods as in the three previous preliminary campaigns. In 1866 his supporters began to suggest to him that the time had come to organize, and in June and July, 1867, he sent a confidential friend to sound the Republicans in the West; he was pleased to be told that Illinois, Wisconsin, Iowa, and Missouri could be counted for him, and that there was a strong feeling against Grant, who loomed up as the probable military candidate. But, just as in 1856, 1860, and 1864, Chase was compelled to face the fact that he roused no enthusiasm among the people, and that he had no strong friends among the leading politicians or public men who would or could prepare the way for him. During 1867 and early 1868 the current ran against him, and in March, 1868, at about the beginning of the impeachment trial, he threw up the contest, and assumed "only the interest of a citizen who loves his country, and desires earnestly the speediest possible restoration." It had by this time become evident, not only that General Grant would be nominated by the Republicans, but that he must be so nominated unless they were willing that he should be the candidate of the Democrats.

After the persistent efforts to make Chase the Republican nominee, it seemed to many of his friends almost treasonable that within a few weeks he should be seeking the Democratic nomination. Nothing in Chase's life has caused such fierce criticism, and nothing has done so much to diminish a well-earned reputation for sagacity, patriotism, and consistency, as his desire for that nomination. But, however faulty Chase's judgment, and however lame his logic, his course is not indefensible. His own explanation was loss of confidence in his old party. "I cannot approve in general," he wrote in September, 1868, "of what the Republican party has done. . . . I hold my old faith in universal suffrage, in reconstruction upon that basis, in universal amnesty, and in inviolate public faith; but I do not believe in military government for American States, nor in military commissions for the trial of American citizens, nor in the subversion of the executive and judicial departments of the general government by Congress, no matter how patriotic the motive may be." To be sure, he had just eagerly sought the support of this faulty organization; but Chase always overestimated the influence which he might have as President in directing and moderating his party, and his indictment of Congress was justified by the intention of the leaders to make that body supreme over both President and Supreme Court.

Neither the question of the form of government, nor even the question of the reconstruction of the

States, was the issue in 1868. In Congress, interest had been transferred from the disabilities of the Southern whites to the possibilities of government under negro suffrage; and the Republican party, with Chase as one of its leaders, stood in the public eye as the defenders of the freedom, the equal rights, and the political privileges of the negroes. How could he put himself into relations with a party whose traditional tenets were against negro equality in any form? The chief justice found himself denounced in savage terms by his old anti-slavery associates for one moment trusting Democrats to do justice to the negro. In his mind, however, had always lain the belief that the Democratic party had by nature anti-slavery principles. Now in 1868 the Democrats in the North were humbled and discouraged, and the Democrats of the South were disfranchised or reduced to impotence. Some of the shrewdest leaders, among them Samuel J. Tilden, favored a new departure, in which the party should accept the results of the war, including the new conditions of the South, as accomplished facts, and should make a stand against the threatened concentration of government in Washington. This was good fighting-ground, and it was upon this basis that overtures were made to Chase to consider the Democratic nomination. The phrase by which he described the new policy was "universal amnesty and universal suffrage," which meant that the Southern white voters were to be restored, but that the negroes should maintain their suffrage side by side with them.

The difficulty with this whole suggestion lay in the obvious fact that negro suffrage, honestly administered, meant that the Southern Democrats should be placed in a permanent minority in most of the Southern States,—and without Southern electoral votes it was folly to think of electing a Democratic President. The strength of the proposition was in the hope that a candidate like Chase would draw into coalition with the Democrats such Republicans as were alarmed at the radicalism of Congress and at the militarism of the Republican candidate. In April, 1868, while the impeachment trial was still pending, Chase indicated his willingness to accept the Democratic nomination, and on May 5, before a final vote by the Senate, he wrote, speaking of earlier years: "I was a Democrat then, too democratic for the Democratic party of those days; for I admitted no exception, on ground of race or color or condition, to the impartial application of Democratic principles to all measures and to all men. Such a Democrat I am to-day."

To many of the Democratic leaders he seemed an opportune candidate, and the chieftains attempted to find some common ground upon which their followers might stand with him. A letter of May 30 to August Belmont contains a candid statement of Chase's position; he held to his conviction of many years that negro suffrage was a necessary condition in the future South, adding: "I would eradicate if possible every root of bitterness. I want to see the Union and the Constitution established in the affections of all the people, and I think that the initiative should be taken by the successful side in the late struggle. I have been and am in favor of so much of the policy of Congress as bases the reorganization of the State governments in the South upon universal suffrage."

For some days before the New York Convention of July, 1868, Chase's nomination seemed likely; the strongest regular Democratic candidate, Pendleton, was found not to control two thirds of the convention, and Horatio Seymour absolutely declined to be considered as a candidate. A provisional platform was drawn up and submitted to Chase, who gave his assent and wrote numerous letters for publication, defining his ground and pledging himself to withdraw the troops from the Southern States. To John Van Buren, son of the late President, who acted as his representative, he took pains to write privately: "I must not be understood as expressing any opinion on questions of constitutional law which may come before the court."

As the date of the convention, July 8, drew near, negotiations grew closer; unfortunately for Chase most of his old and tried friends had no place in a Democratic convention; but Vallandigham of Ohio and other ultra-Democrats favored his nomination, and a majority of the New York delegation had agreed to bring him forward. As the voting proceeded in the convention on July 9, it was clearly seen that Pendleton could not be nominated, and the moment was approaching when the name of the chief justice was to be brought before the assembly. Seymour, the president of the convention, had been most earnest in Chase's behalf, and expected the nomination of the chief justice; but when Pendleton's Ohio leader, General McCook, saw that his favorite could not be chosen, he nominated Seymour, and despite the latter's protestations the nomination was carried with an uproar, Chase's name having barely been mentioned before the convention.

Never in his whole life had Chase come so near to the first step on the way to the presidency. The wrath and indignation of his immediate friends are reflected in a letter from one of his family, who was on the ground: "You have been most cruelly deceived and shamefully used by the man whom you trusted implicitly, and the Country must suffer for his duplicity. . . . Mr. Tilden and Mr. Seymour have done this work, and Mr. Van Buren has been *their tool.*" The real reason why Chase was not nominated was undoubtedly that put into an apothegm by a friend: "Mr. Chase was willing to swallow the Democracy, but not to be swallowed by the Democracy." The principle of negro suffrage, to which he had adhered, and must as an honest man adhere, was too much for the convention, and would have been too much for the voters. The disastrous effect of such a nomination was sufficiently shown in 1872 in the fate of Horace Greeley; and Chase simply escaped a crushing overthrow when the convention refused to put him in nomination.

The impeachment of Andrew Johnson marked the high tide of national feeling as well as of congressional supremacy in reconstruction matters; and when General Grant became President, in March, 1869, there were already evidences of reaction. Notwithstanding the "carpet-bag" governments in the South, the Republican majority in the lower house of Congress was reduced, and the Supreme Court seemed to feel free to decide an accumulation of cases involving the details of reconstruction, and eventually touching the effect of the Fourteenth Amendment. As before, Chase assumed the double function of a public man of large experience and influence who desired to see what he believed to be the principles of the Civil War carried out in legislation, and of the head of the court which had the responsibility of applying that legislation.

This double attitude was a part of Chase's nature. Quite apart from his ambition to be President, he could not stand aloof from the public movement of reconstruction; hence in 1869 and 1870 he took a large part in defending negro suffrage. The radical Republican leaders desired it even more than he did, though for other reasons. Indeed, in 1869 suffrage had been given to the negroes in every Southern State, as a condition of reconstruction; but it was easy to foresee that as soon as the States were left to themselves some of them would surely take away the ballot, with the result of an immediate loss of Republican control. The radical Republican leaders looked on negro suffrage as the basis of their electoral and congressional votes in the South: to passionate reconstructionists, like Charles Sumner and Thaddeus Stevens, negro suffrage meant a final triumph over the hated rebel; to Chase it seemed the means not only of protecting but of ennobling the negro. He championed it earlier than any other public man; from 1862 he urged it in season and out of season; he pleaded for it in the cabinet; and he separated from Lincoln's plan of reconstruction principally because that plan was based on white government. With Sumner he waited on Johnson, immediately on his becoming President, to urge negro suffrage; and the occasion of his opposition to Johnson's reconstruction policy was the President's failure to follow those good counsels. As time went on, the suffrage occupied more and more of his thoughts; he felt sure that Congress would have made easier terms for the Southern States if the South had voluntarily enfranchised the negroes; he was convinced that universal suffrage was everywhere the only safe basis for popular government; and he thought that it was especially necessary in the South, in order to quiet the terrors of the negroes and to bring them back into harmonious relations with their former masters. Indeed, it is probable that for their own purposes the Southern leaders would have done better to accept negro suffrage, and then to organize and influence the negro vote themselves. To secure this blessing, Chase was willing and anxious to have "universal amnesty," that is, the restoration of nearly all the whites to their public rights. In a letter of May 29, 1869, he says: "I have lived to see all men free in America; I have lived to see one currency provided for the people. I hope to live to see universal freedom grounded on universal suffrage, and a national currency perfected into equality with gold. These things are only foundations; future generations must build on them."

Nevertheless, he hesitated when, in 1869, the Fifteenth Amendment was introduced, putting the suffrage into irrepealable form. On April 3, 1869, he wrote to a friend: "After the Fourteenth Amendment was adopted, I thought the suffrage should be left to the States after restoration, and I still think so. Centralization and consolidation have gone far enough and too far. And yet, inasmuch as the proposed Fifteenth Amendment does not prevent the States from imposing suitable qualifications, if qualifications should be found necessary, I incline to wish that it may be ratified. I should have no reservation in that wish if the clause giving Congress power to legislate were left out. I want as little legislation by Congress in respect to the internal concerns of the States as possible." Once decided, however, he supported the amendment heartily, and his influence was strong if not decisive in the Ohio legislature in securing the ratification by that State, and thus completing the three-fourths majority necessary to make the amendment part of the Constitution. When it was duly proclaimed, November 30, 1870, Chase felt that the structure was now complete, and he wrote: "No man can now be found who will restore slavery; a few years hence, if the colored men are wise, it will be impossible to find a man who will avow himself in favor of denying or abridging their right to vote."

Chase's remark about centralization is a key to his general attitude in the court from this time on. It must be remembered that all his life long he had been accustomed to look upon the States as buttressed in impregnable rights. He had always acknowledged the privilege of the States to establish slavery if they chose, and for that very reason had been determined that express constitutional amendments must be secured to deprive them of that right. He had been alarmed both at the immense and unrestrained power exercised by the President during the Civil War, and at the arbitrary power asserted by Congress during reconstruction; and he could see that, if the vitality of the States should be destroyed, the power taken from them must inevitably fall into the hands of the President or of Congress.

No case came before the Supreme Court at this time which involved the right of the individual to freedom. In December, 1865, a negro was formally admitted to the bar of the Supreme Court by Chase's direct influence; and in 1867 he ordered that in the district of North Carolina the marshal should summon negroes as well as whites to serve on the jury. His decision in the *Maryland Apprentice Case* has already been noted. The only slavery cases which came before the Supreme Court involved the enforcement of unexecuted contracts for buying slaves. In the first of these cases (*White* v. *Hart*, 1872) suit was brought for the collection of a note given in 1859, the consideration for which was a slave. Though the Georgia Constitution of 1868 positively denied all jurisdiction for the enforcement of any debt of that kind, the Supreme Court held that neither a state constitution nor a statute could impair the obligation of the contract. In the case of *Osborn* v. *Nicholson*, decided at the same time, the court construed the Thirteenth Amendment, and held that it did not alter contractual rights which had previously accrued. From these decisions the chief justice was the only member of the court to dissent, and his opinion goes back to the same general principle as did his argument in the *Van Zandt Case*, twenty-four years earlier. He held "that contracts for the purchase and sale of slaves were and are against sound morals and justice, and without support except in positive law," and that all laws which supported slavery and slavery contracts were annulled by the Thirteenth and Fourteenth Amendments. The same question came up again in *Bryce* v. *Tabb*, in 1873, and the court took substantially the same ground.

A large group of Supreme Court cases turned upon the effect of the Civil War on the rights of property. In two cases, *United States* v. *Anderson* (1869–70), and the *Protector* (1871), the court passed on the important question as to when the war legally began and ended, but the two decisions did not harmonize. In the first case the court held without dissent that the proclamation of August 20, 1866, was "the first official declaration that we have on the part of the executive that the rebellion was wholly suppressed, and . . . the limitation . . . did not begin to run until the rebellion was suppressed throughout the whole country." In the second case it was held without dissent that "the war did not begin or close at the same time in all the States;" but that it began in the first seven States by the proclamation of blockade, April 19, 1861, and in Virginia and North Carolina by the similar proclamation of April 27, 1861; and that it ceased in twelve States by the proclamation of April 12, 1866, and in Texas by the proclamation of August 25, 1866. In another decision of much importance, *The Grapeshot*, the court upheld provisional courts set up by direction of the President, without any legislative authority, in parts of the seceded States occupied by the federal troops.

Three important decisions expounded the vexed

relation of seceded States to the Union, — the question which had so perplexed Congress. In *Thorington* v. *Smith*, the court without dissent recognized as a fact the existence of Confederate paper notes during the war, and their use in contracts then made. Chase, who drew the opinion, took the ground that the Confederacy "was an actual government of all the insurgent States;" though he refused to recognize it as having been a *de facto* government, obedience to which did not constitute treason to the United States, he did style it a "government of paramount force; . . . the rights and obligations of a belligerent were conceded to it, in its military character, very soon after the war began, from motives of humanity and expediency by the United States." This ground was modified a little later in the case of *United States* v. *Keehler*, in which it was held that "the whole Confederate power must be regarded by us as a usurpation of unlawful authority, incapable of passing valid laws," and that "acts of the Confederate Congress can have no force, as law, in divesting or transferring rights;" and again in *Hickman* v. *Jones, et al.*, when it was held that the recognition of belligerent rights "did not extend to the pretended government of the Confederacy. The intercourse was confined to its military authorities; . . . the act of the Confederate Congress creating the tribunal in question was void. It was as if it were not."

Another group of cases in which Chase took

particular interest related to the border intercourse, which as Secretary of the Treasury he had alternately prohibited and regulated. In *Padelford's Case* (1869–70), the question was raised as to whether Lincoln's amnesty proclamation of December 8, 1863, restored the property rights of a man who had accepted the provisions of that proclamation. The court held that the amnesty did restore him to his rights; and in this instance and also in the case of *United States* v. *Anderson*, the court enforced, and thereby gave its adhesion to, the confiscation acts of 1861–62, and to the acts for the collection of abandoned property, under which the Treasury had taken possession of immense quantities of property. In the case of *Miller* v. *United States*, the court declined to apply the constitutional amendment allowing jury trial and due process of law to those confiscation acts, on the ground that they were not punitive but military acts, exercised under power to declare war and make rules respecting captures. In the case of *Corbett* v. *Nutt* (1870–71), the court refused to apply the principle of the confiscation acts to commercial transactions within the Confederate lines, and thus "to taint with invalidity even the commonest transactions of exchange in the daily life of these people."

These decisions taken together show that the action of the court was both sensible and humane. It refused to hold the internal transactions of individuals within the Confederacy, or those of the Confederate and state governments with individuals, to be simply a mass of futile agreements and restrictions; only so far as acts of individuals or of the Confederacy had been made the means of opposition to the United States were they held illegal and invalid. In this group of decisions there was little dissent, and in no case was Chase among the dissenters.

It was inevitable that the Supreme Court should eventually construe and limit the reconstruction acts so far as they related to the domain of the President. The President's contact with the judiciary power came principally through his pardoning power; and in the Padelford, Klein, and Armstrong cases the court affirmed that his pardon removed any responsibility for an offense connected with the rebellion, and that though an act of Congress might carry the pardon into effect, it could not abridge the President's pardoning power. Though the right of the President to set up provisional courts in the seceded States was approved by the court, Chase could not forget the arbitrary tribunals of the Civil War, to which he had given a reluctant consent when they were founded; and therefore in *Tarbell's Case* (1871), when the Supreme Court denied the power of a state court by *habeas corpus* to release men illegally enlisted in the army, Chase felt it his duty to dissent. This was very nearly the point which had been raised in the Garner controversy in 1856, when as governor of Ohio he had insisted on the power of state *habeas corpus* against federal officials. He now entered his protest in favor of his old principle that "a writ of *habeas corpus* may issue from a state court to inquire into the validity of imprisonment or detention without a sentence of any court whatever, by an officer of the United States," even though the President's proclamation of December, 1863, issued after the adoption of the Fourteenth Amendment, was "a public act of which all courts of the United States are bound to take notice." This decision, however, was not construed to traverse the authority to exclude from office certain classes of persons who had engaged in the rebellion, given to Congress under the Fourteenth Amendment.

In the famous case of *Texas* v. *White*, decided in 1869, the court drew nearer to the fundamental question of the status of the Southern States during the war; the opinion was written by the chief justice, who considered it his most important work on the bench. The critical point before the court was whether Texas was a State in the Union in 1862 and 1865. In a splendid phrase Chase laid down his theory of government: "The Constitution, in all its provisions, looks to an indestructible Union composed of indestructible States. When, therefore, Texas became one of the United States she entered into an indissoluble relation. There was no place for reconstruction, or revocation, except through revolution, or through consent of the States." Hence, he argued, the acts of the seceding legislature were null, for "Texas continued to be a State and a State of the Union." But the chief justice went on to show that although the obligations of Texas were unimpaired, its federal relations were affected, and some of its privileges for the time being forfeited; and that under the power to guarantee to every State a republican form of government Congress had the right to provide for the reconstruction of a State. The decision not only admitted that reconstruction had been constitutionally performed under the acts of Congress, it also recognized, as legitimate and as representing the State, the provisional government which was actually in existence before Texas was readmitted to representation in Congress. Grier, Swayne, and Miller, in dissenting opinions, denied that under the provisional government, subject as it was to military power and deprived of representation in Congress, Texas could be considered as a State in the Union.

The plain effect of this decision was to deny that theory of state suicide to which Chase had earlier given his adhesion; for it asserted that, as soon as the war ended and the people of Texas chose to reconstitute the government, they recovered statehood, though not necessarily complete privileges in the Union, since those involved a question to be decided by the national government. The "Nation" said of the decision: "The Supreme Court has thus in this judgment placed the nation and the State upon exactly the same footing: whatever weakens the one weakens the other; whoever denies the historical origin of the one denies the same origin for the other. This theory gives the greatest security both to the State and to the Union." In the announcement of this decision the court placed itself side by side with Congress and the new President, in affirming that the process of reconstruction had been constitutional, or at least allowable, and could no longer be questioned.

Three years later, in the case of *White* v. *Hart*, (1872), though Chase dissented on one point, he acquiesced in a sweeping approval of the whole system of constitutional reconstruction. "The action of Congress upon the subject," said he, "cannot be inquired into. The case is clearly one in which the judicial is bound to follow the action of the political department of the government, and is concluded by it." Congress had never been quite certain of the constitutional ground upon which it reconstructed the Southern States, and the Supreme Court eliminated most of the prevailing theories. The theory of state suicide it denied resolutely: "At no time were the rebellious States out of the pale of the Union. Their rights under the Constitution were suspended but not destroyed. Their constitutional duties and obligations were unaffected and remained the same." The doctrine of conquered provinces was also denied. "The Constitution," said the court, "assumed that the government and the Union which it created, and the States which it incorporated into the Union, would be indestructible and perpetual."

The decision thus rested squarely upon a modification of the theory of forfeited rights. "A citizen is still a citizen though guilty of crime and visited with punishment. His political rights may be put in abeyance or forfeited."

As might have been expected, so soon as the Southern States were again admitted to seats in Congress there was a tendency in the South to put an end by violence to negro suffrage; hence Congress passed a statute, the so-called Civil Rights Bill, under the Fourteenth and Fifteenth Amendments, to protect the negroes. With reference to this act Chase, in the term of 1871–72, took the unusual step of writing to the judges on his circuit, asking them to send up a divided opinion on a test case for adjudication by the Supreme Court. No such case reached the court during Chase's lifetime, and his judicial activity was now practically over.

A short time before his death, other issues arising out of the amendments were presented to the court in the *Slaughter-house Cases*, which are the most important and far-reaching of the series of reconstruction decisions. The decision was rendered by a nearly divided court: with Field, Bradley, and Swayne, Chase dissented from the opinion of the court; but he was too ill to prepare a statement of his reasons, hence it can only be inferred that he agreed with Field that the Fourteenth Amendment was intended not only to protect the negro's rights, but to remove forever from the States the power of making distinctions between different classes of persons. The case involved the monopoly of the slaughtering business conferred by the legislature of Louisiana; and the counsel whose arguments seemed to find favor with the minority of the court was John A. Campbell, who had resigned from the court in 1861 when his State seceded. His contention was that, by forbidding other butchers to slaughter for the New Orleans market, the government of Louisiana had acted contrary to the Thirteenth Amendment, which prohibited involuntary servitude; and that, in violation of the Fourteenth Amendment, the petitioners, engaged in the business of slaughtering, were deprived of the privileges and immunities of citizens, and were also deprived of their property without due process of law.

The argument drawn from the Thirteenth Amendment was swept away by the court with little more than the remark that "with a microscopic search [to] endeavor to find in it a reference to servitudes which may have been attached to property in certain localities, requires an effort, to say the least of it." The main object of the decision was to consider and construe the Fourteenth Amendment, and the majority of the court put upon it a narrow construction which left to the States most of the powers which they had possessed before the Civil War. They held that historically the amendment was intended to overthrow the Dred Scott decision, for the benefit of the negro race; indeed, that all the amendments were "addressed to the grievances of that race and designed to remedy them." "Where it is declared that Congress shall have the power to enforce that article, was it intended to bring within the power of Congress the entire domain of civil rights, heretofore belonging exclusively to the States?" This reasoning of course withdrew from federal legislation large areas of protective law which had been supposed to be vested in Congress, and it was accepted by the whole country as a withdrawal of powers which would otherwise have been exercised by the national government. In fact, the consciousness of the court that it was acting as a balance-wheel was expressed in the final paragraph of the decision: "But whatever fluctuations may be seen in the history of public opinion on this subject, during the period of our national existence, we think it will be found that this court, so far as its functions require, has always held with a steady and an even hand the balance between State and federal power."

With this decision the Civil War virtually ended, and the Supreme Court reached the height of its conservative influence. During the eight years of his service as chief justice, Chase's influence had been on the whole for moderation, for the continuance of the Union as he had first known it, for the pruning of the excessive powers which had grown out of the Civil War, and for the protection of human rights. Though he could not agree in this final decision, his own influence had long been exerted in the direction which it marked.

CHAPTER XV

FINANCIAL AND LEGAL TENDER DECISIONS

In the previous chapter account has been taken of the principal political decisions of the Supreme Court under Chase's leadership, decisions which dealt with broad questions of human liberty, of arbitrary government, of the methods of protecting civilians, and of the relations of the departments of government with each other; decisions which involved conflicts of jurisdiction between state and national courts, or between civil and military tribunals. Side by side with these judgments came the usual series of ordinary private cases involving property or franchises; but the immense change in the system of public finance caused some of these latter controversies to bring before the court grave constitutional questions growing out of the Civil War. New systems of taxation involved vexed questions of personal rights and of the privileges of the States; the revision of the banking system of the country made necessary new definitions of the power of Congress over corporations; and the government paper currency, and especially the legal-tender notes, furnished a new subject for judicial settlement.

In the most important tax case during the Civil War, *People of New York* v. *Commissioner of Taxes*, 1862, the Supreme Court upheld the exemption from taxation of such United States bonds as formed part of the capital of banks. The reorganized court saw no reason for interfering with the execution of the laws as they stood; and in only one case, *Hepburn* v. *Griswold*, held any part of a financial statute to be unconstitutional. On the contrary, besides many cases in which principles of limitation on state and municipal finance were laid down, the court built up a new system of law based on the national powers of taxation. First by implication and later by specific decisions, it enforced the income tax, the internal revenue, and the modifications of the tariff. In these decisions Chase had the rare opportunity as a justice of the Supreme Court to review judicially and to construe the statutes which he himself had set in motion as an administrative officer. His familiarity with the revenue system gave him a special competency and aided him to strengthen the whole system of national finance.

The first important financial decision was rendered in 1866–67 in the *License Tax Cases*, which turned upon a provision of the internal revenue act of 1864 prohibiting persons from engaging in certain trades or occupations, including those of selling lottery tickets and liquors at retail, until they should have obtained a license. The court held that such legislation was allowable because the licenses were "mere receipts for taxes," and gave no authority to carry on a business which was prohibited by a State; but at the same time the opinions most explicitly set forth that Congress had no power of regulation of commerce or business within the State, except as incidental to the exercise of powers clearly implied from expressly granted powers. Between the argument and the final decision in these cases, Congress by new legislation reiterated the power to stop the exercise of a business till the license was paid, and the court referred incidentally to the new statute with clear approval of its constitutionality.

Three years later the court had occasion again to decide fundamental questions of taxation, and between 1869 and 1871 it rendered three decisions, in all of which may be seen the influence of Chase's identification with the financial measures of the Civil War. The first of these, *Veazie Bank* v. *Fenno*, 1869–70, was a test case upon the most sweeping portion of the national bank legislation, the ten per cent tax on state bank notes, which Chase had so long and so unsuccessfully advocated when Secretary of the Treasury, and which was first imposed by an act of March 3, 1865. The opinion was written by the chief justice, and is in effect a brief history of his purpose and understanding in drafting the national bank legislation. To defend the principle that Congress might prohibit state bank notes under color of taxing them out of existence was difficult, in the face of the long established legal principle that the States might not tax a federal corporation in the same fashion; and the prohibitory tax had always seemed drastic. It was easy to dispose of the contention that the tax was "direct," and therefore must be assessed in proportion to population; but it was more difficult to make out that the United States might tax a franchise granted by a State, and presumably an instrumentality of the State, and might make the tax so excessive as to nullify a power of issuing notes, which was unquestionably possessed by the States. "The first answer to this is," said Chase, "that the judicial cannot prescribe to the legislative departments of the government limitations upon the exercise of its acknowledged powers, and that as a means to provide a currency for the whole country, Congress might restrain the issue of their [the States'] notes." Only two of the justices, Nelson and Davis, dissented, and the principle of the tax has never since been disturbed by Congress or the court.

The *State Tonnage Tax Cases* in 1870–71 had no special relation to civil war finance, though they asserted the superior force of national over state taxes; but in the *Case of the State Tax on Foreign-held Bonds*, in 1872–73, the court by five to four affirmed the important doctrine that a State could not tax bonds held by persons in another State, though secured by property within its limits.

The last of the important tax cases during

Chase's continuance in the court, *Collector* v. *Day*, 1870–71, raised the general question of the constitutionality of the national income tax, which had been laid for the first time in accordance with Chase's suggestions, and had been collected under his supervision. The immediate question was whether an income tax could be levied on the salary of a state officer; and the court held such incomes to be exempt, on the same ground that would prevent a State from taxing the salary of a federal officer. Throughout its decision the court recognized the constitutionality of the income tax as it stood; and the only ordinary financial legislation which it disallowed was a *proviso* in an appropriation act (case of *United States* v. *Klein*), inserted to prevent the proof of claims by persons who had adhered to the Confederacy.

The general result, then, of the decisions which related to the finances of the Civil War was to uphold the legislation of Congress; and in several instances Chase took the opportunity to vindicate his policy by a brief historical and judicial review of the principles and probable reasons of that legislation. The most important decision was that upholding the tax on state bank notes; and that principle has never since been disturbed. The next in consequence was that affirming the income tax. Twenty-five years later, by the narrowest majority, the court practically reversed this decision, and by implication held the statutes of 1861 and 1862 unconstitutional.

Undoubtedly the greatest deviation from the former constitutional principles of the government made during the Civil War was the issue of legal tender notes. It was much contested at the time the first statute was passed in 1862; test cases were made up within a few months which could not be prevented from eventually reaching the Supreme Court; and the history of the issues of government notes from 1862 to 1869 was such as to give pause to some of the early supporters of the legal tender principle. So long as Chase remained in the Treasury he felt it incumbent upon him to defend both the expediency and the constitutionality of the notes. In 1863 the first important test case was made up in New York, although Chase seemed to expect that, notwithstanding the legal tender clause, the state banks might be bound to redeem their outstanding issues in specie. David Dudley Field and S. A. Foote were designated in behalf of the Treasury Department to argue in favor of the constitutionality of the act, and George T. Curtis wrote to Chase to remonstrate on "the improper effort on the part of the administration to influence the court of the State." Both the New York and the Pennsylvania courts speedily affirmed the constitutionality of the legal tender act, and the judges in both States sent messages or letters to Chase to inform him of their decisions. It is plain, therefore, that he was recognized, the country over, as the champion of the constitutionality of the acts, and in a letter of May 18, 1864, he says to a friend:

"I do not agree with you in advocating that the Constitution prohibits the issue of legal tender notes under authority of Congress."

In the same letter Chase goes on to say: "I do agree in the opinion that an inflated paper currency is a great evil, and should be reformed as soon as possible." The sentence really indicates the beginning of the change in his mind, as he saw the dangerous results of the legal tender clause, and when the war was over and he saw the notes still continue, he took alarm, and began to urge the speedy resumption of specie payments. What he had first intended was only to make a provision for a national exigency, to issue $150,000,000, which could be withdrawn as soon as he could place his loans and organize the national bank system; what he saw in 1869 was a prosperous country accepting issues then irredeemable and likely to be unredeemed, and refusing to provide either for their withdrawal or their restoration to a specie basis.

In the original draft of the statute which came from Chase's hands, the issue of notes, even without the legal tender clause, was stated to be for "temporary purposes." As soon as the war was over, Congress, under the efficient lead of Hugh McCulloch, the able Secretary of the Treasury, proceeded to redeem those notes, of which nearly $450,000,000 were then outstanding. December 8, 1865, with but six negative votes, the House voted that it "approved the contraction of currency with a view to as early a resumption of specie payments as the business interest of this country will permit;" and the secretary took advantage of the large income of the government and the sales of military material to withdraw legal tenders as fast as they came into the Treasury. On March 12, 1866, however, Congress limited this necessary process by directing that $10,000,000 of the notes might be retired in six months and $4,000,000 every month from that time on; and even this limited withdrawal was checked by the commercial disasters of 1866 and by reduction of the national income.

Meantime greenbacks circulated everywhere, side by side with the national bank notes, and nothing but more bank currency could take their place. The banks, however, were already looked upon with suspicion as capitalistic monopolies, and on January 22, 1868, the Secretary of the Treasury was directed to reissue legal tenders as they came in, leaving outstanding a maximum of $382,000,000, which was reduced gradually to $346,000,000; this amount was in 1878 made permanent. Johnson outbid Congress, in his last annual message of December, 1868, by proposing that the bondholders be compelled to receive legal tenders in exchange for the face of their bonds, in sixteen annual installments without interest; and though Congress on the last day of Johnson's term voted that the government "solemnly pledges its faith to make provision, at the earliest practical period, for the redemption of the United States notes in coin," it took no steps to redeem that pledge, and a party sprang up which desired to base the national finance on unlimited paper money.

Meanwhile, the Supreme Court had been listening twice over to arguments against the constitutionality of the legal tenders. Grant became President in 1869, and appointed Boutwell his Secretary of the Treasury; it was seen that no remedy for the evils of paper money was likely to go through Congress; and hence the Supreme Court undertook to settle the question by annulling the legal tender legislation and thus compelling a return to a "specie basis." The continuance of a war measure of finance in time of peace seemed to Chase especially unfortunate because, by 1868, the national banks were working so well that they had $300,000,000 of circulation, and had thus justified his original expectation that they would eventually furnish a currency adequate in amount and perfectly secure for all the needs of the country. To his mind, the time had come when the temporary makeshift of the legal tenders might safely give place to a larger national bank currency.

In the term of 1867–68, the case of *Hepburn* v. *Griswold*, involving the constitutionality of the legal tenders, reached the Supreme Court on appeal from the state court of Kentucky. Up to this time, this appears to have been the only decision of a highest state court against the legal validity of the issues. The case was argued and adjourned; and, at the next term, 1868–69, it was reargued, but still no decision was forthcoming. That the chief justice and others of the court felt uneasy, was, however, shown by three important limitations which the court in 1866–69 placed upon the legal tenders. In the case of *Lane County* v. *Oregon*, the court held that the notes were not legal tender for state taxes, because "Congress must have had in contemplation debts originating in contracts or claims carried into judgment and only debts of this character." In the case of *The Bank* v. *Supervisors*, the court took the general ground that the United States notes were "obligations, — therefore strictly securities," and hence excepted from taxation; and, in the case of *Bronson* v. *Rodes*, 1868–69, the court, with one dissent, enforced a contract specifically promising the payment of specie.

These cases not only limited the uses of the legal tenders, by distinctly excepting from the legal tender privilege all express specie contracts: they also treated the notes as evidences of national debt rather than as currency; and, in the last of the cases, the chief justice foreshadowed more sweeping action by the remark: "The quality of these notes as legal tenders belongs to another discussion." At that time, December, 1868, he had already made up his mind to disallow the legal tender clause, and was discussing the question with the other justices over the case of *Hepburn* v. *Griswold*. At length, in December, 1869, the court came to a determination, and directed opinions to be prepared. In addition to the two arguments heard in this case, the question had five times been presented to the court in other cases, which they had chosen to decide on grounds not involving the legal tender controversy. No judicial question was ever more thoroughly discussed: if Chase and his colleagues erred, it was not for want of information, or of argument by distinguished counsel, including a representative of the administration, or of long deliberations by the judges.

Unfortunately the question was so serious, and involved such strong political passions, that when the long expected decision was handed down, February 7, 1870, the court was almost evenly divided; but in this case the chief justice was one of the five who united in declaring that the Constitution had not authorized the issuance of notes which should be legal tender in payment of debts contracted before the statute. Since by the Bronson case the court had recognized as legal all contracts specifying specie, the court might be expected thenceforward to hold that notes could be legal tender only for debts which had been incurred after February 25, 1862, and for which no other medium of payment had been distinctly stated.

The opinion was prepared by Chase, and is practically a legal defense for a change of mind which was founded really on financial and political considerations. The argument makes few references to previous decisions of the court as sustaining its principles; instead, there is an appeal to the general theory of the Constitution, and an argument upon the unfavorable effects of irredeemable paper money. To be sure, he holds that the legal tender act was an impairment of contracts, but he does not dispose of the argument that the federal government might, under some circumstances, impair contracts. The main argument is essentially Jeffersonian: while Chase accepted the familiar constitutional doctrine that Congress might choose the methods of exercising clearly granted powers, he denied that there are any powers, such as the dissenting justices described, resulting from the general nature of the Constitution. On the argument that the legal tender quality was necessary as a war measure, he replied that this was a mistake in the facts, since notes without that quality freely circulated on equal terms with the legal tenders.

Throughout the argument there is almost nothing to suggest that the writer had any special opportunity of knowing the purposes of Congress or judging the necessity of the legal tender clause. But at the end he adds a paragraph evidently intended as a personal justification: "It is not surprising that amid the tumult of the late Civil War, and under the influence of apprehensions for the safety of the republic almost universal, different views, never before entertained by American statesmen or jurists, were adopted by many. The time was not favorable to considerate reflection upon the constitutional limits of legislative or executive authority. If power was assumed from patriotic motives, the assumption found ready justification in patriotic hearts. Many who doubted yielded their doubts; many who did not doubt were silent. Some who were strongly averse to making government notes a legal tender felt themselves constrained to acquiesce in the views of the advocates of the measure. Not a few who then insisted upon its necessity, or acquiesced in that view, have since the return of peace, and under the influence of the calmer time, reconsidered their conclusions, and now concur in those which we have just announced."

Hepburn v. *Griswold* appears to have been selected out of several pending cases, because it turned on a tender of notes in satisfaction of a contract which antedated the first legal tender act. Chase again and again limits the effect of the decision to such contracts; and Justice Grier expressed the opinion that the legal tender act was never intended to cover previous contracts, and that hence the case could be decided without holding that act unconstitutional. But the principles of Chase's decision were just as applicable to later as to earlier contracts; and throughout he is arguing against the whole system. The court was not then ready to go further and apply its principles to contracts then in daily making; but Chase was convinced on that subject also, and shortly drew up an opinion which he expected to file in dissent in another case, maintaining that any creditor who was entitled to "dollars" might insist on coin dollars.

The status of the question in February, 1870, was as follows: the Supreme Court would protect creditors in refusing to accept legal tenders for debts incurred and contracts made before February 25, 1862, or where specie had been specifically promised; hence the legal tender acts were in part unconstitutional; Chief Justice Chase had examined and found insufficient the arguments of Secretary Chase; and it was widely expected that the court would proceed to declare void the whole system of legal tenders.

In the country at large the decision was received as though it meant an immediate dissolution of existing contracts. At that time gold stood at about 120, so that, if the decision held, all debts and obligations would speedily represent one and a fifth times their value as here expressed in greenbacks. This was a weak point for the court, for it set against it the powerful influence of many corporations, especially those, like the Pennsylvania Railroad, with maturing *ante bellum* obligations. As a railroad president wrote to Chase: "How do you suppose the Railroads of the country are to pay their interest in gold and receive only a depreciated currency for their revenues, limited as they are by their charters to a fixed price? Would n't we have a nice time in making Passengers pay their fares in gold?" And another correspondent wrote: "Your decision in regard to legal tenders, if not reversed, is likely to cause the greatest possible distress and ruin among the classes of people already in debt; among the rest, very many widows and orphans owing money on mortgage of real estate of a long date back." To be sure there had been similar distress and loss soon after the time of the passage of the legal tender acts; but that episode was over. The real difficulty with the decision was that it was an attempt to make up for the failure of Congress to bring the country back to a specie basis; in view of the probable shock of an immediate change it seems very unlikely that the decision would ever have been pronounced, had McCulloch been allowed to continue his contraction policy so that the defects of the system might gradually have righted themselves. It was further unfortunate that the court should have taken the responsibility of declaring a statute void even with reference to *ante bellum* contracts. In his opinion Chase said: "This court always approached the consideration of questions of this nature reluctantly; and its constant rule of decision has been, and is, that Acts of Congress must be regarded as constitutional, unless clearly shown to be otherwise." The court might safely have drawn further limitations around the legal tenders; or it might have held the act to be a war measure which would expire by its own virtual limitation when the war was definitely over. To set itself against Congress, against the President, against corporations, and against a popular prejudice, and that by a vote of five to three, was an unsafe experiment. The small effect of the decision in the money markets showed that the great financiers did not believe that the legal tender quality would really be destroyed; and in view of the greenback agitation of the time it was dangerous to hold that a war-time statute might be invalidated, after its work was done; for the same principle might apply in the popular mind to government bonds.

At the time this decision was rendered the court was already in process of reorganization. Grier, one of the five justices who adhered to the decision, resigned before it was formally pronounced, so that strictly speaking the court stood four to three in the decision. The President at once nominated a successor, Strong of Pennsylvania, and also made an additional appointment, shortly before authorized by a statute increasing the number of the associate justices to eight, by designating Bradley of New Jersey. It was Chase's positively expressed belief that through those appointments the court was reorganized with the purpose of securing a reversal of the decision in the *Hepburn* v. *Griswold* case; and President Grant, his Attorney-General, Judge Hoar, and his Secretary of the Treasury, Mr. Boutwell, were openly accused by the press of a conspiracy to "pack the Supreme Court for the purpose of establishing repudiation as a constitutional doctrine."

If by "packing" is to be understood the appointment of men whose views on political questions were likely to be those of the administration, the charge is true, and is equally true of President

Lincoln and of all of his successors down to 1886; for during that whole period no Supreme Court judge was designated who was not of the same political party as the President for the time being. If "packing" means the selection of individuals with a previous understanding of their views on the question of legal tenders, and with instructions to bring about a reversal of the actual decision, the evidence shows that the charge is unfounded. Neither Strong nor Bradley was the first choice of the President. To the new judgeship, created by the act of 1869, the President first nominated Attorney-General Hoar; and when Justice Grier, in December, 1869, gave in his resignation, to take effect on February first, the President nominated as his successor ex-secretary Stanton, who had the support of every Republican member of the Senate, but died four days afterward. The Senate refused to confirm Judge Hoar, and thereupon the President, on February 7, 1870, simultaneously nominated Bradley and Strong.

On February 7, at noon, the court rendered its decision in the *Hepburn* v. *Griswold* case, and the coincidence of date led to a subsequent charge, that the moment the President heard of the decision he took steps to annul it by appointing two faithful supporters of the legal tender act; but Judge Hoar was consulted upon these appointments, and no suggestion was made to him or by him that the legal tender cases bore on the appointments; the members of the cabinet when the nominations were discussed had no knowledge of any "packing;" and it is completely established that, unless by some unprofessional indiscretion of one of the justices, the nature of the decision of the court was not known to the President at the time the two new judges were nominated; and Judge Hoar expected until the decision was announced that Chase would stand for the legality of the legal tenders.

Though the President and the Attorney-General stand absolved from a deliberate purpose of changing a majority of four to three into a minority of four to five, there can be no reasonable doubt that the President and his advisers intended, as vacancies occurred in the court, to fill them with men who would reflect the opinions of the Republican party; and that party had declined to commit itself even to the speedy restoration of the notes to a gold basis. It was true that Strong, as state judge in Pennsylvania, had rendered a decision in favor of the constitutionality of the legal tenders, and so had most of the judges in the sixteen other States before whom the question had come. Yet there was no lack of good lawyers in the Republican party who had not committed themselves upon the question. Had it been the purpose of the President to choose two judges who would balance each other, he could have found two such men; he and his advisers, with few exceptions, desired the legal tender act to stand, and the appointments were generally taken to mean that it would be reaffirmed.

Justice Strong entered the court February 14, and Justice Bradley, March 24; whatever the reason for their appointments, the two new justices were no sooner inducted than they began a dramatic struggle by seeking to call up a pending case upon which the legal tender decision might be reversed in the same term of the court in which it had been rendered. Among the long-standing causes not yet decided was *Lathams* v. *United States*, a suit involving the question of specie contracts. The Lathams had a contract with the United States, executed in 1855, with a stipulation that payments were to be made in "good and lawful money of the coin of the United States;" but Chase, as Secretary of the Treasury, in 1863 refused to pay coin, and tendered greenbacks, which had been received under protest. Suits, claiming the difference in value between greenbacks and gold coin, had been continued, to wait for the decision of the principle in the *Hepburn Case*. Although special leave was given to the United States to appear in the case because it involved the constitutionality of an act of Congress, Chase foresaw trouble and repeatedly announced that no further arguments would be heard on the legal tender question, that having already been decided in the *Hepburn Case*. However, on the second day after Bradley formally took his seat, the new judge reopened the question by urging the court to take up the *Lathams Case*, and suggesting that the legal tender question might thereupon be argued; the three dissentients in the *Hepburn Case* voted with the two incoming judges to hear new arguments, with the plain intention to reverse the recent decision forthwith. Chase and his three adherents protested, stood on the technicalities of the internal rules of the court, and resisted to the utmost; but in vain. When the case came on for argument, however, the counsel for the Lathams, J. M. Carlisle, declined to proceed further, on the ground that the rights of his clients were already protected; and against the protest of Justice Bradley the case was discontinued.

In the course of the proceedings occurred an incident which showed tension and almost hostility between the two factions of the court; the chief justice stated that the court had agreed that the principle of the *Hepburn* v. *Griswold* case should apply to all later cases. Justice Miller thereupon stated that this was not the statement of the court but of the chief justice, and the justices on the bench expressed their differences of memory in unjudicial fashion. The effect of the withdrawal of this case was to prevent the raising of the legal tender question at that time, and the court finally adjourned without further action. But its unsettled state of opinion was well known; and it was confidently predicted that within a few months it would overrule itself.

The expectation that the legal tenders would again be held constitutional was so widespread that the premium on gold was not reduced, and there was no general tendency to specify coin in contracts. Meanwhile the so-called Sheep case (*Knox* v. *Lee*) had long been pending in the court, and it involved the question of contracts subsequent in date to the legal-tender act. The controversy had arisen in March, 1863, and the United States Circuit Court of Texas had held in 1867 that the contract might be satisfied by the payment of greenbacks; at the same time came up the case of *Parker* v. *Davis*, brought up from the Massachusetts state courts, which involved the question of a contract made before 1863. In the term of 1870–71 the United States Supreme Court heard elaborate arguments in these cases; but to listen to argument at all was evidence that the court did not intend to hold itself bound by the decision in the case of *Hepburn* v. *Griswold*. When, on May 1, 1871, a decision was announced, the opinion of the majority of the court was drawn by Justice Strong supported by four other justices, and the chief justice, with the three who had agreed with him in 1870, dissented. But though the decision was announced, the court took the very unusual step of delaying the statement of its reasons. The chief justice was very ill, and unable to write an argument, and the texts of the opinions were therefore not made public till January 15, 1872.

This time the court distinctly faced the question both of *ante bellum* and of later contracts, and the first paragraph contains the essence of the whole argument: "It would be difficult to overestimate the consequences which must follow our decision. They will affect the entire business of the country, and take hold of the possible continued existence of the government. If it be held by this court that Congress had no constitutional power, under any circumstances or in any emergency, to make treasury notes a legal tender for the payment of all debts (a power confessedly possessed by every independent sovereignty other than the United States), the government is without the means of self-preservation which, all must admit, may in certain contingencies become indispensable, even if they were not so when the acts of Congress now called in question were enacted. . . . If, contrary to the expectation of all parties to these contracts, legal tender notes are rendered unavailable, the government has become an instrument of the grossest injustice; all debtors are loaded with an obligation it was never contemplated they should assume; a large percentage is added to every debt, and such must become the demand for gold to satisfy contracts, that ruinous sacrifices, general distress, and bankruptcy may be expected."

The court was careful not to pin itself too closely to specific powers of Congress; instead, it recognized "that general power over currency which has always been an acknowledged attribute of sovereignty in every other civilized country than our own." To this general power the court adds a distinct assertion of the doctrine of resulting powers: "It is allowable to group together any number of them and infer from them all that the power claimed has been conferred." The court also argues very strongly that the legal tender quality was absolutely necessary for the life of the government. "Something revived the drooping faith of the people; something brought immediately to the government's aid the resources of the nation, and something enabled the successful prosecution of the war, and the preservation of the national life. What was it, if not the legal tender enactments?"

Finally, the court left no doubt as to the purpose of its decision. "We hold the acts of Congress constitutional as applied to contracts made either before or after their passage. In so holding we overrule so much of what was decided in *Hepburn* v. *Griswold*, 8 Wallace, 603, as ruled the Acts unwarranted by the Constitution so far as they apply to contracts made before their enactment. That case was decided by a divided court, and by a court having a less number of judges than the law then in existence provided this court shall have. . . . And it is no unprecedented thing in courts of last resort, both in this country and in England, to overrule decisions previously made. We agree this should not be done inconsiderately, but in a case of such far-reaching consequences as the present, thoroughly convinced as we are that Congress has not transgressed its powers, we regard it as our duty so to decide and to affirm both these judgments."

The separate concurring opinion of Bradley was

based not so much on the theory of constitutional government as on what governments ought in the nature of things to be. "It seems to be a self-evident proposition that it (the general government) is invested with all these inherent and implied powers which at the time of adopting the Constitution were generally considered to belong to every government as such." He goes further: Since the States are prohibited from issuing legal tender notes, and there is no express prohibition of the federal government, it must have been expected that it would issue them, and the power to emit treasury notes "has been exercised by the government without question for a large portion of its history. This being conceded, the incidental power of giving such bills the quality of legal tender follows almost as a matter of course. . . . Can the poor man's cattle and horses and corn be thus taken by the government as the public exigency requires it, and cannot the rich man's notes and bonds be in like manner taken to reach the same end?"

For our purposes the most important of the justices' opinions is that filed by the chief justice, which was a disquisition in the familiar vein on the implied powers of Congress and the limitations on Congress. It was impossible for him to ignore the criticism made upon him in the majority opinion, that "even the head of the treasury represented to Congress the necessity for making the new issues legal tender, or rather, declared it impossible to avoid the necessity." The statement was undeniable, and the only manly explanation was that which he made: "Examination and reflection under more propitious circumstances have satisfied him that this opinion was erroneous, and he does not hesitate to declare it. He would do so just as unhesitatingly if his favor to the legal tender clause had been at that time decided, and his opinion as to the constitutionality of the measure clear."

Chase's attitude upon the legal tenders is one of the critical points in his life, and involves three distinct questions, — the ultimate argument as to the constitutionality of the statutes, the argument as presented by the Supreme Court, and the responsibility for his change of mind. The question of constitutionality goes to the very bottom of the national authority. We have already seen that no suggestion of legal-tender notes had ever been taken up by a responsible administrator till Chase's letter to the Committee of Ways and Means in February, 1862, although treasury notes had been very familiar. Perhaps the argument over the constitutionality of forced issues may best be put in the form that it not only would have been held unconstitutional by the Supreme Court before the Civil War, but would have been contrary to the principles of government then established; but that during and after the Civil War it was constitutional because the government had changed its foundations. Both Congress and the President had freely departed in many directions from any power reasonably implied in the Constitution, but at the end of the Civil War most of these extraordinary powers lapsed, from the cessation of the circumstances which called them out; and by 1871 reconstruction was practically ended, and thus another group of assailable acts ceased to have force. The legal tender issue was one of the few large extensions of national powers that continued still to have the same influence in time of peace; and Chase's effort was to restore that power also to ante-bellum conditions. Had he been able to carry with him a decided majority of the court, it is probable that the country would have acquiesced; but the division showed the powerful influence on public life and private finances caused by the changes which had been brought about by the creation of the notes.

The arguments in both the Hepburn and Legal-Tender cases were really less legal than political. Neither side was able to find a series of consistent precedents either in state or national decisions; and both majority and minority opinions consist in the first place of elaborate essays on the nature of government in general and especially on the federal government, with appropriate quotations from Marshall's decisions; and in the second place of long and often passionate arguments as to what was most expedient for the welfare of the country during the Civil War. It is noteworthy that both sides avoided the issue of treating the legal tenders as simply a war measure which ceased to have force when the war was over, but preferred to discuss the nature of legal tenders as incidental to the regulation of the currency and to general financial powers. In dignity and logic the chief justice was superior to his opponents, and pointed out with clearness the danger of the principle, announced by the majority, that the government might perform certain acts, because they were usual among sovereign powers. Throughout the discussion is evident also the curious feeling of the sanctity of legal tender notes, because they were supposed to have performed a great service in time of war. This was perhaps a result of the rising tide of demagogism in the country, which threatened to make wholly irredeemable the already depreciated paper notes, on precisely the ground stated by Justice Bradley, — the comparison of "the poor man's cattle and houses" with "the rich man's notes and bonds."

As to Chase's change of mind, his own statement in his two opinions is his best defense. Perhaps he might have said more; he might have urged that he was returning to the convictions of a lifetime, disturbed for the time being by the anxieties of his secretaryship. When the justices descanted on the importance of the national currency, Chase could have replied that the permanent national currency ought not to be, and was not intended to be, composed of government notes with the legal tender quality, but of national bank notes, which could do their work without any such support. That sober judgment which absolves Lincoln for his assumption of hitherto undreamed powers, and approves the progressive changes in his point of view towards both national and rebellious governments, must also apply to Chase. In 1869 he saw results of his own action which he could not see seven years before.

Yet his attitude on the legal tenders was unfortunate, both for his reputation and for the welfare of the country; and his connection with the issue of the legal tenders put it out of his power to help in the restoration of the government to the sounder financial principles for which he was so ardent. His own honesty stood in his way, for he could not convince people that he had in 1862 assented to a measure really fraught with danger to the country; and when he found that he could count on but five judges out of eight, it would have been politic to proceed on the lines of the Bronson and Oregon cases, setting up all the limitations possible on the exercise of the power, but leaving the legal tenders where they were. Undoubtedly Chase's judgment was better in 1869 than in 1862; the country would have been better off if it had not insisted on the legal tender act; and it would have been better off if it could have accepted the judgment of 1869; but that judgment was pronounced with an incomplete court, which in the nature of things must speedily be remodeled, and it would have been wiser not to provoke the issue of a reversal.

The reputation and prestige of the court necessarily suffered from the sudden change of front, a change of which there has been but one subsequent instance. "The rehearing," said the "Nation" in 1871, "on the first point, is an acknowledgment by the court of the soundness of the arithmetical view of its powers, *e. g.*, that the claims of its decisions to popular respect depend for their validity on the number of judges who concur in them. Considering that Congress has the right to increase the number of judges at pleasure, it is hardly short of suicidal for the court to give any countenance to the notion that nine judges have power which seven have not, or that a majority of three could give weight to a judgment which a majority of one could not give it. We therefore look on the reopening of the question of the applicability of the legal-tender act to contracts made before February, 1862, as a great misfortune."

Chase's service on the Supreme Court was for many reasons onerous: the docket was long and the decisions many and intricate; his circuit court business was also harassing, and his feeling of responsibility in public affairs kept him upon a continual strain. The contest over the legal tender decision in the spring of 1870 was especially trying, for it seemed to him an attempt to undo the most important service which the court had rendered the country. He was a man of strong and aggressive health, but he never spared himself or distributed his work so as to keep up his highest efficiency. In August, 1870, he was seized with paralysis. Though the attack was severe, he gradually improved, but was not able to take his place on the bench during the term of 1870–71. During 1871 he spent a considerable part of his time in health resorts, east and west, and even contemplated going abroad. He did, however, sit with the court during the terms of 1871–72 and 1872–73, and prepared many opinions, but he felt exhausted and would have been glad to retire altogether had the law given the privilege at an earlier age than seventy years.

An evidence that he had lost his keenness of observation and discrimination was his continued hope of the Democratic nomination in 1872. Many obscure correspondents during 1869, 1870, and 1871 assured him of their support, while Cassius M. Clay got twenty leading Democrats to agree to stand by him. Chase could no longer claim to be a Republican: he was much disappointed in General Grant, and would have been glad to aid in his defeat. In March, 1872, he pulled some wires for the Cincinnati Liberal Convention, and wrote in accustomed phraseology that he did not seek a nomination, but "if those who agree with me in principles think that my nomination will promote the interests of the country, I shall not refuse the use of my name." When Greeley was nominated he announced his purpose of voting for him. "I am," he wrote, "as you are aware, a Democrat, separated in nothing from the

Democrats of the Jackson and Benton school, except my convictions on the slavery question in times past, and now by nothing."

In the spring of 1873 he appeared noticeably older and weaker; though he felt great interest in the Slaughter House cases, he was not able to prepare a dissenting opinion. Indeed, he began to look forward to his end, and chose Judge Warden to be his biographer; in his hands he placed his most confidential journals and correspondence, and to him he talked freely about the events of his life. On May 6, 1873, a second shock of paralysis came upon him while in New York. He never recovered consciousness, and died, May 7, 1873, at the premature age of sixty-five.

CHAPTER XVI

THE MAN

CHASE'S public life has now been reviewed, and it remains to sum up the things which made him so strong a personality, so distinguished a man, and so important a statesman. In person he was one of the most striking men of his time. More than six feet tall, with a broad and majestic form, strongly carved and individual features, a keen eye, and resolute although opinionated mouth, he always made an impression of strength, readiness, and power. In massiveness and appearance of reserve strength he is comparable with Webster, whom he somewhat resembled in feature. A little conscious of his own advantages of person, he was always careful to set them off with appropriate dress. In manner he was agreeable but never deferential. Most people who met him admired his incisiveness and force, but he did not hold back his opinions, and was not always considerate in expressing them. Among his own friends he was genial, and even warm-hearted and affectionate, but he had a strong sense of what was due him, and sometimes his temper got the better of his judgment, and he would break out into reproaches. He wrote a great deal with his own hand as well as through secretaries, and his handwriting, never remarkably legible, at last became difficult to read. He was methodical in his habits, but was too busy to hold himself to any routine, and his papers abound in journals and letter-books begun but not completed.

Chase was always fond of building houses and laying out grounds, and in the course of his life owned four or five different houses: two in Cincinnati, both of which were sources of expense long after he had ceased to occupy them; the handsome house which he built in Columbus while governor; and finally his estate of Edgewood, about two miles west of the Capitol at Washington. This estate of fifty-five acres with a broad, old-fashioned house, crowning a hill, though it absorbed plenty of money for repairs and improvements, turned out in the end to have been one of the few good investments that he made. He took great pleasure in planning and occupying it, and though not very far from the Capitol, it was at that time quite outside the city, and served him as a country residence.

Throughout his life Chase suffered inconvenience and loss because he could not make up his mind to turn into cash a sufficient part of his property to extinguish his debts. Some parts of his real estate he was unable to sell until his youngest daughter reached her majority, in 1865, inasmuch as she had an interest in it; and it was not until about 1867 that the sales of real estate in Cincinnati and Brooklyn cleared him of long-standing debts. Then for a time he was prosperous. He had some railroad and telegraph stock which suddenly became valuable, and at one time he held in his possession marketable securities to the value of nearly $50,000; but in his private finances he never was happy. On the advice of one of his oldest and shrewdest friends, Joshua Hanna, he put a little money into gold mining stock, with the usual result that the stamp mill was always "just about to start up."

Ever since his first days in the Treasury he had retained a warm personal friendship for Jay Cooke, the great Philadelphia banker, as well as for his brother, H. D. Cooke of Washington, who later became his executor. Jay Cooke made a large fortune, partly out of his extensive banking business, partly out of his deserved profits from the agency for the sale of government bonds, and partly through his interest in the Northern Pacific Railroad. For Chase's own finances this friendship was disastrous. He had several times protested against offers of Mr. Cooke to enrich him against his will, and in 1868 declined to accept certain stock which Cooke informed him had paid for itself through the simple process of charging Chase with the cost price of the securities and selling them out at an advance without his having furnished any money, given any directions, or assumed any responsibility. On this episode Chase wrote: "I shall never cease to be glad and grateful that I laid down for myself the rule, after Congress gave me such great powers, enabling me to raise and depress values very largely at my discretion, that I would have nothing to do, directly or indirectly, with speculations or transactions, in gold or securities of any sort, for my own or anybody's private benefit."

He did, however, accept Cooke's advice on certain cash investments which proved profitable, and in December, 1869, turned over to him cash and cash securities to the value of $40,000, for which he took $50,000 of Northern Pacific bonds at 80, — they were then paying seven per cent. The investment was speculative and eventually proved a heavy loss, as did also an investment of $9000 in Potomac Ferry stock which the Cookes carried for him on their books for six years, till it had by interest charges accumulated to $14,000. Notwithstanding an excellent salary as chief justice and considerable revenues from his investments, the executors of the chief justice found little to show at the end of his eight years' service, except the estate of Edgewood. His daughters, however, both married men of property, and were not dependent upon him.

One reason why Chase rarely had ready money was his generosity towards his poor relations. Year after year he sent money to certain pensioners whose lot he raised out of misery into comfort. Throughout his early life brothers, sisters, nephews, and nieces looked to him for counsel, and sometimes for support; and he was subject to many calls for charity and public subscriptions.

Chase was a man of warm attachments, and in the twenty years that he lived a widower he suffered for the lack of his wife's companionship, sympathy, and counsel. Many people predicted that he would marry a fourth time; and there were several ladies in whom he took a cautious interest, and one who was thought by his friends to be selected. His grown daughter was not likely to feel enthusiastic over a fourth marriage; and when this lady came by invitation to visit at his house she did not find a warm atmosphere, and the visit was never repeated. He had little inclination to change his estate again, for so long as he lived his daughters continued to be his greatest human interest and happiness. The attachment of the brilliant young Senator Sprague for Miss Chase became evident soon after they went to Washington in 1861, and they were married in much state. Sprague was afterwards governor of Rhode Island, was a warm supporter of Chase in his presidential aspirations, and cordially welcomed him to his home and his circle of friends in Rhode Island; and it was for many years the custom of the secretary and of the chief justice to spend at least part of the summer at Narragansett Pier, though he was also fond of the White Mountains. His younger daughter, Nettie, was married, March 23, 1871, to Mr. W. S. Hoyt of New York, and both sisters remained not only attached to their father, but in close relations with him, and shared in his interests and his career.

No account of Mr. Chase could be complete which ignored the remarkable connection of Kate Chase, later Mrs. Sprague, with her father's public life. Young, remarkably beautiful, regal, and captivating, she made it her business in life to establish cordial relations with his political friends, and she was a gracious hostess for the hospitality which her father enjoyed giving; ambassadors, senators, and politicians were eager for her good-will and willing to promise her aid, and Mrs. Lincoln had battles royal with her for (as she said) coming to the receptions at the White House as a guest and holding court on her own account. She had a resolute purpose to bring about her father's nomination in 1864, and perhaps her influence held her father to his opposition to Lincoln. Indeed, this remarkable woman was generally considered to be a political force of magnitude, and she is the only woman in the history of the United States who has had such public influence. She felt keenly indignant with Lincoln for letting her father leave the Treasury, and jokingly accused Sumner on the day of the nomination of the chief justice of being in a plot to "shelve her father." The influence and spirit of his daughter again held Chase up to his strife for the presidency in 1868. She was virtually his manager in New York, and competent judges have believed that had she been able to go into the convention and make her combinations on the spot she would have secured his nomination.

Within his family Chase unbent from that Jove-like serenity which distinguished him, and was an interesting and lovable man. Throughout his life he wrote frequently to his children with sympathy, interest, and good sense. His numerous kindred were welcomed to his house. Perhaps he needed a more robustious atmosphere; perhaps his public life would have been freer from mistake had he lived more with other public men and been more subject to the virile criticism of less admiring associates.

Chase was a man who cared very much for the favorable opinion of other people, and who loved to serve and advise his friends. He genuinely liked men and women, liked to be among them, liked to be well thought of by them; and he had many devoted friends, especially among younger men. For instance, he enjoyed the cordial regard of the young, brilliant, and rising public man, James A. Garfield. He was pleased with the blunt, straightforward respect of men like Edward L. Pierce, with whom he was in correspondence for more than twenty years. From Major Dwight Bannister, of Iowa, Chase received almost chivalric tokens of his interest, for he offered to throw up his profession that he might take care of Chase in his last illness. He had the power of attaching such men and making them lifelong correspondents, admirers, and political aids.

To men more nearly of his own age and position in life Chase was less attractive. Upright, honorable, kindly, accustomed from his birth up to associating with the best in the land, Chase yet seemed throughout his life unable to form warm friendships with other public men. In the galaxy of the great men of the Civil War period, his only intimate personal friend was Charles Sumner. John Jay, of New York, wrote often, and had a very cordial interest and respect for him, but they were seldom thrown together. Among his associates in the cabinet Chase had not one intimate friend, not even Stanton. In Congress Fessenden of Maine most nearly represented his views and became his worthy successor, but in the House in the crisis of the taxation, currency, and bank discussions, the only member of large influence who was personally attached to him seems to have been Ashley, and his championship was at that time of little service. Among the Republican war governors, not one was an ardent supporter of Chase at any time, and even in the Supreme Court there appears to have been no one with whom Chase was familiar; while the coterie of leading Republican politicians, Ben Wade, Thaddeus Stevens, and the rest, were openly hostile to him. Though in abilities and reputation Chase surpassed all these men, his warmest and most devoted political friends were for the most part men who merged their political identity in his, and both in 1864 and 1868 he could not stir the levers through which public sentiment works its will. Politically and even socially he was throughout a *novus homo*. Notwithstanding his excellent social and professional start in Washington and Cincinnati he took a side in the anti-slavery contest which, in the minds of many aristocratic people, set him among fanatics and persons of imperfect social instincts. To defend negroes, to appear before the Supreme Court as their champion, to tell them that they ought to have a ballot, was to create against himself that social prejudice which was felt in equal measure by Charles Sumner.

Nor was Chase at any time in his life genuinely popular. He was submitted to an election by ballot but twice, in the Ohio campaigns of 1855 and 1857, and in the second of these contests his majority was very narrow. He had a certain Roman aggressive virtue about him, a Cato-like consciousness of uprightness, which somehow vexed and repelled the ordinary voter, and was one reason for his lack of personal relations with other public men. But on the other hand, he had not the *bonhomie*, the power of putting himself in relations with the average man, which carried a man like Abraham Lincoln beyond all questions of social prejudice. Chase was a representative neither of the traditional aristocratic classes nor of the laborer; and his splendid championship of the cause of the negro did little to endear him to the masses, yet gave him a radical reputation which did not commend him to the leaders.

Few men leave behind them such minute memoranda of their private lives as those which are open to the biographer of Chase. Mr. Warden knew no other use to make of the mass of his diaries and correspondence than to print the most private and sacred passages with the rest. But the character of the man stands both the test of his printed journals and of his immense unpublished correspondence. He was by nature religious, not only maintaining the formal observances of religious worship in his family, but holding to the faith of the Christian. He was a man of sobriety of character, whose jokes were clumsy, whose conversation was almost painfully decorous, and whose letters even to intimates, were stately and sometimes obviously intended for posterity. He was a truthful man from top to toe; perhaps he was over-anxious to defend himself, to deprecate or forestall criticism; but deceit was not in him, and his worst enemies might accuse him of being too blunt, but not of an unworthy finesse. In the course of his life he knew much violent abuse, and was often accused of getting his senatorship by a political job, but the terms of the combination in the Ohio legislature of 1849 were known to everybody at the time, and involved no concealment nor dishonesty.

Chase was a man of varied interests, who always had many irons in the fire, and was harassed by the effort to keep them all hot; but he was a painstaking lawyer, a careful and considerate senator, a hard-working secretary, and a thoughtful judge. Perhaps what he most lacked was healthful pessimism; he had always too much preliminary confidence that everything was to be for the best, and a corresponding sinking of heart when his plans miscarried. His greatest fault was a lifelong habit of self-introspection, to assure himself how upright were his purposes; but his belief in himself does not lessen the truth that the roots of his private character were a strong sense of duty and a high standard of conduct.

While the great variety of his life experiences did much to make Chase a broad and far-seeing man, it is unfortunate for his reputation as a jurist that he had so short a time of service on the bench, and allowed so much of his energies during that period to go into political and personal questions. Chase had the foundations of great judicial eminence: as a lawyer he was industrious and painstaking; his mind had the habit of throwing aside unimportant things right and left, so that he might get at the essential questions; he saw broad relations, and at the same time had a power of discrimination which enabled him to apply effective precedents and to get rid of comparisons which were not really parallel.

In judicial style Chase has little of Marshall's marvelous art of arrangement, and of luminous, unmistakable statement of great principles in a literary form. His opinions lacked method, and did not clearly reveal the progress of the argument in his own mind; but his law was safe, conservative, and respectable, if never brilliant; and the decisions of the Supreme Court during his incumbency in general show consistency and an accretion of principles which harmonize with each other.

The exact character of his influence on the Supreme Court is difficult to determine, and little light is thrown upon it by the official tributes paid by his colleagues after his death. The reorganization of the court from 1865 to 1870 brought heartburnings and some dissensions, although the public saw little of these troubles until the explosion over the legal tender decisions; and in that crisis the pressure of the majority was resisted by Chase not very gracefully or graciously. Indeed, Chase's best judicial service was given in the four years from 1865 to 1869, while he was still in the fullness of his powers, and before the court stood before the country as a divided and disagreeing body. Chase's greatest opinion was that in the *Texas* v. *White* case, which shows such power of compressed historical statement and such application of great principles to the problems of the Civil War, that his admirers must wish that he had lived to render a series of such decisions, for in them he would have gone upon the roll of the greatest American jurists. Even in his brief experience his reputation remains that of a sound, hard-headed, well-informed, well-trained jurist. He stands below Jay and Marshall and Story; but in general qualities and services as a judge he has an honorable place among the judges who have sat upon the Supreme Bench.

Into his public life Chase carried the characteristics which marked his private life: the same sense of duty and the same optimism, tempered in later life by his own experience, the same restless spirit of hard work, the same application of a high standard. He was a great man, who would have left a greater impression upon his contemporaries had he been content to do one piece of work at a time, and to give to it his whole mind. His conception of public life was that of public service; that he should have handled hundreds of millions of dollars without any part of it sticking to his fingers was hardly a subject for the self-congratulation which he bestowed upon it; but it was an achievement to administer the Treasury during the Civil War without giving to any of his friends a hint which would have enabled them to make money in private speculation. His acts as a public servant he understood to be for the public welfare. In the midst of a venal and corrupt period, when even some of his colleagues were suspected of putting good things in the way of their friends, Chase remained honest. He had an immense opportunity through his control of the border trade, and doubtless permits to trade were often issued to inferior men; but he intended that that difficult business should be honestly carried through, and was not more deceived than must have been the case with any administrator dealing with the seizure of private property in the midst of such turmoil.

Chase had also the honesty of expressing unpopular opinions and adhering to them when it seemed likely to be to his own hurt. A few times in his life he shifted his beliefs, once when he went into the Liberty party in 1842, once when he changed ground on the question of resisting secession by force in 1861, and once on the constitutionality of legal tenders. But certainly the first and the third of these changes were likely to bring him nothing but ill-will and difficulty. For the great prize of the presidency, which always eluded him, he made long and astute preparations beforehand, but he was not at any time willing to change his opinions in order to win votes, nor to compel his subordinate officials to work for his political advancement.

As a politician Chase lacked conciliation and alertness; yet he did first and last win many votes for the measures and the men whom he supported. He was in large degree an opportunist. In the Kansas-Nebraska Bill, where his qualities as a man were perhaps more clearly revealed than in any other episode of his life, he did everything that could be done to modify the bill, except to give up the principles upon which his objection was founded. However strong his sense of his own judgment he was willing to yield in details, and to work with other men. If he yielded to Congress on the legal tenders, Congress yielded to him on internal revenue, on methods of collection, and especially on the national bank system; and as a constructive statesman Chase must ever stand among the greatest Americans.

Chase saw more clearly than any other public man of his time, except Lincoln, the importance, the necessity, and the moral effect of sticking to a consistent principle. He entered public life as an anti-slavery man, and nothing ever drew him aside from what he conceived to be the right of the bondman, and the parallel right of the community to be freed from bondage. In this respect he stood far above William H. Seward, a man whose career was in many respects like his own. In the dark months of 1860 and 1861, both men were inclined to give up the strenuous opposition to secession,— Seward, because he believed the Southern States were not in earnest; and Chase, because he could not at once see that the future freedom of the continent depended upon striking at the Confederacy before it was completed. The national banking system was Chase's creation, and from 1861 to 1864 he thought of it continuously, losing no opportunity of showing how much it was needed; and eventually his principles triumphed. Beginning with the conviction that the self-control of the States in their own concerns was necessary for freedom in the North, Chase never divested himself of the belief that it was best to leave even the Southern States after reorganization to manage their own affairs; and at his death he stood on the great question of state rights about where he had stood thirty years earlier. Other men of his time had changed their minds, and Chase was not the man to be bound forever by a partial conception arrived at early in life; his view was simply that it lay in the nature of man to misuse the powers of government if too much were assembled in the national part of the American system.

Why is it that a man so large, so farsighted, so upright, whose principles were so excellent, should have failed to leave an impression of supereminence? One reason is that the times were not so favorable for the reputation of a civilian as of a military man; but a still stronger reason is that Lincoln, in the public mind, so overtopped all other statesmen. There were plenty of striking civilians during the Civil War, and Chase came into relations with most of them; but their reputations are all stunted by the greatness of that most overpowering personality. Charles Francis Adams, Stanton, Seward, Sumner, and Thaddeus Stevens, would all have shone more brightly in earlier or later times. They are the men with whom Chase is to be compared; and not one of them has such claims to our admiration as he. A fierce and implacable radical in his younger days, Chase came to have a spirit of moderation, and a conception that there was possibly another side to the controversy, which could never enter into the minds of Sumner and Stevens. In breadth of view and insight into the conditions of the country he certainly surpassed Adams; in balance and in power of working with other men as instrumentalities Stanton was far his inferior; and the whole course of the Civil War and Reconstruction showed that he had in his mind a basis of solid conviction which was lacking in the fiery, more astute, and genial Seward.

The truth of this statement does not take away the fact that in his own lifetime Chase had fewer warm friends and admirers than almost any one of these rivals, and that somehow he repeatedly gave an impression of smallness in small matters, which dimmed his reputation. This came first of all from his measuring himself with Lincoln, and in that unhappy difference he did not show a great man's appreciation of another great man's character and personality. Little men, buzzing newspaper correspondents, disappointed candidates for office, and unsuccessful generals, might have been expected to carp at Lincoln's oddities of manner and slowness in making up his mind, but it was reasonable to expect a broader view and a loyal sympathy from a man like Chase, so closely associated with the President, so cognizant of the tremendous economic and political difficulties which beset him.

It is not a defense to say that for some years Chase thought that his own experience and long service as an anti-slavery man gave him a deeper insight than Lincoln possessed. In the crisis of 1862 and the supreme effort of 1864 he ought to have taken his place as Lincoln's strongest and most generous supporter. That he did not is due to two defects in his make-up: he lacked a sense of proportion and he lacked imagination. It was not in him to see that in 1864 the question was not of military success, nor of putting at the head of affairs a man of great intelligence and good judgment, — that is, Chase himself, — but in uniting the country in its final, desperate effort under the headship of the one man who by that time could unite the country. Again, Chase's lack of humor put him out of relations with the President. They never understood each other; Seward, though far inferior to Chase in the conduct of his own public business, and though a much weaker element in the relations of the administration to the country, could obliterate himself and be content to be a lieutenant of the greater man; but Chase in his whole life could not learn the lesson of subordination. He never looked upon himself as under the directions of the President; he always considered Lincoln to be only a *primus inter pares*, and his conception of the Lincoln administration was that it ought to be a collegiate body in which the strong intellects were to shape a majority. Had Chase shown towards Lincoln the kind of patriotic fidelity which General Sherman showed towards Grant, his name might have gone down linked indissolubly with that of the greatest American, instead of standing as a representative of discontent and protest against his president and his chief.

Another reason for the disappointment which Americans have felt not only in Chase, but in all the leaders of the Civil War, both civil and military, is that we no longer realize the tremendous task which settled down upon them. Lincoln was wise enough to write: "I have made mistakes;" and yet we feel impatience with the unsuccessful generals and the imperfect statesmen. This generation measures the last by results which the wisest throughout the world did not in that day foresee. It seemed simply common sense for foreign observers in 1861 to predict that the Union would be permanently divided by secession; no American, North or South, was justified in confidence that the North could be united for a single year's campaign, until the firing upon Fort Sumter raised a storm of wrath and resistance; and even then a large minority in the North was opposed to the war, and a small minority ventured to express its dissent. Is it reasonable to hold Chase and Seward and Stanton, Grant, Halleck, and Buell, Adams and Sumner, responsible because they could not look forward even half a year into the future? A Napoleon could have broken up the Southern confederacy in three months, but he could not have organized the moral forces of the Union to remove the causes of secession and restore mutual respect. Whatever the defects of the American public system, it did bring to the front in the great crisis of the slavery conflict those Americans who were best able to understand both their own countrymen and the problems which had to be solved. So far as they failed, there were no others who could have better succeeded.

"There is one glory of the sun, and another

glory of the moon, and another glory of the stars: for one star differeth from another star in glory." Let not Lincoln's surpassing power to gather within his own mind the purposes of the American people dim our admiration for the men who surrounded him! Of these men there may have been abler statesmen than Chase, and there certainly were more agreeable companions, but none of them contributed so much to the stock of American political ideas as he, both before, during, and after the Civil War. At first an obscure member of a little group of anti-slavery politicians, he came to something like headship of that party in the campaign of 1848. He was the first efficient anti-slavery senator, and in his management of the opposition to the Kansas-Nebraska Bill showed great qualities as a parliamentary leader. He came forward as secretary of the treasury in the midst of chaos, and made suggestions and developed financial ideas which may have been imperfect, but which were so clear and definite that Congress was compelled to adopt most of them. Almost single-handed he began the attack upon the sixteen hundred state banks which were the entrenched fortresses of a vicious system, and compelled both bankers and congressmen to accept a better scheme. More than any other man he seized upon the conditions of the Civil War as leading straight to the legal and political freedom of the negro, and to him more than to any one else is due that system of negro suffrage which he advocated, not because he thought it was ideal, but because he saw no halfway place in giving to the negro his long-usurped rights. In his latest years he well used his opportunity to stand for the principle of limited powers, as against the conception of a sovereign legislature, both in the States and the Union.

Chase could never have been a father of his country; he was rather one of those elder brethren who freely suggest, criticise, and complain, and who by the rectitude of their own lives, and by their upholding of high standards, influence the children as they grow up. No man of his time had a stronger conception of the moral issues involved in the Civil War; none showed greater courage and resolution; none came nearer to doing the thing for which he existed. The underlying idea of his public life was to bring the law up to the moral standards of the country, and to make both moral standards and law apply to black men as well as to white men. He had ambitions which sometimes dimmed his understanding and led him into injustice, but his life was sincerely given to the service of his country. Lincoln was a keen knower of men, and nobody had better opportunity to observe Chase's deficiencies; and Lincoln said of him: "Chase is about one and a half times bigger than any other man that I ever knew."

SUMMARY OF THE NATIONAL

	1860–61	1861–62
Revenues.		
Customs	39,582,000	49,056,000
Direct Tax		1,795,000
Internal Revenue		
Income Tax		
Miscellaneous	892,000	932,000
Public Land	871,000	152,000
Total	41,345,000	51,935,000
Payments.		
Ordinary civil expenses . .	26,947,000	24,511,000
Army	22,981,000	394,368,000
Navy	12,429,000	42,675,000
Interest on debt	4,000,000	13,190,000
Total	66,357,000	474,744,000
Debt Outstanding.	June 30, 1861	June 30, 1862
Funded Loans 6 per cent . .	39,773,000	100,754,000
Funded Loans 5 per cent . .	30,483,000	30,483,000
7-3/10 per cent Notes . . .		122,837,000
Treasury Notes	20,611,000	2,849,000
Demand Notes		53,040,000
Legal Tenders		96,620,000
Temporary Deposits		57,746,000
Certificates of Indebtedness .		49,882,000
Fractional and Postal Currency		
Total	90,867,000	514,211,000

The figures are in every case the nearest thousand to the full figures; hence the totals do not always tally exactly with the items.

FINANCES, BY FISCAL YEARS, 1860–1866

1862–63	1863–64	1864–65	1865–66
69,059,000	102,316,000	84,928,000	179,047,000
1,485,000	475,000	1,201,000	1,975,000
37,185,000	94,822,000	188,897,000	248,333,000
456,000	14,919,000	20,567,000	60,894,000
3,047,000	47,511,000	32,978,000	67,119,000
167,000	588,000	997,000	665,000
111,399,000	260,633,000	329,568,000	558,033,000
27,470,000	35,024,000	59,024,000	59,909,000
599,299,000	690,792,000	1,031,323,000	284,450,000
63,211,000	85,733,000	122,568,000	43,324,000
24,730,000	53,685,000	77,398,000	133,068,000
714,710,000	865,234,000	1,290,313,000	520,751,000
June 30, 1863	June 30, 1864	June 30, 1865	June 30, 1866
257,085,000	672,162,000	771,324,000	891,246,000
30,483,000	102,509,000	200,634,000	198,800,000
139,971,000	109,356,000	810,766,000	945,553,000
895,000	168,750,000	236,213,000	162,584,000
3,351,000	781,000	473,000	272,000
387,644,000	431,179,000	433,687,000	400,619,000
162,385,000	72,330,000	89,717,000	120,176,000
156,784,000	160,729,000	115,772,000	26,391,000
20,192,000	22,895,000	25,006,000	27,071,000
1,098,790,000	1,740,691,000	2,682,592,000	2,772,712,000

The footing for June 30, 1866, is about 11 millions less than the official total, because the gold certificates were not included here.

BANKS AND CURRENCY, 1860–1866

	1860–61	1861–62	1862–63	1863–64	1864–65	1865–66
STATE BANKS.	Jan. 1, 1861	Jan. 1, 1862	Jan. 1, 1863			
Number	1601	1492	1466	?	?	
Capital	429,593,000	418,140,000	405,046,000	?	78,866,000	
Notes	202,006,000	183,792,000	238,677,000	?	?	
NATIONAL BANKS.			Nov. 1363	Nov. 1864	Oct. 1865	Oct. 1866
Number	None	None	134	584	1566	1647
Capital	"	"	*7,185,000	108,965,000	395,728,000	417,245,000
Notes	"	"	†6,000,000	65,865,000	190,847,000	292,672,000
TOTAL PAPER OUTSTANDING:	Jan. 1, 1861	June 30, 1862	June 30, 1863	June 30, 1864	June 30, 1865	June 30, 1866
Demand Notes	None	53,040,000	3,351,000	781,000	473,000	272,000
Legal Tenders	None	96,620,000	387,644,000	431,179,000	432,687,000	400,619,000
State Bank Notes	202,006,000	†183,000,000	†240,000,000	†150,000,000	†40,000,000	†10,000,000
National Bank Notes . . .	None	None	†6,000,000	†50,000,000	†175,000,000	†265,000,000
Fractional Currency . . .	None	None	30,192,000	22,895,000	25,996,000	27,771,000
Total	†202,000,000	†303,000,000	†667,000,000	†655,000,000	†674,000,000	†704,000,000

The figures are throughout in the nearest thousands. * For 60 Banks only. † Estimates.

INDEX

INDEX

One of the founding fathers of professional history in the United States, ALBERT BUSHNELL HART (1854-1943) taught at Harvard for sixty years and served as President of the American Historical Association and the American Political Science Association. He was the editor of the 28-volume American Nation Series, which provided a foundation for the study of American history for half a century. He was also the author of an exceedingly large number of pioneering works that reflected the new scientific and institutional approach to the field, among them his biography of Chase; *Slavery and Abolition, 1831-1841; American History Told by Contemporaries;* and *Harper's Atlas of American History.*

G. S. BORITT, Associate Professor of History at Memphis State University, is the author of *Lincoln and the Economics of the American Dream.* He is a Fellow of Harvard University, the Henry E. Huntington Library and Art Gallery, the Newberry Library, the Social Science Research Council, and the American Philosophical Society.